MARK SATIN

NEW OPTIONS FOR AMERICA

The Second American Experiment Has Begun

Foreword by Marilyn Ferguson

D1445296

The Press
at
California State University, Fresno

This book is dedicated to the memory of my mother

Selma Rosen Satin

who tried to tell me to look before I leaped

and wasn't here when I clambered back up again...

...and it was put together with deep appreciation for the NEW OPTIONS staffers and consultants who, over the years, and in their many different ways, helped me leap more gracefully:

Shelley Alpern
L. Robin Cahn
Chip Craver
Roger Craver
Karen Flaherty
Denise Hamler
Baker Johnson
Judith Leckrone
Art Levine
George Lizama
Ralph Meima
Richard Perl

Roger Pritchard
Mary Coleman-Ragsdale
Gail Richards
Grace Sannino
Marc Sarkady
Andrew Schmookler
Sherri Schultz
D. Wayne Silby
Sylvia Tognetti
Caroline Udall
Marcella Wolfe
Elaine Zablocki

CONTENTS

Preface

The Second American Experiment Has Begun

As *New Options* readers know, only about five percent of my newsletter consists of my own views. We hear from thinkers and activists on each topic under discussion; we read guest articles by members of our 100-person Board of Advisors; we hear from you, the reader, in voices ranging from dour to enraged.

The *New Options* family includes Greens and Republicans, libertarians and Democrats. It can't be typed politically (unless you want to call "post-conservative, post-liberal, post-socialist" a political type!). And that is as it should be, for any practical vision of a decentralist, globally responsible society demands voices as broad gauge and diverse as possible.

But there is one thing that all our people do share: a certain temperament, a certain manner of being in the world. One way I like to put it is that the members of the *New Options* community— be they carefully-coiffed bankers or frizzy-haired community organizers—are all early participants in the Second American Experiment.

The First American Experiment began in the mid-1700s, and by its own criteria, at least, has been a smashing "success":

• *Economic growth:* We proved that an economy could grow seemingly forever.

• *The welfare state:* We proved that a society could be held together by giving people more and more rights, more and more "entitlements."

• *Policing the world:* We proved that a nation could become so powerful and awe-inspiring that it could successfully police the whole world.

The participants in the Second American Experiment have differing views on the First Experiment. Some—those carefully-coiffed bankers, perhaps—think it was a noble and brilliant experiment that is no longer sustainable. Others—those frizzy-haired organizers, perhaps—think it was ignoble and wrong-headed from the start.

If you want to dig deeply into these two views, read Andrew Schmookler's *The Parable of the Tribes* (1984) for the first, and Riane Eisler's *The Chalice and the Blade* (1987) for the second. Both Schmookler and Eisler are dyed-in-the-wool Second Experimenters. You'll have plenty of fun.

But the larger point—and the point that concerns us in this book—is that all participants in the Second Experiment are convinced that the First Experiment is no longer wise. Here are some of the questions they've been asking:

• *Beyond economic growth:* What are the long-term consequences of an ever-expanding economic pie? Aren't they rather, um, scary—especially if everybody on Earth wants to live as we do?

• *Beyond the welfare state:* How valuable are "rights" in the absence of felt responsibilities? How can people be encouraged to do more for themselves and their communities?

• *Beyond being the world's policeman:* How should we interact with other nations and peoples—especially now that we're moving into a multipolar world in which economic as well as military power will be decisive?

Important questions, all! (And that's just scratching the surface.)

But the Second American Experiment does not consist only, or even primarily, of asking such questions. What makes it important—what makes it a real Experiment, and not just another intellectual exercise—is that its participants are also articulating policy proposals and creating organizations.

And that experience is not leaving them untouched. If the First Experiment produced that well-known American archetype, the "rugged individual," the Second Experiment is producing not its socialistic opposite—a selfless individual—but a new American archetype, which I call the "caring individual" (see Chapter 21).

Because our national politicians and mainstream media are still obsessed with the First Experiment, the Second Experiment is as obscure now as the First may have been in the mid-1700s. But if you look and listen long enough, you will not only be convinced of its reality. You will be excited, even awed, by its potential for good.

Through *New Options,* I have spent seven years tracing the outlines of the Second American Experiment. I have interviewed over 500 key thinkers and activists, visited over 100 organizations. Now, in this book, I've arranged some of my best articles so you can see the Second Experiment in all its promise and fragility.

Part One introduces you to some of the key issues and organizations. Parts Two, Three and Four look at some of the Second Experiment's alternatives to economic growth, the welfare state and policing-the-world, respectively. And Part Five argues that the Second Experiment is farther along than you might think, and than even some of its activists think.

This is not a propaganda book. *New Options* is often constructively-critical of Second Experiment ideas and organizations, and that has not always endeared us to the Experimenters.

Still—I admit it—after you finish this book I hope you'll want to see yourself as a participant in that Second Experiment...as a truly "caring individual" who wants to add his or her own five percent to the mix.

Foreword

---

by Marilyn Ferguson

"Be outrageous," someone once said. "It's the only place that isn't crowded."

In the sense that Mark Satin has been walking the edge since he was a teenage newspaper columnist, he is outrageous. In the sense that he has defined and redefined his philosophy without apology, Mark Satin surprises us. Yet it becomes ever more evident that such bold, self-defining people are the only antidote for a society sick from a prolonged diet of appearances.

In these pages Mark proposes that it's time for Americans to adopt the creative attitude of the nation's founders. In that spirit he offers a number of imaginative possibilities—what we might call unconventional wisdom. Are these ideas do-able? A few years ago knowledgeable people thought that Ted Turner was crazy to think there would be an audience for an all-news television network.

In a way, Mark's life is as instructive as his writings. In the tradition of Buckminster Fuller he seems to be living his life as an experiment.

At 14 he convinced the editor of the *Red River Scene* (Moorhead, Minnesota) to let him write a newspaper column on teenage affairs. Living in a small town, he was dreaming of city lights—and parks and buildings and roadways. He read books by social critics like Lewis Mumford, Paul Goodman and Jane Jacobs and conceived of a career as a city planner. He would create a city that would inspire people to be citizens of a different kind.

He went off to college to be instructed. But toward the end of the first semester the dean broke the news. City planners were not expected to be visionary, he told Mark; they were lucky to get the sewers laid properly.

By then Mark had a new passion. He dropped out of college in the winter of 1965 to work for civil rights in Mississippi.

Back at school he became one of the hotter heads in the SDS chapter. As he recalls it, "The more radical I became, the more people seemed to like me. Soon I'd convinced myself that the U.S. was so evil that even *living* here was participating in the Viet Nam war." After his sophomore year he emigrated to Canada. At 20 he launched and directed the Toronto Anti-Draft Programme and wrote an underground best-seller, *Manual for Draft-Age Immigrants to Canada.*

"After a couple of years I began to realize the seriousness of my emigration," Mark says now. "Unless there was amnesty, I'd be stuck there forever. Partly to ward off my pain and regret, I decided that ambition was the root of all evil."

During the anti-ambition experiment he hitchhiked across Canada 16 times, indulged in the current equivalent of wine-women-and-song, and tried his hand at union organizing and underground journalism. Finally, while writing an article about a supposedly oppressed group of workers, "something snapped. I had to confront the fact that I no longer believed my own Marxist rhetoric."

Until then he had been approaching life in terms of abstract collectives rather than trying to understand himself. Suddenly he saw relevance in writers he had rejected as too apolitical or "spiritual": E. F. Schumacher, Ivan Illich, J. Krishnamurti. Out of this exploration came an autobiographical novel, *Confessions of a Young Exile,* published by Gage/Macmillan of Canada. The author was highly critical of his protagonist, who appeared to be having fun, "showing himself brave and strong and radical," Mark recalls, but was "sliding down a slippery slope," haunted by a subliminal suspicion that nothing really made sense.

The advance from the novel and odd jobs paid the bills for another experiment. Mark wrote a pamphlet, *New Age Politics,* printed 500 copies and took them to the World Symposium on Humanity in Vancouver in 1976. The pamphlet sold out in four days and was featured in the *Toronto Star.* A Canadian publisher contracted for a book-length version, which was released in 1978. A still longer version was later issued in the U.S. by Delta/Dell.

FOREWORD

After President Jimmy Carter granted amnesty to American expatriates Mark spent a year giving talks and workshops on the book, then another year traveling the U.S. by Greyhound bus. He was determined to meet people who were working and thinking differently. He was laying the groundwork for the New World Alliance, a national political organization based in Washington, D.C. For three years he served on the staff.

The New World Alliance "governing council" met semi-annually to discuss strategies for social transformation. After four or five such meetings Mark realized how little practical action comes out of intoxicating rhetoric. He decided to do one thing that seemed practical and concrete—start a national political newsletter.

He calculated that he needed $90,000 for the undertaking. When he appealed to New World Alliance members and others who had participated in his workshops, 517 individuals donated a total of $91,000. In 1989 his eight-page monthly newsletter, *New Options,* won the *Utne Reader* "Alternative Press Award for General Excellence." As Mark says, the constant feedback from readers "drew me to subjects—tax policy and school reform, for example—that I'd had little patience for when I wanted the world to change overnight."

It has been said that the difference between successful people and most others is that successful people "fail" more often. In other words, experiments always yield information. Mark's life—a series of experiments—shows that it's important for all of us to rediscover the importance of commitment and experiment.

Mark is beginning to view his life trajectory with a little more compassion. He likes to say he's living evidence of "what you can do with determination and no fancy credentials or resources." And yet he did have one priceless resource: the courage of his conviction.

In certain esoteric systems, the Fool is considered the most advanced level of spiritual attainment. The Fool, in this light, is trusting enough to throw himself headlong into life. The Fool makes mistakes—and thereby makes discoveries. This is a book of such discoveries.

PART ONE

DARKNESS VISIBLE AND SEEDS OF HOPE

The easiest way to define the Second American Experiment is by saying what it is not, and in the first two articles I do just that.

In "Two Conferences, One Generation," which was a gut-wrenching piece for me to write (you'll see why), I put some distance between the Second Experiment and the extreme political left and right—as well as between the Second Experiment and the inept anti-politics of the New Age movement. In "The Democrats Won't Save Us" I put some distance between the Second Experiment and all three wings of the Democratic party.

But NEW OPTIONS *never* focuses solely on the negative, and in both articles I also talk about new political possibilities and alignments.

The next two pieces are about groups that can be said to represent the idealistic and pragmatic poles of the Second Experiment. (Or call them the post-socialist and post-conservative poles, if you like.) "Last Chance Saloon" is a constructively-critical account of the 1989 national gathering of the U.S. Greens—a burningly idealistic organization whose members are trying to put the Second Experiment on the national political agenda. "Buy Our Way to Freedom" reports on an attempt by Tony Brown, the African-American television journalist, to put some Second Experiment values—e.g., self-reliance, decentralism, ethnic awareness—to work in the real world. One effect of my article was to inspire a meeting between Brown and some of the white advocates of economic self-reliance featured in NEW OPTIONS.

Linking the idealistic and pragmatic poles is the Second Experiment's overriding commitment to the human potential and spiritual health of Americans. More than any political publication I know, NEW OPTIONS has done pieces on such subjects as child-rearing, values, spirituality, "visioning," pre-schools, and self-esteem. (The late Carl Rogers, a founder of humanistic psychology, was one of our first supporters and Advisors.)

In "Promoting Self-Esteem" I look at California State Assemblyman John Vasconcellos's claim that self-esteem is the key political issue for the 21st century. His claim might or might not be exaggerated, but at least it takes our political attention away from ideology and economic growth and *things* and puts it where it should be: on our health and happiness.

1 Two Conferences, One Generation

October 1987

We attended two conferences this month that, between them, cast a powerful searchlight on the Vietnam generation as it struggles to develop a post-liberal, post-socialist politics.

On Oct. 17-18, at the "Second Thoughts" conference in Washington, D.C., over a dozen former civil rights and anti-war activists got together to explain (to over 200 journalists and movement-conservatives and political seekers of all stripes) why they'd given up on the Far Left and re-joined the political mainstream.

On Oct. 23-24, at the "New Synthesis" conference in New York City, over 60 academics and activists got together to discuss launching a "think-tank" that could translate innovative postliberal/Green/transformational ideas into concrete policy proposals that policymakers and journalists could understand and use.

Since coming back to the mainstream, the ex-radicals at the Second Thoughts conference had amassed a great deal of personal power. One is a TV personality, two are best-selling authors, two work for big-league think tanks, one teaches at Harvard. But in the process, they'd mostly quite consciously abandoned not just their leftism but their original visionary idealism as well—often in the name of "maturity."

The people at the New Synthesis conference had not abandoned their decentralist/globally responsible ideals; most of them had spent the last two decades refining and "operationalizing" them. But they had not amassed much power, and as the weekend wore on it became clear that the fledgling think-tank had nowhere to turn for the resources it would need.

And isn't that one of the tragedies of the Vietnam generation—that among those of us who've worked to go beyond the political left, some of us have power without original vision, and others of us have vision without power?

But there are signs that this "tragedy" is going to be less than permanent.

I. Like a bad dream

Sitting at the Second Thoughts conference was . . . excruciating. I kept having to leave the gaudy Grand Hyatt hotel, with its endless chandeliers and mirrors, to pace around outside.

And it wasn't just because the business of the conference—the terrible relentless recounting of our "youthful"-but-not-innocent political mistakes—cut to the quick. Up on stage, the hosts (and organizers of the conference) were Peter Collier and David Horowitz, editors of *Ramparts* when it was setting the tone for late-Sixties political radicalism: the kind of radicalism that preached that fascism was about to arrive in America, and that the violence of the Weathermen was fully justified.

Of all the publications I'd read in the 60s, *Ramparts* was the one that had made the deepest impression on me, the one that had done most to convince me that the USA and everything about it was decadent and corrupt and *I* was decadent and corrupt (since I wasn't "oppressed") and if I had any integrity I'd better do what I could to keep from profiting from America's awful ways. And

3

so I emigrated to Canada at the age of 19—a hardened Marxist revolutionary, I told myself bravely; and that's where I had to stay until President Carter's amnesty, 11 years and many lost opportunities later.

And there they were again, Collier and Horowitz, like in a bad recurring dream; a bit larger at the waists but still basically the same; still berating me, still telling me how recalcitrant I was; only now I wasn't a privileged bourgeois oaf but someone who hadn't sufficiently recanted his past, someone who hadn't sufficiently adopted the right-wing political agenda that was all that was keeping us from slipping into the cleverly-disguised "neo-communism" of the "solidarity left."

I am not exaggerating. Throughout the conference, Collier and Horowitz's statements seemed calculated to be as outrageous as possible. At various times during the two days, Horowitz called leftism an "infantile disorder"—claimed that "it was the left that introduced drugs into America"—asserted that there are "many fifth-column types" in Congress—called Congressman John Conyers "pro-communist"—and pontificated that "Hatred of self, and by extension of one's country, is the root of the radical cause."

The ploy worked. Collier and Horowitz managed to dominate the press accounts of the conference. Their performance not only played well in the mainstream press (which feeds on bitterness and controversy), but provided a convenient handle for the leftist press which had its own reasons for wanting the conference to appear to have been dominated by the rabid right.

But it wasn't so. Despite the conference's right-wing sponsors (fabulously wealthy foundations like Coors, Olin and Scaife), most of the rest of the speakers struck a decidedly different note. Most of the rest of them spoke in a considered, nuanced, and utterly genuine way about the mistakes they'd made in the Sixties and the lessons they'd learned, or hoped they'd learned.

Everyone who lived through the Sixties should have forced themselves to sit in the front row, as I did, and listen to the inner music of the speakers, and try to look into their eyes.

You'd have heard Jeff Herf, former SDS leader at the University of Wisconsin, explaining that his second thoughts began when he was finally able to admit to himself that Vietnam turned out to be as bad as the right-wing said it would be. "The boat people, the Cambodian holocaust and the Vietnamese Gulag were not what we expected.''

And you'd have heard David Ifshin, former radical president of the National Students Association, raging at how Vietnam ''decimated'' our generation and how ''so many of us are gone,'' casualties of drugs or crazy politics or broken dreams.

And Carol Iannone, feminist scholar, bravely insisting that her goal now is ''true intellectual and emotional freedom'' for women even if that freedom proves disruptive, in practice, to the official liberal feminist agenda.

And Joshua Muravchik, former chair of the Young People's Socialist League, arguing that it's not arrogance to wish democracy on other people.

And above all Stephen Schwartz, ex-Trotskyist, lamenting how he was a promising professional poet until the late 60s when he was guilted into dropping his poetry and becoming a manual worker (for 11 years). Part of the heritage of the 60s, he explained, was leaving your professional-intellectual work and becoming part of the ''great movement of history.''

And so we didn't professionally form ourselves, said Schwartz. We simply ran out onto the streets and we felt the streets would go on forever. We'd pass out leaflets for years and at the age of 90 we'd have accomplished nothing with our lives but we'd be ''great people'' because we'd have passed out all those leaflets.

The rejection of our intellectual lives, Schwartz cried, the Great Refusal to develop our personal capacities, has not only crippled our careers; it's crippled our generation itself.

Could you have looked Schwartz in the eye?

II. Time passes

Five days later I was sitting on the top floor of a building just across from the U.N., waiting for the ''New Synthesis Think Tank'' conference to begin. Despite the hard metal chairs, I felt as comfortable at this conference as I felt uneasy at the other; almost too comfortable. Then I realized why. I had been there before. The room was where the New World Alliance had held its party, the night before it launched its short-lived career as the first national ''New Age'' political organization.

And here I was, eight years later, with another group hoping to launch a national postliberal/Green/transformational (there was still no widely-accepted term) political organization. If anything, it was an even more representative body. There were leading-edge activists. There were academics from non-elite universities. There were "socially responsible" businesspeople.

We gathered ourselves into a big circle, just like we did in Alliance days, and as we went around the circle introducing ourselves it struck me how we'd *aged* since then. Time had had its way with us, I felt; and I knew that others of us were feeling that too; and were hoping against hope that the convenors of the conference (principally Belden Paulson, a major player in the Conference Group on Transformational Politics of the American Political Science Association, and Gordon Davidson and Corinne McLaughlin, founders of an intentional community in western Massachusetts), could help take us the next step beyond immersion in our separate paths.

They tried. They devised a program that allowed us to approach the think-tank idea systematically and intelligently. They scheduled a rich mix of talks, video presentations, freewheeling plenary discussions and small-group exercises. But in the end, the effort sputtered. We were able to reach little agreement on who the think-tank should represent. . . or, even, on the wisdom of *having* a formal, more-or-less traditional think tank.

Belden Paulson argued for the traditional kind of think-tank. In his major Saturday morning presentation, he told us he'd spent a great deal of time visiting successful think-tanks like Heritage, Cato and Brookings, and they all seemed to do one key thing: bring together a mass of knowledge and insight for policymakers and the media. It got him to thinking: Wouldn't such an operation help us get *our* ideas into the public policy debate? Then he visited his Congressperson, Jim Moody (D-Wisc.), who began lecturing him: Look, I get all this stuff from Heritage! But where are you guys? Where are you holistic thinkers?

Paulson's speech was received with a great deal of affection. But the conference generated almost as many alternative visions of the think-tank as there were participants.

Hazel Henderson, futurist and "anti-economist," offered the most detailed alternative in her keynote speech. She challenged the notion that there are power centers that can be manipulated and changed. Instead of "petitioning the powerful," she said, let's "link all the existing forces" that might be receptive to our message (among them: the "TV constituency" and the Vietnam generation). And let's recognize our strengths! We have nearly everything in place, in the alternative and transformational movement. "All we need is to create a little more density with our networking," and things will begin to "precipitate."

That was virtual heresy to Lester Milbrath, professor at State University of New York-Buffalo and author of *Environmentalists* (1984). According to Milbrath, we have a *long, long* way to go. We not only have to found a Heritage-like think tank, we need to found an umbrella organization, an "Institute for a New Society," that can do think-tanking, networking, reaching out to the general public. . . .

Paulson's and Milbrath's visions were heresy to Michaela Walsh, president of Women's World Banking. Walsh reminded us that, at a conference in Copenhagen in 1980, U.S. women tried to centralize the global women's movement. Their efforts failed, and the global women's network "is now stronger than ever, partly as a result."

Judi White, of the Institute for Cultural Affairs, preferred "a more expansive model" than going to policymakers. She'd do education and create "dialogues" among the general public.

Robert Gilman, editor of *In Context,* wanted a think tank that would provide technical assistance to local groups—assistance that could help *them* have a bigger impact on policymakers and the media.

There was no attempt to synthesize these different formulations, in part because there was no pressing need: Major funding was nowhere in sight. In the various discussions on resources, plenty of suggestions were laid on the table. One person suggested that we "share our rolodexes"—another that "one of us really needs to make this their full-time project"—another that "the think tank could make money building non-toxic houses." You know—those kinds of suggestions.

III. Smile on your brother

Superficially, the Second Thoughts and New Synthesis conferences—and the political subcultures they represented—could not have been more different. And yet, they had more in common than a superficial observer might be led to believe.

Above all, the people at both conferences came from the *same family.* Not just in the sense that they both came from the same generation, but in the sense that they both came out of the late 1960s political left.

The late 60s left had had a traumatic effect on both groups but in different ways.

Among the presenters at the Second Thoughts conference, the effect had been to create a deep suspicion of vision and idealism. At one point Jeff Herf spoke of the "need for a non-utopian politics" in the U.S.

Among the people at the New Synthesis conference, the effect had been to create a deep suspicion of power; especially organized power. During the discussion on the nature of the think tank, one person said this: "Why don't we think of *ourselves—each* of us— as a think tank? We can take responsibility for getting our own ideas to Congresspeople and media and let *them* broadcast them out. . . ." Nobody laughed.

It is now 12 years since Saigon became Ho Chi Minh City. Is it too much to expect that these two wounded fragments of the Vietnam generation will some day—before they reach senility— discover that they need each other's strengths, and try to initiate some kind of dialogue?

To some extent, they've already begun seeking each other out. Some of the New Synthesis types are discovering some of the Second Thoughters' books—e.g., Julius Lester's *All Is Well* (1976), in which the former civil rights spokesman discusses his growth through Marxism to a "spiritually aware" politics. In the Second Thoughters' favorite magazine, *The New Republic,* Charles Paul Freund recently wrote, "If the New Age can dump its loonies, a political move is coming" (Oct. 19)—the first time The *New Republic* had acknowledged a political dimension to the "New Age."

Another reason the two groups might start talking to each other is they share the same sparring partner: the traditional political left. The report on the U.S. Green conference in the July 29 *U.S. Guardian* was every bit as malicious as the report on the Second Thoughts conference in the Nov. 2 *Nation.*

But the best argument in favor of a future dialogue between the two groups may be the argument of necessity. The ex-radicals have all kinds of insights into the "right relationship" between power and innocence. The New Agers have preserved the decentralist/globally responsible vision that animated the social change movement in its pre-Horowitz, pre-Weatherman, pre-guilt-tripping phase. And it is only by overcoming its fears—of vision *and* of power—that any fragment of the Vietnam generation can finally learn to express its vision in a politically powerful way.

2   The Democrats Won't Save Us

September 1988

For much of the Democratic National Convention, held in Atlanta June 18-21, I felt sick. There was a pain in my side, and it hurt so much it made me dizzy.

I didn't understand the source of the pain. But I had a clue. For my whole adult life I'd thought of myself as an outsider. I thought significant social change could only happen outside the two-party system, and I carried around a very satisfying picture of the two major parties as hypocritical, racist, sexist, mean-spirited, etc. Now here I was at my first convention and I had to admit that the scene was very different from what I expected.

I'd thought that only social change groups fostered real inclusiveness and diversity, but the Democratic convention was more diverse than any social change group I'd ever been part of. I'd thought that only spiritual or humanistic-psychology groups were capable of establishing environments of real sharing, but the quality of listening in some of the state delegate caucuses matched anything I'd been exposed to in 25 years of Searching.

How could I have been such a fool, I thought, through my pain.

World-weary press. Some of it was clearly my doing. But some of it was the media's doing. They tell you so little. Even in 1988, even at Atlanta, the vast majority of the 15,000 reporters in attendance weren't doing their jobs.

The vast majority of them hung out all day at the Georgia World Congress Center, a mammoth sterile warehouse of a building next to the Omni (where the televised, evening sessions were held). All day long, while dozens of caucuses and receptions were taking place around town, you could see them at the Center, eating the free food, reading the occasional press release and engaging in cynical banter. Dave Barry of the *Miami Herald* had the courage to joke about it: "The giant press facility has become a very grim place indeed, with journalists gazing glumly at vast expanses of press releases... Things finally got so bad that some members of the press, in desperation, resorted to ACTUALLY LEAVING THE PRESS FACILITY..."

Because most reporters failed to do their legwork, the Democratic convention was not how it seemed:

• It seemed choreographed. In fact, it was incredibly vibrant.

• Dukakis seemed conventional, Jackson seemed exciting. In fact, Dukakis could spearhead the first major Democratic departure from New Deal ideology. And Jackson is in most ways a very conventional liberal Democrat.

• The basic division in the Democratic party seemed to be between pragmatists and change agents. In fact, three major factions are competing for supremacy. And all three factions share the same basic assumptions. And none of those assumptions are particularly uplifting.

I. Choreographed?

Everyone said the convention was timid and choreographed—everyone from the *Washington Post* to the *Northern Sun News* (Minneapolis's alternative monthly). The parts on TV *were* choreographed. But if you attended the state delegate caucuses, the interest-group caucuses and the receptions, which began at eight in the morning and continued full-blast until just before "prime time," you'd have known the convention was brimming with passionate life.

The platform debate in the Omni—on tax policy, no first use (of nuclear weapons), and Palestinian statehood—was pompous and superficial. And the delegates knew it. They "voted with their mouths and feet" by talking loudly and running around throughout the proceedings.

But if you'd attended the Women's Caucus earlier that day— and over 800 delegates did (out of approx. 4,000)—you'd have been treated to an electric debate on all three issues. *And anyone could have gone up to the microphone and participated.*

That debate saw the bravest single performance of the convention. Madeleine Albright and other Dukakis "heavies" were weighing in with arguments against no first use, and Claire Greensfelder, Bay Area peace activist, was trying to refute them. Bella Abzug—chair of the session and bullish as ever—began deriding Greensfelder for her lack of expertise (a devastating charge in a roomful of self-consciously "professional" women). But Greensfelder refused to back down: "I don't think I need to be an expert to be up there. . . . All I can say is we shouldn't necessarily listen to the experts whether they're men *or* women, but listen within—to ourselves. . . ."

If the Women's Caucus was electric and bruising, the Gay and Lesbian Caucus was forever gentle. Evenly divided between Dukakis and Jackson delegates, whenever passions ran too high someone would tell a joke, or someone who fundamentally disagreed with you would say, "I think that's a good point, and it's well-taken."

The most disappointing interest-group gathering was the Peace Caucus. The Monday session was advertised as a debate on no first use, and over 200 delegates showed up. But there was no audience participation and no real debate. Superficial arguments were presented with rhetorical flourishes by a galaxy of "stars" (Congresspeople, organizational leaders, etc.), most of whom didn't even stay in the room but simply came in to have their say and then went out again. We didn't even get to ask questions of the "stars." Is the peace movement so eager to achieve mainstream respectability that it's selling its soul?

The mainstream press enjoyed bashing the Democratic delegates—pointing out how they were richer than the general public, better educated, more "permissive," etc. The alternative movement did the same thing in its own way. "We Need a People's Party, Not a Businessmen's Convention," read one protester's sign outside the Omni.

Most of the Democratic delegates *were* well-off (55% had household incomes of $50,000 or more); most of them *were* well-educated (46% had been to graduate school). But those were hardly the most important things about them.

For example: Twenty-seven percent of the delegates were non-white, 49% female, 48% under 45 and 33% divorced or widowed or single. I wouldn't be surprised if this was the most demographically balanced convention of *any* political party—mainstream or "oppositional"—in American history.

The Jesse Jackson hospitality room was on the 10th floor of the posh Marriott Marquis Hotel. You could go up there and see a steady stream of black people, from every walk of life, peering out at the atrium and listening to the jazz pianist and sampling the exquisite salad. The sense of accomplishment and quiet pride in that room could have raised the Titanic.

Waiting for the New York delegation to come to order one morning, I was deeply moved by the casual ambience—so different from what you saw of the delegates on TV. Fewer than half the men were in suits and ties, and message T-shirts were everywhere ("Win Jesse Win"; "Palestinian Statehood Now"). There were blacks with gold pendants and blue jeans, sleepy-looking women with hip-hugging dresses. Everyone seemed to be talking at once, and their voices seemed to be coming from a deep place. They called out to and touched each other with ease.

Perhaps because it was smaller, the Louisiana delegate caucus maintained an easy intimacy and camaraderie even after it got down to business. Two of the youngest delegates were asked to get up and say something about the "youth movement" they were hoping to get going among Louisiana Democrats. One was male, one was female; both of them were black. They got a standing ovation, and some of the people standing up for them were some of the same kinds of people that chased civil rights workers' cars down back country roads 25 years ago. The young man took the microphone and everybody laughed and hooted: "Chauvinist!" He kept his poise and his sense of humor. The young woman spoke next and said, "I allowed him to speak first 'cause I initiated all this...." More laughter, more cheers.

II. "We are the future!"

But for all the good human connecting, for all the passion and caring, it wasn't enough. Something was still missing. My side still hurt.

On the second day of the convention I made my way to the empty parking lot outside the convention facilities. The parking lot was the sanctioned staging area for protest demonstrations, and Dr. Leonora B. Fulani and the New Alliance Party were out in force (Fulani, a 38-year-old black activist, is the Alliance's candidate for president).

As I arrived, a pick-up truck turned into the parking lot, then pulled out again, and the sparse crowd of protesters began shouting, "We beat back the Klan!" Speaker after speaker tried to tell people that the Klan and the police and the Democratic party were just different aspects of the same rotten system. One of Fulani's lieutenants shouted into the microphone, "This is a fascist state!"

A bevy of protesters displayed an enormous sign: "No Business as Usual—No Matter What It Takes."

I felt badly for the majority of the protesters—mostly 15-to 20-year olds whose emotions were being manipulated by the New Alliance organizers for their own ends. Then I realized with a start that I was just as alienated—and just as credulous—when I was that age. My alienation and credulity didn't end until long after I'd walked away from my career and emigrated to Canada, ostensibly to protest the war, really to punish myself for being middle-class.

It took me 11 years to get back to the U.S. How many of these kids' lives would be equally twisted, I wondered, by the likes of the New Alliance Party?

A chant came up from the crowd: "Not the bomb, *we're* the future! Not the bomb, *we're* the future!"

III. The candidates

The mainstream press almost unanimously agrees with Dukakis's now-famous assertion that the 1988 election—and, by extension, Dukakis himself—"is about competence, not ideology." Even the left press agrees, though it's less happy about the situation.

The press couldn't be more wrong. Dukakis is the first Democratic nominee in my lifetime that just might rewrite traditional Democratic ideology.

For the last 15 years or so—ever since the 1974 (post-Watergate) election—a new breed of governor has been coming to power across the U.S. Economically sophisticated, these "new" governors are less interested in rebuilding our industrial base than in moving us on to a post-industrial, communications-era economy. Socially committed, they're less interested in proposing big government/New Deal solutions to our social problems than in using government as a kind of facilitator.

They might not build much housing for the poor—but they'd help get needed capital to community development organizations and neighborhood banks and housing co-ops in poor areas.

On the Democratic side, the most prominent and successful of these "new governors" are Jim Blanchard of Michigan, who addressed the convention; Bill Clinton of Arkansas, who nominated Dukakis; and Dukakis himself.

The hot book on the new governors is David Osborne's *Laboratories of Democracy,* 1988. Osborne concludes that the new governors offer the glimmerings of a "new paradigm" (his term). "To boil it down to a slogan, if the thesis was government as solution [McGovernism] and the antithesis was government as problem [Reaganism], the synthesis is government as partner....

"Traditional liberals in Massachusetts attack Dukakis for not raising welfare benefits to the poverty line. Dukakis responds that such a move would destroy incentives to work, and that the better path is more investment in education, training, job placement, and low-income housing. Does this put Dukakis to the left or right of his critics? The answer is that it puts him within a different paradigm."

Just as the mainstream and alternative press sees Dukakis as he'd like to be seen (as a moderate), so does the press see Jackson as *he'd* like to be seen—as the radical, the change agent, the treeshaker. But if you paid close attention to his nominating speech, and his proposed platform planks, and the attitudes of his delegates, chances are you'd have a different view. For all his moving words, at the 1988 convention Jackson emerged as a very conventional big government politician.

In his minority report to the Democratic platform, Jackson called for doubling the amount of federal money spent on education—without bothering to say how the money should be used, or suggesting any changes in the *ways* we educate our children!

Similarly, he proposed a government-run national health program—without once mentioning the need to incorporate holistic or preventive approaches into the program.

He proposed adopting a policy of "no first use" of nuclear weapons—without saying how we would help defend Europe if the Soviet Union invaded. Would we beef up our conventional forces (far more expensive than nukes) to deal with this possibility? Would we change over to some kind of "alternative" or nonviolent military strategy? If you want to be a change agent, you can't just say "no" on defense.

IV. Three factions, one worldview

Because the media took what the candidates were saying about themselves at face value, they saw the convention as a battle between pragmatists and change agents. But if you hung out at the convention and trusted your eyes and ears, you'd have concluded that there were three major factions competing for supremacy. Call them "left-liberals," "reform-liberals" and "moderates."

The left-liberals' key word is *fairness* or *compassion.* In 1980, their presidential candidate was Ted Kennedy; in 1984, Jesse Jackson and Walter Mondale. The real significance of the 1988 Democratic campaign may be that, through it, Jackson took unchallenged control of this faction of the party and moved it further to the left.

The reform-liberals' key word is *management* or *innovation.* In 1980 their presidential candidate was Jerry Brown; in 1984, Gary Hart. In 1988, the reform-liberals experienced (some might say, suffered) a sea-change. They were no longer outsiders challenging the left-liberal and moderate establishments. They had displaced the left-liberals as part of the establishment.

The moderates' key word is *strength*—as in "military strength." In 1980 (but not 1976) their candidate was Jimmy Carter; in 1984, John Glenn. In 1988, Lloyd Bentsen is their man.

All three factions liked to speak of "balance." It might have been the second most frequently used word (after "family"). The media was impressed by the "balance" the Democrats had been able to achieve between and among their various groups.

In his brilliant new book, *Out of Weakness* (1988), political philosopher Andrew Schmookler says, "It is balance that the warrior spirit within us has lacked." But there was something not satisfying about the "balance" at the Democratic convention; something not quite right.

The reason is simple. All three factions are unbalanced in the *same way*. All are based on the *same assumptions*. To be unkind, all are based on Schmookler's "warrior spirit within us." Just think:

• All assume that economic growth should continue forever—despite the limited carrying capacity of the Earth.

• All assume we should maintain an overly commercialized society in which getting and spending—not being and experiencing—is the be-all and end-all.

• All assume we are superior to animals and other life-forms and should continue to dominate them for our own short-term benefit.

• All assume that the full-employment economy (i.e., distributing income via "jobs") should continue indefinitely—even though many of the jobs we're paid for *now* could disappear without a trace, and much of the work we're not paid for (like community organizing and raising our kids) is crucial.

• All assume our own citizens' *wants* are more pressing than the rest of the world's *needs*.

• All assume that simpler lifestyles, gentler on the Earth, leaving us much more time for learning and sharing and growing, can hardly be a political goal.

V. A longing

Those were some assumptions shared by the Democrats in Atlanta. But there were other assumptions—genuinely "balancing" assumptions—that came out here and there.

I think of the South Carolina delegate who urged patience with the Democratic party because "under the surface" it was "spiritually evolving."

I think of the New York delegate—hard at work in Dukakis's trailer—convinced of the need to develop empathy for the Earth.

I think of the Georgia delegate who claimed to be looking for the "next step" beyond feminism and environmentalism.

I think of Bruce Babbitt turning to a small select audience with a pained look in his eye, and saying: As the American system ripples across Asia and even the Soviet Union, do we have the capacity to look ourselves in the mirror and ask, What kind of an example are we setting?

Most of all I think of all the receptions and parties I went to where people would turn to me and say things like, "What are you doing here? This isn't important," or, "So how much longer do you think we can keep it all going?," or, "This is crazy, isn't it?"

Beneath the surface of the convention, then, besides the dominant assumptions of the three major factions were some very contrary assumptions. Behind many of the contrary assumptions was a longing for such values as simplicity, ecological wisdom, global responsibility, and a focus on the long-term future.

Can such values—call them Green or New Age values—be brought in to the Democratic party in a substantial way? For all that I was impressed with the intelligence and energy and dedication of party activists; for all that I'd *like* to say "yes" and finally feel part of the mainstream and get rid of this pain in my side; the truth is that I can't see it happening anytime soon.

The reason is not that the Democratic party establishment is hostile to such values. It would be, but if we got far enough to arouse their hostility we'd have already won two-thirds of the battle. The reason is deeper and sadder. The vast majority of Democrats have personally bought into the assumptions of the three major factions.

You could see it in the passive way most Democrats accepted the direction of the Dukakis and Jackson floor leaders on every issue.

You could hear it in the nominating speeches for Jackson and Dukakis, with their inescapable underlying theme: "He'll save us."

You could see it in the way the Democrats stared at Hollywood stars such as Morgan Fairchild and Ed Begley, Jr., when they came into the room. You could tell they wanted that same status and power and privilege for themselves.

The Democrats need to add a Green or New Age leg to the three-legged (three-factioned) table that they've been setting for the American people. Eventually, perhaps, they will. And then they'll have a chance to bring this society into real balance. But first they're going to have to develop the self-awareness and self-esteem (some dare call it spiritual confidence) needed to pay close attention to what's in their hearts—and to share those deeper messages in a public and political way.

For the foreseeable future it remains with us, innovators and experimenters and pioneers, to give shape and substance to that fourth "leg." And tens of thousands of us are doing that every day, in groups as courageous and varied as The Association for Humanistic Psychology, Greenpeace, Center for Innovative Diplomacy, Cultural Survival, Elmwood Institute, Co-op America, Renew America, People for the Ethical Treatment of Animals....

For the foreseeable future I am just going to have to continue to live with that pain in my side. And we are all going to have to continue to live with the pain of knowing how wide is the gap between what we are as a society and what we could and should be.

3   Last Chance Saloon

June 1987

For 25 years I've tried to build an organization that could put my values—call them the values of the idealistic fragment of the Sixties generation—into the mainstream political debate. I've been a civil rights worker, a campus president of SDS, a founder of the Toronto Anti-Draft Programme, a founder of the New World Alliance...the list goes on and on.

Now I'm in my 40s, and when I can't sleep I catch myself wondering: What good did it do, really?

In many professions, those of us who were forever changed by the civil rights movement and the Vietnam war have begun to change things for the better. In politics, though, it's a different story. The Democrats and Republicans seem as unchangeable as ever. We don't even have an organization like Common Cause or Moral Majority to call our own.

What's the problem? Why haven't we been able to launch a permanent, competent organization that reflects our values? Will we ever? To provide some answers to those questions, I flew out to the second national U.S. Green gathering June 21-25 at the University of Oregon campus in Eugene, Oregon.

For five years, the U.S. Greens had been trying to launch a permanent, competent political organization, and I was one of only five people who'd been to all three of the Greens' national meetings. I knew that quite a few Greens felt—as I did—that their group represented our generation's last chance to affect the mainstream political debate. Walking slowly across campus one night, one of them told me that being in the Green movement now was akin to sitting in the Last Chance Saloon. We might never get another.

•   •   •

If you stood in the middle of the University of Oregon campus and watched the Greens arrive, with their T-shirts and blue jeans and casual manner, you might have thought you were seeing the students arrive. But if you walked closer you'd have seen some gray in their hair.

The average age of the Greens at the gathering was just over 40. Fewer than 10% of them were under 30—an ironic twist on the old Sixties slogan, "Don't trust anyone over 30."

But if they were middle aged, they were hardly settled down. Only two out of seven were married—as compared to nearly two out of three for the country as a whole. Remarkably, another two out of seven were divorced and had never remarried—as compared to only 7% for the country as a whole.

Many of them had exchanged some of their income-earning power for "meaningful" jobs or simple lifestyles. Just consider: About two-thirds of them had spent some time in graduate school. But their median household income was under $25,000 a year! The average household income for people with five years of college is over $58,000 a year now.

All these statistics suggest that the Greens gathered in Eugene had been deeply influenced by the idealistic values of the Sixties. A second reading suggests that they might have been not just shaped by the Sixties, but wounded by them, too. Both the strengths and the wounds would become apparent during the gathering.

I. A stiff drink

Before the main event, there was a mini-Interregional Committee (IC) meeting that revealed a lot about the internal workings of the organization.

The IC is basically the "people's congress" of the Greens. It consists of delegates from the regional Green groups. The ICs are famous for their storminess and lack of clarity, and this one proved to be no exception, though I was told it wasn't nearly as frustrating as some.

For hours and hours, in a long, narrow room, the delegates wrangled over structure and bylaws. At one point a rather elegant-looking structure was discussed at length, and some delegates went away thinking it had been agreed to in principle; others were adamant that it had not been.

In addition, a "clearinghouse coordinator"—in effect, an executive director—was chosen to replace the outgoing coordinator,

Dee Berry. On the first day of the IC meeting, the Search Committee described its two leading candidates, both of them gentle and sensitive men. But it was clear from the body language that the Search Committee wasn't entirely happy with either.

Both candidates had led "a very Green life," as one Committee member put it. But both lacked qualities that Greens found very difficult, even embarrassing, to put into words. "The necessary pizzazz," is how one Committee member eventually blurted it out.

The next day the Committee stunned the IC by announcing it had decided to recommend neither of its finalists, but, instead, a third person—Mindy Lorenz, a vigorous and articulate Green activist from Los Angeles. Lorenz accepted the position contingent on the IC's willingness to pay her a full-time salary and move the clearinghouse from Kansas City to Eugene (the IC had located the clearinghouse in the Midwest as a way of telling Middle America, "We're with you").

With minimal discussion, the Search Committee's recommendation was consensed upon—as were Lorenz's conditions—and everyone cheered wildly.

I enjoyed the IC's enthusiasm. But I couldn't help noticing that during the discussion nobody asked Lorenz to describe her sense of what the priorities of the clearinghouse should be. And nobody asked an even more obvious question: Since we could barely pay Dee Berry $200 a month, how were we going to pay Lorenz many times that?

Few people questioned the wisdom of moving the clearinghouse from Kansas City to Eugene—a pretty, out-of-the-way college town that happens to be one of the 10 whitest cities (of over 100,000 inhabitants) in the country.

Already a couple of local chapters are up in arms over the Search Committee's process and the IC's decision. One of their objections: Who knows how many other good people would have applied for the job, had they known the clearinghouse could be moved to a place like Eugene?

And while we're on the subject of sins of omission: Nobody told the two finalists what was going on until it was all over. Their barely-suppressed bitterness and hurt was a constant presence for the rest of the gathering. It isn't always pretty at the Last Chance Saloon.

It was a relief and a delight to go from the IC meeting to the lawn outside the Student Union building where the opening speeches were about to begin.

About 250 people were spread out along the lawn, on the steps, under the trees. I hung out among them, listening to the speeches and remembering why I believed in Green politics.

We need to break away from politics as protest, shouted John Rensenbrink, the gray-haired political science professor who coordinates the Greens' platform-writing process. We've got to redefine political struggle as the act of taking responsibility for our lives—and our communities. And in the process we've got to totally redefine such ancient political goals as "power" and "victory."

Charles Betz, from the Left Greens, argued for a consistently "anti-capitalist," consistently "oppositional" politics. His concepts came across as wooden and over-abstract, as if they'd all come out of musty texts and not from his experience of the world.

Equally one-dimensional was Joseph Sisto, a consultant to some of the Fortune 500 companies. He informed us that if we demonstrated "love and understanding" when dealing with corporate leaders and political parties, we'd almost surely be successful.

Danny Moses' closing speech set the tone for the best of the gathering. Moses, an editor at Sierra Club Books, presented us with a jazz-like sequence of some of the wonderful and horrible things going on in the world.

He had high praise for Lois Gibbs's Citizens Clearinghouse for Hazardous Wastes, with its "4,600 grassroots groups"; he delivered a devastating (but rhetoric-free) critique of genetic engineering. And he ended with Bob Marley's great plea, "Won't you help to sing/these songs of freedom." Every Green was ready.

II. Groping forward

Our first two days were spent largely in "working groups." The Green gathering had been called primarily to write the first draft of the Greens' political platform, and 19 working groups were set up to draft each of the sections of the platform.

I chose to take part in the "strategy" group, in part because it was the largest and contained many of the Greens' heavy hitters. The facilitator, Sam Kaner, made his living helping everyone from corporations to social change groups develop consensus decision-making processes. He was a big bear of a man with just the blend of authoritativeness and gentleness that could keep the strategy group from tearing itself apart.

He had his work cut out for him. After a couple of hours it was clear we had very different visions of the future—or at least, very different ways of expressing them.

Brian Tokar, author of a book explaining Green politics from an eco-anarchist point of view, said our movement's task was to empower communities. George Katsiaficas, author of a book on the global student movement circa 1968, wanted a more pressingly global focus.

Genevieve Marcus, a former co-candidate for governor of California (she'd run with her husband), tried to put things as simply as possible by saying our task was to create a "healthy, sustainable world." Carl Boggs, author of a book on contemporary radical political movements, worried that many Greens' visions were too simplistic. He especially lamented the lack of economic-class analyses.

No one could have figured out what was really being said in the room—no one could have picked up on all the subtle thrusts and parries (New Left vs. New Age, anarchist vs. socialist, etc.)—without having spent at least three years in the alternative political wars. An IQ of 130 or more would have helped, too.

We were stumbling toward a point where we could begin to discuss strategy in some detail—but there wasn't time. So before the meeting ended we scheduled four "mini-working groups" for anyone who wanted to continue meeting later that day. Once again, as always, those who were most willing to give up their free time— those who were most willing to ignore their personal needs and attend more meetings than anyone else—would end up having the most say.

The mini-working groups were lively two-and three-hour affairs held under the trees. And the next day we came in rarin' to discuss all kinds of strategic possibilities for the Green movement.

We weren't willing to vote on them (that would have been too "adversarial"), but we did take a "straw poll," which felt like voting to me. The top three: "No elections on any level without first networking among like-minded groups"; "[Support] Green information transfer"; "Focus on local presence."

Significantly, none of the 30-plus proposals received a majority of "No" votes (other possibilities included "High priority," "Low priority" and "Further discussion needed"). So as several people pointed out, the results could have been interpreted not as enshrining the top 3-5 proposals, but as encouraging and empowering virtually everyone to do what they felt needed to be done.

Unfortunately, that was not to be. That kind of suggestion (coming mostly from women) was routinely ignored, and the final strategy document was full of explicit and implicit "shoulds" and "shouldn'ts."

III. Two big divisions

The division between "political Greens" and "spiritual Greens" that some detected at the first Green gathering was nowhere to be found at Eugene. Some of the most constructive statements on Green spirituality were made by members of the Left Green Network, the left-wing caucus within the Greens; and some of the most politically sophisticated analyses came from post-socialist and "New Age" Greens.

A couple of big differences of opinion did surface at Eugene, however. One had to do with whether our problems are due to "capitalism" or "industrialism."

At the hugely successful "Economics Forum," several Greens made the case for treating capitalism as prime. They argued that capitalism—"a global system increasingly seeking control over all the planet's markets and resources"—is the dominant force in the world, and if we failed to challenge it head-on we'd never be able to build a just society. In their view, the industrial system is a product of capitalism.

Other Greens at the Economics Forum argued that industrialism is a broader concept than capitalism. In their view, both modern capitalism and modern socialism are biased in favor of the industrial system (giantism, hierarchy, economic growth, technological drivenness, etc.)—though neither needs to be.

The "industrialism" position has intriguing post-socialist implications. Lorna Salzman, from New York City, put her finger on one when she argued that empowering people and communities—not redistributing wealth—should be first on our agenda. Mitch Chanelis, from Boston, identified another when he drew a crucial distinction not between capitalism and socialism but between "monopoly capital" and "free enterprise."

The latter is what we want, he said—fair competition among many different kinds of small and medium-sized producers. Whether we call it true capitalism, human-scale socialism or some third thing makes little difference.

The other big division at Eugene was between those who wanted to focus strictly on local politics (at least for now) and those who wanted to focus on national politics—as well as local politics—as soon as possible.

On the surface, it's amazing that anyone would object to a national political effort. The time is ripe. Even *Time Magazine*, even the big corporations, are beginning to admit that the planet is in danger.

At Eugene, Dee Berry made a moving plea for "multi-level movement building," and Adriane Carr, from Canada, pointed out that her country's fledgling national Green party inspired the Canadian media to pay attention to the Green message.

But many objections were raised. Some feared an early focus on national work would keep us from ever creating a local presence. "The strength of the Greens is that we encourage and even require activists to work at the local level," said Larry Martin, from the Potomac Valley bioregion.

Other Greens said we didn't have the resources to run for national office. Still others said we'd be tempted to trim our sails to public opinion even before we raised them.

Some of the Greens' international guests got caught up—almost despite themselves—in the national/local debates, they were that intense. Wilhelm Knabe, a tall and silver-haired Green member of the West German *Bundestag,* told a plenary session that he could understand our reluctance to form a national party. But consider the international importance of the U.S., he pleaded; consider the urgency of the situation of the planet. Imagine the difference that just a decent Environmental Protection Agency could make....

IV. Contact high

On the second-to-last day of the gathering, representatives of each of the 19 working groups stood up before all 250 of us and summarized their policy statements and asked for feedback. But there wasn't time to respond in any depth—and a few people seemed to hog the microphones. Basically we just had to passively sit there.

At any other conference we might have rebelled. But all of us knew we were sitting in the Last Chance Saloon—all of us sensed that if we weren't able to come out of this gathering with a draft document (and a reputation for civility), we'd probably never again have a chance to build a political organization based on our ideals.

So we all sat there politely, listening to the presentations, daydreaming, taking roundabout trips to the water fountain. . . . When a professor from the University of Wisconsin started going on and on about land use policy, I really thought I'd fall asleep.

Suddenly there was commotion at the door, shouting, electricity in the air! Thirty people burst into the auditorium—mostly male teen-agers with long hair and headbands. They were carrying a 24-foot-long imitation marijuana cigarette made of canvas and hay—the spitting image of the real thing. And they were chanting, "We smoke pot and we like it a lot! We smoke pot and we like it a lot!"

That woke us up in a hurry. Some of us shouted back, some of us felt panicky, some of us got really mad. Ironically, many of us had spoken up for direct action during the course of the conference. But we'd never guess that anyone would practice direct action *on us,* and it was clear that it made most of us just as uncomfortable as it did The Establishment.

The unruly teen-agers—most of them participants in a big "National Smoke-In" held in Eugene that weekend—were armed with a message. You guys are selling your generation out, they shouted. All you people look like you smoke dope, and here you are making demands for everybody but yourselves. Your platform has got to demand HEMP RIGHTS—legalization of marijuana!

The kids had hit a nerve. Besides fear and hostility, I detected a kind of embarrassed shock of recognition. Those kids could have been us 20 years ago. And in some ways they were right. . . .

For a couple of minutes, it looked like our whole session would have to adjourn. But, miraculously, our chief facilitator, Caroline Estes, managed to restore order—by including the direct-actionists into our process. They were invited to stay and listen to our speakers. They were invited to send a spokesperson up to address us (for five minutes). And they were invited to attend our picnic afterwards.

Their speaker, a long-time activist for "hemp rights," was forceful and factual—though probably most of us still balked at putting legalization of marijuana into our platform. (We knew what the media would do with that one.) And they did come to our picnic, to which they made a couple of unique contributions.

V. Platform-to-be

Our last day was even more formal and constrained—and we were just as well-behaved. Reps from each of the working groups read their final policy statements and asked the delegates to "consense" to parts or all of them. (Delegates could also choose to "block consensus" or to "stand aside.")

The statements—along with the degree of support for each— would be printed in a special edition of the Green newsletter; gone over assiduously by the local Green groups; and finalized at the Greens' next gathering, in Estes Park, Colo., 1990.

Remarkably, no statement was blocked by more than about 10% of the delegates. No statement was even "stood aside for" by more than about 20% of the delegates.

The statements were of uneven quality and reflected many different political tendencies within the Green orbit.

Some managed to summarize, credibly and succinctly, just what made the Greens different—and worth watching. The Greens' emphasis on ecological wisdom, as distinct from economic growth, was nowhere better expressed than in the "forests" statement: "The principle that forests have an intrinsic value in and of themselves, over and above their economic value, is the foundation of the Green program for forestry."

Their emphasis on personal and social responsibility—not just social responsibility, as per most movement groups (and the West German Greens)—came out in the "ecofeminist" statement. On the one hand, it called for "proportional representation of gender and race." On the other hand, it said this: "Men and women need to take responsibility for their own participatory style and emotional process."

Traditional capitalism *and* traditional socialism call for top-down, centralized solutions to our problems. At their best, the Greens call for solutions that empower people, communities and regions. The "food" statement got it right, calling for "an ecologically based sustainable agriculture system that moves as rapidly as possible towards regional/bioregional self-reliance." Similarly, the "energy" statement speaks of "ultimately render[ing] individuals and communities energy self-sufficient."

Both "economics" statements came out against such underrecognized (by Democrats and Republicans) social ills as "massive overconsumption of products and resources," "addictive consumerism," and our "perpetual growth imperative." And both sought to promote everything from "simpler, self-reliant lifestyles" to "an equitable distribution of basic goods and services." One was rather socialist in its approach, the other was a bit more entrepreneurial, going so far as to speak of our "loss of personal...initiative" in the corporate-dominated present.

There were some problems with the Greens' draft document. There was some mind-numbing rhetoric (e.g., "Through education we engender and, at the same time, become products of social and pedagogical relations"). Sometimes people wrote their pet explanations into the document, as if they were writing a thesis: "Greens need to understand Patriarchy as the root cause of our current oppressive structures throughout the world."

Too much of the text was abstract, philosophical. Like the 1988 Democratic platform, it was long on values and code words, short on real world examples. Some key subjects, such as transportation and foreign policy, were left out entirely!

But on the whole, the document is a major achievement. No U.S. political platform comes as close to embodying the ideals of the alternative movements of the Sixties, Seventies and Eighties. And no platform includes anything like the Greens' statement on spirituality.

VI. Thinking it through

There were plenty of reasons for Greens to celebrate their achievements at Eugene, and in three long evaluation sessions following the gathering about 60 exhausted but enthusiastic participants did just that.

Irene Diamond, a well-known ecofeminist, praised the quality of the dialogue in some of the working groups. Brian Tokar praised the "strength and clarity" of the policy statements. Marcia Dickinson, from Kansas City, couldn't believe how close to consensus we were on so many statements.

Danny Moses may have put his finger on the most significant positive achievement of the gathering when he said, "There's been the achievement of a kind of psychological solidarity; a feeling of bonding with each other in a way that is critical to the work we want to do together. The Green movement is more present, now, because of this....

"The feeling takes me back to the times I cherish and the work we did in the early 60s in the civil rights movement, which was an 'inspirited' movement—one in which spirit and analysis worked hand in hand to produce great results."

Although the participants were right to congratulate themselves on many things, they were also right to look at some other things with a cooler eye.

Women/men. Virtually everyone agreed that this was one of the few conferences they'd been to where women were heard— not just listened to—by men. In part that was due to the Last Chance Saloon phenomenon—everyone was on their best behavior. In part also it was due to the sensitivity of the facilitators. For example, at the strategy working group Kaner said he'd try not to let "yang energy" dominate the room.

But behind the scenes, all was not bliss. According to my sources, many women discussed among themselves how unhappy many of the Green men seemed to be. Some men concluded that many of the Green women were 20 pounds overweight, and fretted about "what that meant."

Some women felt that they—and their perspectives—were largely shut out. At one evaluation, Anne Conway, from Los Angeles, said she felt many men cared more about being heard than about participating in a dialogue. She could tell, she said, because there was "no eye contact" from many of them. She wanted "compassion" to be added to the list of key Green values.

One of the bravest evaluations—and to my mind one of the truest—came from Dee Berry. She said what was missing in our process was not the "female" but the "positive male."

She said we'd spent much of the gathering talking and talking, going around and around. She said our movement desperately needed positive male energy—the moving forward, the making rules we could all follow.

We didn't allow the men at the gathering to be positive males, she said. We forced them to act like women. And some acted like negative (aggressive) males and others acted like women. But we ignored the positive male just like we ignored the youth, the Native Americans, and so much more.

Guilt. The "social justice" working group produced a strongly worded statement on such diverse topics as advertising, population control, abortion, heterosexism, dying, and anti-racism. Much of it is excellent. However, parts of it are riddled with traces of guilt and self-contempt.

Nothing good is said about men in the section on (heterosexual) men—nothing; and if you believe the text, it's a wonder we're able to get up in the morning.

The anti-racism section doesn't say what's perfectly obvious out on the street—that the various races in this country desperately need to learn about each other and from each other. It doesn't speak of mutual learning at all. Instead, it's all one-way (and all in the unctuous tones of political correctness): "We especially challenge people of European ancestry to accept their responsibility to confront racism. . . . We actively seek [the] leadership and wisdom of ["people of color"]. . . ."

These weren't just quirks of the social justice working group. Time after time, when racial issues came up at the gathering, it was as if people retreated into a politically correct shell. Our words were "correct" but our hearts and minds were God-knows-where.

For example, I attended the Native American session out on the lawn, and it was the only session I attended at the entire gathering where not one critical question was asked. Guy Chichester, from Vermont, explained it to me this way: "We were there to listen!" But my response was, Were "we" there at all? It was incredible—all these white people (not a few of them Jews whose ancestors had fled from the pogroms) being held responsible for the sins of the Puritans, for Chrissake, and just *sitting* there silently, staring down at the ground.

For hundreds of years, most whites saw people of color as symbols of darkness and evil. Now, apparently, many of us oh-so-well-meaning white people see them as symbols of our *own* darkness, our *own* evil. How long will it be before we begin to see them as just people?

To tell when that begins to happen in the Greens, watch for two things. Their social justice statement will address real problems in the black and Hispanic communities. And their interracial dialogues will be characterized by a sharing of politically uncensored thoughts and feelings—on all sides.

Money. There was another subject that caused a kind of fog to descend on the gathering. That was the whole subject of money and fund-raising.

It wasn't as if we didn't know how important the subject was. At the IC meeting, Dee Berry gave a report that made it clear that—despite her willingness to work for $100-200 a month—the Green clearinghouse was on its last legs financially, with no real help in sight. Jim Richmond, Berry's assistant, put it almost plaintively at one of the evaluations: The clearinghouse might not last long enough to move to Eugene next spring!

It is bizarre—and revealing—that the Greens are having financial problems at all. When the organization tried a membership drive two years ago, it sent a poorly written, poorly designed and poorly printed direct mail package to 5,000 names on the *Utne Reader* mailing list. The response rate was over 6%—about three times what financially successful organizations usually get.

You don't have to be a marketing genius to see that the Greens are sitting on a gold mine. With results like that, an intelligent direct mail campaign could easily bring in 100,000 members (Common Cause and People for the American Way both have over 200,000 members, and neither has the electric appeal of the Greens). At $20 per member, that's $2 million a year. If even one-fifth of them chose to join their local chapters, that's 20,000 new Green activists, campaign workers and direct-actionists. But the IC isn't willing to appropriate any more money for direct mail.

There are many reasons for that—just as there are many reasons why the organization (now five years old) has still not applied for non-profit status from the IRS. But the underlying reason is simple: Many Greens are ambivalent about the very act of fund-raising.

Talk to them at length and you'll hear there's something suspicious about it, something grubby, something vaguely elitist, something too "Washington, D.C." Like the proverbial businessman who developed a better mousetrap, many Greens seem to believe, in their heart of hearts, that if they just develop a better political platform the world will beat a path to their door.

In sensitive 20 year olds, these attitudes are understandable, even endearing. In 40 year olds they're considerably less so. Forty year olds should know that there are only two ways of raising money for an organization—from members or from rich people. And that the former is a lot more in keeping with "Green values," even if it means you've got to learn business and marketing skills (aka "capitalist skills," aka "industrial methods") in the process.

Process. Nobody doubted that the design committee for the gathering did the best it could. I watched one planning group spend three hours on the tiniest details of one plenary meeting (and they'd been up till three a.m. the night before discussing that same meeting). But people's unhappiness with the process was rampant.

Even the facilitators had doubts and criticisms, and after the gathering they were happy to share them with me.

"This particular design—where you had a minimum amount of time together in groups, and a maximum amount of time doing 'right-brain' activities, or at least relaxing and seeing sights—just didn't seem to be appropriate for the task at hand," Caroline Estes said. "People didn't have enough time to think about their policy statements or to get good feedback from the plenaries."

Why the inappropriate design? "We have so many conferences that focus on the left brain, there may have been an over-emphasis here on the other. . . .

"Also, the Greens have rejected a lot of what they consider to be manipulative politics. So they're trying to use the least amount of structure they can get away with, to keep from manipulating people. But I think they're missing the point. The point isn't minimal process, minimal structure; the point is appropriate process, appropriate structure."

Sam Kaner saw a different problem. "The biggest problem I saw in the design of the process was we didn't educate participants to the underlying principles that are necessary in order to do a consensus process.

"Unanimity isn't just the decision rule in consensus; it serves a larger purpose. That purpose is to make sure that every person has participated, full out. And the value of supporting full participation is that it forces a group to come up with interesting, creative, sophisticated solutions. Because the solutions, by definition, have to incorporate a lot of different points of view.

"The designers of the next Green gathering have a major issue to confront. They can set up processes that will force people to make 'either-or' choices on policies and programs. Or they can set up processes that will help people analyze their differences until they reach a new level and can make 'both-and' choices. Choices that take all people's views into account."

VII. The planet is calling

With no money, few members, a national office-to-be in Oregon, no designated leaders or spokespeople, incessant internal squabbling, and a political document that's long on philosophy and short on specifics—how do the Greens expect to get their message across to the American people?

Their ideal is to reach people through their deeds at the local level. But they have a parallel and so far much more successful strategy, unconscious and unacknowledged though it may be. It is a classic American political strategy. It is a media strategy.

That is: They count on the alternative media to wildly exaggerate their importance. And it does.

There were reporters at Eugene from the *L.A. Weekly, Mother Jones, New Age Journal,* Pacific News Service, Pacifica Radio, *Utne Reader, Zeta Magazine,* and many other key alternative outlets. I could have gone to the national NOW conference, I could have gone to the national NAACP conference. But instead, I came to Eugene. Why? For the same reason most of the other reporters came. We wanted the Greens to succeed so much that we couldn't stay away.

Because we share the Greens' hopes and dreams and experience of the world, we find it almost impossible to be "objective" about them. Worse, we find it difficult not to cheer them on, sometimes in ways that border on the unethical.

For example, many alternative periodicals reported the attendance at the 1987 Green gathering to be about 1,500. After all, that's what the organizers said it was. But anyone who used their eyes knew that that was a wildly inflated figure. In fact, registration was around 400, and no more than about 200 other souls poked into our meetings.

Or, for example, many alternative periodicals have reported that the Greens have "more than 200" local chapters. That's what the Greens say—and that's what we want to believe. It sounds so good! But a simple phone call reveals that fewer than 40 local chapters have paid their dues this year.

At Eugene, the temptation to paint a rosy picture was especially great. The bitterness that characterized parts of the first two major Green meetings was nowhere to be seen (neither were most of the antagonists from those meetings), and the worldwide Green movement is growing by leaps and bounds. On the last few days in Eugene there were even some Greens who played the role of "spin doctor," giving interviews to the alternative press in which they put the best "spin" possible on the events that transpired there.

One supportive way of covering the Greens is to buy into their exaggerated claims. Another way is to present, fairly, both the strengths and weaknesses of the organization, and hope that people rally around the strengths and seek to correct the weaknesses.

I think the kinds of things that need to be corrected are clear:

• Money will not simply come to you if you're doing the right thing. A sophisticated fund-raising strategy needs to be put in place ASAP. Its centerpiece should be a massive ongoing membership campaign. No members, no resources, no clout. No members, no resources, and you're just doing "recreational politics," as Boston politician Mel King likes to put it.

• Similarly, the organization needs to get a grip on its overblown Sixties fears of hierarchy, structure and leadership (even while continuing to experiment with new processes and forms). These fears of "Big Daddy," in Rensenbrink's telling phrase, are holding the Greens back a lot more than the capitalist system is holding them back!

• The organization needs to be made appealing to people of color—not to mention businessmen, factory workers and people like our parents (to name three more missing ingredients). That means becoming less like a club for certain personality-types and temperaments...even while *strengthening* some of the practices that make the Greens "inspirited."

All that will be hard. But when all is said and done, I can't believe it won't happen. Too many good people are involved—too many special, caring, dedicated people—for us to not finally launch that "permanent, competent political organization" that will project our values into the mainstream.

True, too many of us may fear power and success. True, too many of us may want to be large frogs in a small Green pond. True, too many of us are still acting out—in our 40s.

But one thing I've learned, in over 25 years in the social change movement, is never to underestimate the power of context. Deep down inside, the Greens know they're sitting in the Last Chance Saloon—and it's not just their own last chance. The planet itself is at stake. And is calling upon us to grow up, already.

4   Buy Our Way to Freedom

November 1986

What is the next step beyond the civil rights movement? Three Saturdays ago, over 200 black people and one white reporter crowded into a beautiful old Baptist church in inner-city D.C. to find out if the "Buy Freedom" campaign is any part of the answer.

Buy Freedom was launched late last year by Tony Brown, a prominent black television journalist (his weekly program, "Tony Brown's Journal," is aired on over 100 PBS stations). Its goal: encourage blacks to spend up to 50% of their income on black businesses. Its rationale: only by keeping much of their money in their own communities, will blacks be able to achieve economic parity with whites.

I. The color of freedom

The crowd drifts in slowly and begins to take its seats. Most of the men come in alone; most of the women come in with other women. It's a largely middle-class crowd, well-dressed and self-possessed, and when Tony Brown begins to speak (one of the 100-plus speeches he'll be giving this year for the Buy Freedom campaign) you could have heard a pin drop.

The civil rights movement has been a gigantic success, he shouts in a staccato, hectoring, verging-on-indignant tone of voice. *You can go into any dress shop you want. Try on new clothes. Move into any white neighborhood. You can fly in their airplanes, stay in their hotels. What is your problem? You can't afford it!* [knowing laughter].

We have won the first phase of the rights revolution; we have won the civil rights phase. Move on to the second phase—the [self-help phase]. Our problem is [no longer] white people; our problem is not having what white people have.

To say Brown's speech was riveting would be an understatement. Imagine Stokely Carmichael with an M.B.A. Imagine Farrakhan without the dark side.

Nobody's going to share power with you [willingly]. Nobody gave the Jews power. They used to have a sign on the beach down in Miami, "No Jews and dogs allowed." The Jews bought the beach [startled laughter]. *You can't find any anti-Semitism down there any more. They took care of anti-Semitism the same way we're going to have to take care of racism—[through] economics....*

Again and again, Brown says that what he is advocating is not an economic boycott and is not anti-white. He wants blacks to stop thinking of themselves as victims and to start thinking of themselves the way all other Americans think of themselves—as producers and consumers.

Ladies and gentlemen, we are not poor, and we are not a minority. We are a cultural-economic market that has been trained to behave as a poor minority. There are more blacks in America than Canadians in Canada, and as many blacks in America as Poles in Poland. Last year we earned in excess of $200 billion. We spent in excess of $180 billion....

Today we are 11% of the population. We buy 18% of the barbeque, 20% of the rice, 26% of the Cadillac cars. 56% of us own our own homes, 26% of us travel exclusively by airplane, 40% of all records purchased are purchased by black teens. . . . If you took blacks out of America, Wall Street would collapse last week! [laughter and cheers].

Why is it, then, that we have that much money, but we do not have what whites have? Simple. Whites spend their money with whites, and blacks spend their money with whites [laughter].

Every other ethnic and racial group in America turns their money over in their own communities from five to 12 times before one penny leaves. They spend their money at a 360-degree angle so [pounds podium] *it comes right back to them. In the black community, we turn our money over with one another less than once. We spend it at an 180-degree angle: directly away from ourselves.*

How can you have what white people have? Just be simple and logical about our condition. How can you have what I have with you spending 95% on me and 5% on yourself? Blacks spend 6.6% of their money with another black person—a black business or professional. We spend almost 95% of our money outside our neighborhoods.

You earn $100 a week and I earn $100 a week. You give me $95. I'm living on $195 and you're living on $5. How can your house be as big as mine? How can your car be as big as mine? How can your IQ be as high as mine? They cannot be. There is no way you can violate the basic laws of economics, and have freedom! The only color of freedom is green.

II. The work of freedom

Brown doesn't come into black communities in a vacuum. Typically there's a Buy Freedom network already in place, or about to be put in place.

The Buy Freedom movement's founding convention took place last year in Cleveland. Delegates from all 50 states discussed and ratified a "Freedom Plan," a multi-year plan designed to move black America in the direction of community independence. So far the movement has experienced mixed results. "We did well where we attracted serious, hard-working leadership,'' one Buy Freedom volunteer recently reported. "[We] could not follow through where we attracted the self-promoters and opportunists. But that problem is being resolved.''

In black communities across the U.S., the movement is attempting to identify and recruit "Freedom Businesses.'' To become a Freedom Business, it is not enough merely to be black-owned. All Freedom Businesses must take a five-point pledge to: treat all customers with courtesy; offer competitive prices; give price discounts (if possible); create new jobs (when possible); and become involved in the life of the black community.

Effie Smith is one of Washington, D.C.'s five Buy Freedom volunteer coordinators. According to Smith, over 100 D.C. businesses have become Freedom Businesses so far. They range from automobile repair shops to banks, liquor stores to law firms. Each Freedom Business displays a Freedom Seal in its window (a green dollar sign with the slogan "Buy Freedom'') and is listed in a Buy Freedom business directory. "Over the next couple of months,'' Smith told NEW OPTIONS, "we will be having Freedom Breakfasts just with the Freedom Businesses. They will be able to sit around very informally and talk over business ventures or problems that they might be having, and help each other out. . . .''

But are speeches and directories and "networking'' enough to convince the black community to change its age-old buying habits? When we expressed our skepticism to Effie Smith, she would have none of it. "I do think that the time is right,'' she said, "and people are very perceptive of the idea right now. That is definitely going to be our future.''

•   •   •

Smith's and Brown's ideas are rooted in a long political-intellectual tradition in the black community—the tradition of economic nationalism. In one article, Brown traces the lineage of "economic self-help and ethnic nationalism'' back to Carter G. Woodson, Marcus Garvey and Booker T. Washington. (Note that this is not the standard civil-rights lineage, which gives pride of place to W.E.B. Du Bois.) But neither Brown, nor any other spokesperson for the Buy Freedom movement, appears to be aware that there is a parallel tradition among white economists and development consultants—the tradition of economic decentralization and community self-reliance.

In the 1950s, a creative alliance developed between various civil rights leaders in the black community and "progressive" elements in the white community. That alliance went on to set the political agenda for the 1960s. In our time, it is not far-fetched to imagine that a similarly creative alliance could develop between various economic nationalists in the black community, and advocates of economic decentralization and community self-reliance in the white community.

5 Promoting Self-Esteem: Political Priority #1?

May 1990

When the California Task Force to Promote Self-Esteem was set up three years ago, most commentators' reactions to it were predictable. Leftists accused it of being New Age mouthwash; rightists accused it of being a waste of taxpayers' money. Garry Trudeau had a field day lampooning it in *Doonesbury*.

This January the Task Force published its final report, and it was clear from people's reactions that it had won a measure of credibility. There was a nice editorial in the *Boston Globe*. There were some fair-minded articles in big-city newspapers. The country didn't exactly stand up and take notice, but one could be forgiven for thinking that it should have.

I. Reasons to believe

One reason the Task Force won some credibility was because of its own processes. It held public hearings across California.

It commissioned an intelligent book by seven UC professors summarizing the research on self-esteem and social behavior (*The Social Importance of Self-Esteem,* 1989). Perhaps most impressive, it will not evolve into a bureaucracy—on June 30 it will dissolve and be replaced by a private advocacy group, Self-Esteem Central.

Some of the credit also has to go to the Task Force's makeup—27 people chosen from over 400 applicants (more than had applied to be on any other commission in California history). The group not only included 15 Republicans and 12 Democrats; it ranged from the fundamentalist Christian school principal to the gay therapist, from the L.A. police sergeant to the Asian Planned Parenthood director.

But most of the credit has to be given to John Vasconcellos, chair of the powerful Ways and Means Committee of the California Assembly and initiator of the legislation for the Task Force. Vasconcellos worked tirelessly for years to get the legislation approved. He spoke out all over the state and, recently, he's been speaking out all over the country on behalf of the notion that self-esteem is the key to many of our social problems.

Vasconcellos is not your ordinary politician. He practices self-disclosure with a vengeance. "I was a dutiful, well-behaved, frightened kid," he told reporters during a recent visit to Philadelphia. "We were so heavily Catholic—the whole 'I'm a sinner, I'm evil, I'm not worthy' breast-beating thing. It was crippling. When I was in my 30s, I came apart at the seams."

He sought therapy from California's humanistic psychologists. One thing they did was encourage him to vent his frustration and rage, and long-time California Assembly watchers recall that, many years ago, floor monitors had to be regularly assigned to calm him down. His coming-apart was tolerated partly because he explained it all so carefully to the voters, and partly because the therapies worked: he radiates a personal comfort now, and he has become one of the few members of the Assembly whom all factions can turn to when the going gets rough.

So when Vasconcellos tells you about the use-value of self-esteem, you know you're not hearing somebody's abstract intellectual theory. Couple his integrity with the Task Force report and the many successful school programs built around self-esteem and you have the makings of what Vasconcellos and others have begun to call a self-esteem *movement*. . .a movement they feel will be every bit as good for us as the women's and environmental movements.

We spoke with Vasconcellos last week from his office in Sacramento. Of all the dozens of recommendations in the report, we asked him, which two were the most important? "First, that every *prospective parent* ought to be prepared to become a presence that nurtures the self in the child. And second, that every *teacher* ought to be prepared to be the same."

We asked him to be even more specific, and he referred us to some of the recommendations in the report: "develop a statewide media campaign"; "make courses on child rearing available to all"; "course work in self-esteem should be required as a part of ongoing in-service training for all educators."

When we asked him what the chances were of getting any of this adopted, his tone changed from missionary to grave: "Well, the chances are complex. Anything that costs money is out, because we're going to be $3.6 billion in the red next year.

"Still, I think we've got a good chance of incorporating some of the dimensions of the report into some of the ongoing practices in this state. I'm going to introduce a series of resolutions in the Assembly that's going to ask every school to incorporate the relevant recommendations, and every mental health program and every prison and department of corrections. I would expect I'd get pretty strong support for that."

In his talks and writings, Vasconcellos makes four dramatic claims for self-esteem. We asked him about each of them:

• **It's the key to solving our social problems.** "What I've been saying," Vasconcellos told us, "is self-esteem amounts to a 'social vaccine.' It provides us with the strength not to be vulnerable to dropping out or getting pregnant too soon or getting violent or addicted. . . . I called Jonas Salk and *he* said that was an appropriate metaphor!"

• **It's the key to our economic development.** "It's a new strategic vision for the development of human capital," he says. "Healthy self-esteeming persons are more likely to become productive, creative and responsible employees."

• **It's the key to community.** "It is my sense that only a self-esteeming person can truly relate across lines of race and gender comfortably, and not want everyone to be 'just like me' so they can feel okay."

• **It can reframe the political dialogue.** "The ideal of the right is that of the individual becoming able to take care of him- or herself. The ideal of the left is that we ought to be active in...leading people to better lives. The self-esteem movement merges both ideals."

II. Not so fast, bub

To Vasconcellos, the perspective above seems like only common sense. But to many others it's misguided at best.

For one thing, the book of research summaries that the Task Force commissioned, *The Social Importance of Self-Esteem,* did *not* find the clear causal effects between self-esteem and social problems that the Task Force assumed it would. In the book's introduction, prominent sociologist Neil J. Smelser states, "The news most consistently reported...is that the associations between self-esteem and its expected consequences are mixed, insignificant, or absent."

Garry Trudeau seized on this in a February 20, 1990 *Doonesbury.* He had Boopsie, channeling Hunk-Ra, state, "Hear this! The intellectual foundation for this report, the academic research, DOES NOT SUPPORT ITS FINDINGS!... Our leaders knew this and ignored it!"

We called David Shannahoff-Khalsa, the research scientist and Task Force member from Del Mar, Calif., who'd been communicating with Trudeau and whose ideas are reflected in the strip (and who's even pictured in the Jan. 12, 1988 strip), and asked him to say more.

"I did not sign the Task Force report because to me it was fraudulent," he said. "It covered up the key findings [of the academic researchers].

"Vasconcellos knew personally that the chapters of the academic book did not substantiate his thesis. I heard him *say,* after he had just finished reviewing them, that if the Legislature found out what was written there they'd cut the funding to the Task Force."

We asked Vasconcellos to respond to these criticisms, and he did—with passion!

"The book's been used against us," said Vasconcellos, "but only by those people who think the book is all there is.

"The book wasn't the end of [the Task Force's] search! They did, like, nine public hearings from the north of the state down to San Diego; they had experts in from all over the country; they did lots of reading and research of their own. And they concluded from *all* that that there was enough evidence to make the claim of a causal relationship and a 'social vaccine.'"

Another kind of criticism came from people who think people's self-esteem *should* and *must* be bound up with real achievements, real accomplishments.

Syndicated black columnist William Raspberry recently distinguished between "self-esteem, which can thrive on the sugary diet of self-affirmation—'I am a good person,'" and "self-respect, [which] is both an acknowledgement of personal responsibility and an assertion of one's ability to meet that responsibility." Raspberry goes so far as to suggest that self-esteem can get in the way of self-respect, since it denies people the chance to prove themselves by "measuring up."

Garry Trudeau's feelings are roughly similar. "Trudeau told me about a study that looked at students' proficiency at math in the developed nations," Shannahoff-Khalsa told NEW OPTIONS. "There were two findings that he brought to my attention. One being that the Koreans did better than students from every other country, while students from the U.S. were at the bottom. When the same students were asked how well they *thought* they did, the U.S. students ranked themselves at the top and the Koreans ranked themselves at the bottom.

"So our students feel very good about themselves—but they don't function very well. They are not proficient, they are deluded...."

What does Vasconcellos think of those criticisms? "You know, David proved to be the most uncompromising, dogmatic person on the Task Force...."

No, no: What does Vasconcellos think of those *criticisms?* "It's a common belief that we're not worth much," he told us, "and so you go out and you work hard and become saved. It's kind of the Calvinist model.

"That's not my bias. That's what I lived with for a long time and...didn't 'live with' at all, OK, 'cause you can't live with it.

I think the human being is *inherently* worthy and inclined towards good. And if we know that and proceed from that knowledge, we'll learn and express and relate and produce. But you don't 'get' self-esteem by going out and doing something good for somebody. The good proceeds from the self-esteem.

To say self-esteem proceeds from achievement, that's real dangerous, it's getting into competition, and those who don't 'win' can't be esteemed.''

Several left-liberal thinkers have raised a different objection to the report.

''The larger issue is that [self-esteem] problems are rooted in the economy,'' says Utah psychologist Roger Schultz.

''More than half the jobs created last year pay $7,000 or less,'' says San Jose State University professor Roy Christman, ''and so it follows that people at the bottom of the totem pole aren't going to feel good about themselves....''

''That's a self-fulfilling prophecy,'' Vasconcellos told us.

''That doesn't mean people should be allowed to languish at the bottom of the totem pole. My record is one of a lot of activity to reach out to people who are the dispossessed and uncomfortable! But we need to do it in a way that gives them more than material goods. We need to give them material things but also encouragement to become able to protect themselves and take charge of their lives.

''Self-esteem is really a matter of empowerment. I don't think that's been emphasized enough.''

•   •   •

After we finished this article, we felt deeply moved by the sincerity and intelligence and commitment of all those we had talked to. But we were also somewhat sad.

For the arguments about self-esteem we'd been privy to were arguments that deserved to be at the very forefront of the American political debate. But in fact, they are not even a significant part of it.

How long, oh, how long America, will it be before you admit that people's feelings about themselves are as real—and as politically potent—as the amount of money they have?

PART TWO

BEYOND ECONOMIC GROWTH

Despite their surface differences, all our major national politicians have the same underlying economic goal: to make the economy grow and grow and grow.

Even their rhetoric differs little on this issue. During the 1988 election, Bush, the conservative, pledged to ''sustain America's economic growth.'' Dukakis, the liberal, said he was ''committed to vibrant and sustained economic growth.''

That rhetoric is repeated—often even more insistently—by our major political periodicals. *The Nation, The Progressive, The New Republic, National Review*. . . all want to get this country GROWING again.

None of them suggests that most of us can already meet our genuine material needs.

None of them suggests that our larger socioeconomic problems may have more to do with distribution than ''growth,'' more to do with values than economics.

None of them suggests that what we're getting now, from our overheated economy, may be less than what we're giving up as human beings by keeping it all GROWING.

Over the last decade or so, a small but devoted band of social scientists, activists and entrepreneurs—participants, all, in the Second American Experiment—have begun to envision an economy focused not on growth so much as on ''health,'' ''vitality,'' ''community,'' ''regeneration'' and/or ''sustainability.'' In this section I try to show how practical and attractive their vision can be.

The first three pieces touch on those old standbys of economics: labor, land and capital, respectively. In ''Should We

Protect *Jobs*—or Redefine *Work?*'' and "Small, Organic Farms Can Solve the Farm Crisis,'' I show that a society focusing on ends other than growth can be efficient as well as humanly satisfying. In "Rebuilding America—the Old-Fashioned Way,'' I suggest that community-oriented local banks can be the source for much of the capital that a decentralist, ecological and human growth-oriented society might need. We wouldn't have to look to Germany or Japan if our goal were human growth rather than economic growth.

"It's Overdue!—An Income Tax That's Simple and Fair'' is about the specter that haunts us every April, the federal tax system. It implies that a simple flat tax with a substantial ($15,000 per adult) personal exemption would do more good, overall, than the tax system we have now, which is twisted around in a thousand different ways to produce economic growth.

The last piece, "To Balance the Budget, Build a Sustainable Society,'' is an attempt to sum up the economic thrust of the whole Second Experiment. It not only shows how we can eliminate the federal deficit (which most economists think we need for "growth's'' sake), it shows how we can become healthier and happier in the process.

6 Should We Protect *Jobs*—or Redefine *Work?*

October 1985

At last the Democrats think they've found an economic issue with which to defeat the Republicans. They have become the party of protectionist trade legislation, leaving the free trade arguments to President Reagan. Right now the Democrats are sponsoring a bill that would put a 25% surcharge on imports from Japan, South Korea, Taiwan and Brazil.

What tends to be forgotten, amidst all the partisan hoopla, is that most Democrats support protectionism and most Republicans support free trade for the same basic reason: to maximize the number of jobs in the U.S. Their tactics may differ but the goal—full employment—is the same.

Because of the consensus on full employment, certain observations rarely break in to the public political dialogue. These include: that under no conceivable circumstances can we ever achieve genuine full employment; that even if full employment were possible, it might not be desirable in the new kind of society we are entering; and that even today, most of the useful work we do is not structured into paying "jobs."

These observations are being made by a handful of innovative economic thinkers today. Their names are not exactly household words: for example, James Block, Anna Christensen, Charles Handy, David Macarov, Anne Miller and James Robertson. But their ideas deserve to be better known. Let's call them the "Reframing Economists," because their goal is to create new frameworks for key issues.

On this issue, they appear to be suggesting that we worry less about preserving jobs and more about empowering people to do socially useful work. They are suggesting that we distinguish "work" from "jobs," and that we give everyone who "works" a subsistence income.

I. Beyond full employment

The Re-framing Economists have developed a powerful critique of the conventional full-employment economy. At the heart of their critique is the belief that full employment is no longer *possible*.

According to Israeli economic thinker David Macarov, our governments cannot *afford* to create enough jobs. "With about 10 million people unemployed in the U.S., creating jobs for them [all] would cost $171 billion [per year]." He cites an International Labor Organization estimate that a *billion* new jobs would have to be created by the year 2000 to achieve full employment worldwide.

According to futurist Willis Harman, production of "sufficient" goods and services can now be handled "with ease." According to British economist Tom Stonier, only 10% of the labor force is needed to provide all our essential needs.

According to Swedish futurist Anna Christensen, "If we accept the new labor-saving technology, then most wage labor will simply disappear. If we do not accept it, then wage labor loses the special productivity which forms the basis of its existence."

But even if it were *possible* to return to the days of full employment, say the Re-framing Economists, it is no longer *desirable*.

According to Macarov, machines will soon be able to do most jobs better, faster and cheaper than most people. So why should people be "condemned to difficult, demeaning, unsatisfying work as a condition for financial maintenance?"

According to British economist Charles Handy, "We would be in danger of demeaning the concept of a job if it were seen as something for which society [might] not ordinarily pay."

According to DePaul University political scientist James Block, "The goal of traditional full employment prevents [our coming to grips with such problems as] giant bureaucracies, make-work programs, job featherbedding, [planned obsolescence], and unproductive labor such as advertising."

According to Swedish economist Gunnar Adler-Karlsson, "If we are going to have any solidarity in practice with the poorer nations, we cannot egoistically maintain all jobs for ourselves in the West."

In the past, thinkers and activists who criticized the job-centered society would have proposed some kind of "leisure society" as their alternative. Not the Re-framing Economists. They tend to see the leisure society as inherently oppressive and elitist.

In a well-received speech to The Other Economic Summit (a grassroots version of the annual "economic summit" of the seven richest nations), British economist James Robertson said he sees a time—if current trends continue—when "only a minority of citizens will be employed. These will be highly skilled, highly responsible, highly regarded, and highly paid members of a technocratic elite. The rest of the population will have no useful work to do, and will live lives of leisure."

Robertson goes on to make the essential political point about this kind of society: "In contrast to the typical industrial society, split between a superior minority of employers and an inferior majority of employees, the so-called leisure society would be split between a superior minority of workers and an inferior majority of drones.''

II. Time to redefine work

There is an emerging alternative to jobs-centeredness and leisure-centeredness. Handy puts it well when he says, ''We must look beyond employment not to unemployment or boundless leisure but to a new view of work, of which the job is only a part.''

The key insight here is that the ''jobs economy'' is only one part of the whole economy—and not the largest part, at that.

The Re-framing Economists tend to go to great lengths to explain this. Handy's explanation is one of the simplest and clearest. He distinguishes among *organized work, gift work* and *pocket money work.*

• **Organized work** is jobs in industry, commerce and services and comprises the vast bulk of the GNP. But it represents less than half the effort we expend on keeping the society running smoothly—less than 50% of the work that goes into what Handy calls the ''total economy.''

• **Gift work** is the work we do for love (for ourselves or others)—arts and crafts, homemaking, growing vegetables, ''do it yourself''—as well as the work we do supplementing the social services, like Meals on Wheels. ''None of this gift work is priced in our present society,'' Handy told a gathering of post-liberal thinkers in England. ''Nor is it reckoned with in economists' thinking. Yet it represents 50% of the country's total economy, and without its contribution society would suffer.''

• **Pocket money work** is work done for others and charged for, but generally not recorded on people's tax forms—work like selling produce by the roadside or doing the odd maintenance job. ''Organized work is so highly priced today that a great many essential jobs would get left undone were it not for the pocket money economy.''

The bottom line is this: a great deal of socially useful work cannot be easily structured into jobs (''organized work''). Arizona economist Robert Theobald gives some examples: ''child-nurturing, self-discovery and expression, care of the sick and old, community support and development."

It makes sense to the Re-framing Economists that we re-organize the economy so people can do useful work whether or not it can be structured into jobs. Robertson envisions a society "in which increasing numbers of people [can] organize useful and rewarding activity for themselves. . . . Instead of an employment society or a leisure society, the post-industrial society will be an ownwork society."

III. Separating "jobs" from income

To pave the way for an economy of "socially useful work" rather than make-work jobs, most of the Re-framing Economists are calling for a guaranteed subsistence income of some kind.

"There are some very elaborate basic income schemes," Handy told the Findhorn community earlier this year. "But a very simple one would be to pay everybody, say, $4,500 a year, which of course is not enough for most people. On anything you earn above that, you automatically pay 50%, so there's still an incentive to earn more money."

Some innovative economists have proposed refinements of that basic scheme. For example, the British Ecology party calls for weighting the payments "in favor of the less densely populated areas." British Economist Anne Miller calls for tying the payments to aggregate output—so if output begins to fall, the guaranteed income would also fall.

Other economists have proposed significantly different schemes. For example, Harman would have the government provide support not to everyone, but to all those "who have demonstrated an ability to hold structured jobs but who want to carry out some project of manifest social merit. Such activities could include study and research, providing educational opportunities for the elderly, beautifying the environment, carrying out a social experiment. . . ."

Most of the Re-framing Economists are confident that we can separate "jobs" from subsistence income in our time. Many of them have suggested plausible strategies to get us there.

Harman suggests a strategy based largely on changes in education. He'd have us educate for a society in which "learning, fulfillment and becoming human are the primary goals."

Robertson and his collaborator, Alison Pritchard, would start with the unions. "First, [the union movement] could facilitate the inevitable contraction of formal employment, [but] on terms that are favorable to the affected employees.... Second, the unions could represent the interests of people working outside formal employment. For example, they might provide technical and legal advice to protect them against exploitation."

Block envisions a quasi-populist strategy—"one that, as a start, demands automation, increased efficiency, and the elimination of useless work.... A broad constituency will refuse to make more sacrifices.... Ironically, a program demonstrating our resolve to limit work could restore optimal productivity where policies rooted in our commitment to work cannot."

An ideal strategy would surely combine elements of all three approaches. But before we focus too much on strategy we'd better succeed at redefining work—so it can never again be seen as "radical" or "progressive" to angrily demand jobs for all.

7 Small, Organic Farms Can Solve the Farm Crisis

December 1985

There are not one but two farm crises. The "official" farm crisis is bad enough—and no genuine solutions have been forthcoming from the traditional left or right. The "unofficial" crisis is typically ignored by policymakers from both sides.

The official farm crisis—soaring farm debt, dramatically increasing numbers of farm foreclosures—is in part a *result* of the farm policies that have been enacted over the last two decades.

These policies are hopelessly contradictory. For example, tax policies are designed to help big farmers get bigger, and to encourage surplus production on marginal lands (e.g., about 3% of our wheat is grown with federally subsidized water!). At the same time, farmers are paid to *not* plant crops. In 1983, subsidies to farmers from that year's farm program totalled $32 billion. That's $12 billion more than the *net earnings* of farmers!

In response to this situation, many conservatives are calling for a "free market" in agriculture. The response is understandable, but the effect would be to wipe out all but the 100-200,000 biggest farmers. As for the traditional liberals, here, as in so many other areas, they have become the party of the status quo. They don't want anyone to have to leave farming, and they are prepared to continue to provide massive subsidies to ensure the continuation of "farming as usual."

Unfortunately for the prospects of "farming as usual," a hidden farm crisis is brewing—"hidden" because it is rarely addressed by traditional liberals or conservatives. It consists of the following:

• Our agricultural lands lose 4.8 billion tons of topsoil annually to erosion—enough to cover all the cropland of New England with one foot of earth.

• To maintain high crop yields, we apply an average of 111 pounds of synthetic fertilizer per acre of cropland each year— about 210 pounds for every person in the U.S.!

• In the past 15 years, while pesticide use has gone up 140%, crop loss to insects has *increased* more than 40%!

• More than 75% of the food we eat is processed in some way.

• The average molecule of processed food in this country travels *1,300 miles* before being eaten.

Fortunately for us all, some people are addressing *both* farm crises—and are doing so in constructive and innovative ways. But they're not well known in Washington, to say the least. They include such people as Chuck Hassebrook, at the Center for Rural Affairs in Nebraska; Wes and Dana Jackson, at the Land Institute in Kansas; and Ellen Pahl, at Community Regeneration in Pennsylvania. We like to call them the "Re-framing Agriculturalists," because their work, taken together, is creating a whole new framework for understanding agricultural issues.

If you put together what the Re-framing Agriculturalists have been saying, it is this: to solve the farm crisis, we need to achieve at least six interrelated goals. We need to increase farmers' profits. We need to establish more small farms. We need to put more people on the land. We need to adopt sustainable agricultural practices. We need to achieve regional self-reliance in food. And we need to increase the nutritional quality of food.

It's a visionary agenda, but given the "hidden" farm crisis, it may also be our only realistic one.

Increase farmers' profits. The obvious way to increase farmers' profits is to increase the prices people pay for farm goods. Some Congressional populists would have the federal government impose rigid farm-by-farm quotas on production. The idea is to lower production enough to drive up prices. However, most of the Re-framing Agriculturalists are searching for methods that would keep the government out of the business of policing farm production, and would keep prices from going up in the supermarkets (to the detriment of the urban poor).

Spokespeople like Ellen Pahl are making the point that organic farming and local marketing could—all by themselves—increase farmers' profits substantially. "If all farmers were to cut their input costs by farming regeneratively," Pahl told NEW OPTIONS, "savings in fertilizer alone would be enough to provide over one million farms with the present average farm income. And with less input costs, interest payments would decrease as well. . . . If there were more local markets for a more diversified crops-and-animal production system, farmers would earn more for their products because there would be fewer middlemen than in the transcontinental distribution system we currently use.

Break up the big farms. Food production is becoming concentrated in fewer and fewer hands. Currently 1% of farmland owners control 30% of all farmland.

There would be some justification for this Banana Republic-like development if it could be shown that there are "economies of scale" in agriculture. But there are none. According to Chuck Hassebrook and others at the Center for Rural Affairs, most types of farms come close to "theoretical technical perfection" while they are small. For example, a typical Midwestern corn and soybeans farm achieves 90% of its potential efficiency with 300 acres under cultivation. Production efficiency may actually *decline* as farms grow larger than this. It is only the tax structure of American agriculture that makes it possible for larger farms to reap greater profits. It is entirely shameless in this. For example, the individual farmer with a taxable income of $50,000 pays 40%, while the rate for corporate farms is 17%.

The Re-framing Agriculturalists have proposed a number of measures that would, in effect, break up the large farms and permit their division into many small ones. They would, to begin with, tax family-sized farms at the same rate as corporate farms, or even at a lower rate. Jefferson is frequently quoted on this score: "[Let us] exempt all [property] from taxation below a certain point, and tax the higher portions of property in geometric progression as they rise."

Marty Strange, a colleague of Hassebrook's, would eliminate the use of tax deductions that heavily favor large farms (e.g. those that encourage purchases of heavy farm equipment, and those that encourage the sale of capital assets like land and breeding stock). Medard Gabel, a colleague of Pahl's, would put a $25,000 limit on the amount of subsidy any one farmer could receive.

Bring in more farmers. Most advocates of family-sized farms are seeking to "maintain" or "preserve" the number of farmers now on the land. Often they'll admit they're motivated mainly by sentiment. The Re-framing Agriculturalists would bring more people onto the land—millions more. And they'd do so for reasons that are eminently practical.

The main one is that you can't have organic agriculture without more people—a point well made by Dana Jackson in conversation with NEW OPTIONS: "You can't farm well without caring. We need a better eyes-per-acre ratio to take care of land well."

"Increased labor requirements on 'organic' farms [might] range from 2% for apple production in the Northeast to 111% for corn production in Iowa," says one Community Regeneration study. "Changing the average size of the U.S. farm to 300 acres [from 430 today] would create over one million additional farms employing [nearly] 1.4 million people—two million if the additional farms were [organic]" ("Jobs for Americans," 1984).

The Great Fear in Rural America is that more farmers would mean less income per farmer. Not so, say the Re-framing Agriculturalists. According to Pahl, billions of dollars of energy savings would result from market decentralization and decreased farm size. Moreover, "If the billions of dollars of subsidies that the taxpayer/consumer is currently paying to the large farmers were

54

removed, and these tax revenues were given back to the consumer, the actual price paid for food might indeed be *less.* ''

There are about as many proposals for attracting more people to farming as there are Re-framing Agriculturalists. Hassebrook told NEW OPTIONS that the Farmers Home Administration (FmHA) should return to its original purpose of providing reduced-interest loans to low-income and beginning farmers (over the years it's drifted into the role of providing "emergency" credit to cushion expanding farms from financial risk!) Other Re-framers are pursuing a more exclusively market-oriented approach. Let's figure out how to make small plots profitable again, they seem to be saying, and new farmers will come running.

In Alabama, Booker T. Whatley, recently retired professor at Tuskegee, is figuring out how to turn a tiny, 25-acre farm into a moneymaker. (Among his suggestions so far: it must have a year-round cash flow from crops that mature sequentially, and it must sell its crops to signed-up "members" to assure a steady flow of customers.) In Missouri, activist Chris Hitt is establishing a network of "training farms" to introduce beginning farmers to organic agriculture *and* to business. "Farmers were all entrepreneurs once—they had to be," he told NEW OPTIONS. "We're trying to get entrepreneurship back into farming again."

Promote organic farming. It should be obvious by now that the centerpiece of the Re-framers' proposals is the promotion of a largely organic (a.k.a. "sustainable" or "regenerative") farming system in the U.S.

Pahl and Gabel would hope to achieve this simply by creating a level playing-field for organic agriculture. They are convinced that, "Without subsidies, the small number of large farms would not be able to produce the crops that they do with the costs they presently have, and there would be more farms and more people in farming."

Michael Luick, an Iowa farm activist, would have state governments play a more explicit pro-organic role. Here is one of his model proposals: "The Iowa Department of Agriculture should declare an eventual phase-out of the general use of pesticides, herbicides, and artificial fertilizers over a 10-year period."

Encourage self-reliance. A final goal for the Re-framing Agriculturalists is to achieve regional self-reliance in food production. It sounds impractical, even romantic, but the Re-framers' rationale is hard-headed as can be. "A more regenerative, regional food system would not have the long distance transportation bills to pay that our present food system does," Pahl told NEW OPTIONS. "Nearly $21 billion is spent just moving food in the U.S.—amounting to $344 per family." Other Re-framers emphasize that regional markets could provide fresher and more nutritious food.

How to create regional self-reliance? Simply moving to an organic system would help, since most organic systems would require farmers to plant a variety of crops, not just one or two. Farmers' markets are catching on and can certainly help. In addition, farmers need to market their crops much more systematically to local and regional outlets. "You have got to start with the marketplace," Hitt told NEW OPTIONS. "If the farmers were connected in a tangible, real way with the local and regional wholesalers and retailers, that would do more than any single thing to get American farming back on track."

The genius of the Re-framing Agriculturalists' program is that it is internally consistent. Small farms can be worked organically. Organic farms require fewer costly inputs, meaning farm profits can rise, meaning more people will want to go into farming. Organic farms require more farmers than large, mechanized farms. Organic produce is nutritionally sound. Fresh, nutritionally sound produce can find markets close to home.

To move toward the Re-framers' program, it will be necessary for the traditional left and right to take the "hidden" farm crisis into account. And it will be necessary for decentralist/globally responsible, Greenish advocates to have the courage of their convictions and insist on the interconnected, inseparable nature of their proposals, even if that puts them at odds with most of the farmers' own organizations.

8   Rebuilding America—the Old-Fashioned Way

March 1988

The Democratic presidential candidates have big plans for "rebuilding" America. Paul Simon would launch public works programs. Michael Dukakis would offer grants and tax subsidies to businesses. Richard Gephardt would offer a pinch of Simon, a spoonful of Dukakis, and protective tariffs as well.

The trouble with these proposals is that it's not enough to create more housing and more businesses, it's not enough to grease the already-existing wheels. We need to create the right kind of housing, the right kinds of businesses. We need to ask: How can we encourage, not housing in general, but attractive, affordable, even (sometimes) co-operative housing? How can we encourage, not business in general, but human-scale socially responsible businesses? Above-all, we need to ask: How can ordinary people be empowered to help rebuild America?

Not only are none of the presidential candidates asking such questions, neither are any of our "oppositional" political groups. Citizen Action and Democratic Socialists of America have no basic quarrel with Simon's and Dukakis's approaches; in fact, some of their members helped hammer them out. The U.S. Greens might have some objections—even some alternatives—but so far they've failed to express them, choosing instead to spend the election year passionately debating such matters as "social" vs. "deep" ecology.

There is an emerging alternative to the big government-big business-big labor kind of "rebuilding" of America. Its basic strategy is to get investment capital out of the hands of the big banks, the big brokerage houses, the multinationals, etc., and into the hands of the communities. Its greatest champions are neither politicians nor oppositional political groups, but—remarkably—bankers; or more specifically, those few bankers who describe themselves as "community development bankers," or "socially responsible bankers," or some such.

We spent the last month talking with some of these New Bankers, especially at the bank that—everyone agrees—best practices what all these bankers preach: South Shore Bank of Chicago. One of the first things we noticed is that they all started out in fields *other* than banking:

- **Ronald Gryzwinski,** 52, chairman of the board of Shorebank Corporation (South Shore's holding company), used to sell computers;

- **Joan Shapiro,** 45, senior vice president at South Shore, used to teach literature, theater and dance. "Like many women of my generation, I am a generalist," she told NEW OPTIONS;

- **Dorris Pickens,** president of The Neighborhood Institute (Shorebank's non-profit affiliate), had been a community activist. "I loved community work, and I love the neighborhood," she says;

- **Mary Houghton,** 47, president of Shorebank Corporation, has a master's degree in international relations;

- **Lyndon Comstock,** 37, principal organizer for the New York City-based Community Capital Bank, was a full-time anti-war activist in the 60s, "then I was involved with developing housing and small business co-ops in the early 70s both in Michigan and the Bay Area...."

All these people can, and usually do, look like traditional bankers; Gryzwinski and Comstock are even semi-bald, like in the old left-wing cartoons of bankers. But just try typing them as left or right. Wasn't that Shapiro we saw at the New Synthesis Think Tank conference a few months back (Chapter One)? Wasn't Community Capital's program director at the Green gathering last summer?

I. Miracle on 71st Street

South Shore Bank doesn't *look* out of the ordinary—modernistic white concrete on the outside, corporate purple-and-lavender on the inside. True: there's wallpaper, not paint, on some of the walls, and enough potted plants to serve as a statement of some kind. But it's the "Development Deposits" that separate South Shore from all other banks. It's the Development Deposits that support South Shore's innovative urban lending program—which has directed over $85 million in credit to neighborhood residents to rehabilitate run-down housing, pay college tuition and finance small businesses and non-profit organizations.

"By definition," Shapiro told NEW OPTIONS, "a Development Deposit is any deposit that comes to the bank from outside its immediate neighborhood. Forty percent of South Shore's deposits are Development Deposits. . . . Right now it's about a $59 *million* portfolio.

"Now, why would some middle class person in Fargo or Tucson or San Francisco put money in a medium-sized bank on the South Side of Chicago? The answer is that those people *care* about what's happening to their money, what it's being used for."

According to Shapiro, Development Depositors need make no financial sacrifices. "The vast majority of the deposits in this portfolio are market-rate deposits. Our money market account will equal *or exceed* that of other national indexes; our CDs would be fully competitive with the national market. . . ."

The default rate on South Shore's loans is less than 2%. "So you *don't* lose your shirt making loans in low-to moderate-income communities," says Shapiro. "If you make a long-term commitment to it, if you put your best loan officers to it, you're going to have a very strong portfolio.

We asked Shapiro to tell us the difference between Development Deposits and the various "social investment" funds like Calvert and Working Assets. We could tell she didn't want to say anything that would reflect poorly on her friends and colleagues at the funds. But she did say this: "The social investment funds invest in paper and securities of national intermediaries. South Shore invests directly in the community. So part of the difference is the distance of the investment from the actual direct impact."

A second basic difference, of course, is that investments in South Shore's Development Deposits are FDIC insured up to $100,000.

A third difference is that the social investment funds employ largely negative social screens. They *refuse* to invest in South Africa, nuclear power, etc. Banks like South Shore *affirmatively* direct capital to community-based businesses and non-profits.

In our opinion, that's the biggest difference of all. It may be more glamorous to "refuse" to invest in nuclear power than to help make credit available to small-fry housing developers. But the former only says ''no!'' to what's wrong with America, the latter also says ''yes!'' to what's emerging and right.

II. Follow the Dodgers

Two blocks from Brooklyn's Seventh Avenue subway station is a Baptist stone church with green trim. Inside, everything's creaky and there's a lovely old musty church smell. You'd never guess that, somewhere within, in a room big enough to accommodate five desks, Lyndon Comstock and his co-workers are preparing to launch the Community Capital Bank—New York's version of South Shore Bank.

''What we now have is a staff of five people,'' Comstock told NEW OPTIONS, ''an advisory board, a board of directors that's in formation. . . . What has to happen [next] is we have to file our charter application. Putting the charter application in is what really starts the clock ticking on the rest of the process leading up to the doors opening.'' The doors should open by 1991—probably somewhere along Flatbush Avenue, which is where the Brooklyn Dodgers used to play.

Why does Comstock think he'll succeed in replicating South Shore Bank when no one else has even tried? South Shore had a difficult time raising the initial equity capital. They got it from foundations and to some extent churches and a couple of corporations. And furthermore, they started out with a very small amount of true equity. The rest of it was all out on loan, which was bad. I mean, they were really undercapitalized. And then when the prime rate leaped to 20%—and their loan was at prime—that was a big problem for them. All that must have been discouraging to people.

''We're trying a different tack for raising capital from what they took, and it's partly because we're in a different time. We're going to go and raise capital from the socially responsible investment (SRI) market.

''The SRI market didn't exist in [1973]. We're going to try to tap that market for what will be the *first-ever public offering of common stock to be sold explicitly on social grounds as well as financial grounds. . . .* I think that market is ready for it.

"It's not that we aren't going to try to get some equity capital from the institutions as well [in fact, $2 million from corporations, foundations and the like, $3 million from individual investors–ed.]. But the problem has been that trying to get *enough* capital out of the institutions has been quite difficult, unless you've got a sensational track record like South Shore now has.

"We're devising a direct-mail program, an educational program—there's a real network developing around our ideal— plus there's all the investment advisors and brokers who belong to the Social Investment Forum. . . . So for the right proposals, I think the equity funding will start becoming available."

III. Out of Bangladesh

The New Bankers are not just trying to get money to socially-responsible housing developers and business people. They're also trying to get money to ordinary people for use in their own tiny ventures.

In this country, of course, only those of us with collateral are able to get business loans—a phenomenon immortalized in the folk saying, "Them that has, gets." But in Bangladesh, the Grameen Bank has been making tiny business loans to villagers, and over the last three years various of the New Bankers have been travelling abroad to see how the Bangladeshis do it.

And now, Dorris Pickens in Chicago and Mary Houghton in Arkansas are about to help implement loan programs based on the Grameen model. (How many other American "professionals" have proved themselves willing to learn from the Third World?)

"In Arkansas we're going to run a program called the Good Faith Fund," Houghton told NEW OPTIONS. "It will have a half million dollars capital and be lodged in our non-profit. And be staffed by an 'enterprise agent' whose job it will be to organize 'borrowing groups' of people who either are or would like to be self-employed. And these borrowing groups will work modeled exactly on how they are in Bangladesh.

"So if you live in a small town in Arkansas and you want to borrow small amounts of short-term capital, you'll have to go find four other people who are motivated and interested in the same way you are. You'll have to meet with them regularly. And then you and your buddies in the group will decide which two of you should draw down the first loans.

"You'll be eligible to borrow say $1,000 to begin with, maximally say about $5,000. And after the first two people borrowing are repaying as agreed, the next two people—say maybe 2-3 months later—will borrow. And if all four people are paying back as agreed, then the fifth will borrow.

"And everybody will know that the next time around they'll be able to borrow a higher amount. But they will never be able to borrow again unless everybody is paying as agreed, or unless they clean up the debt of the defaulter.

"What all this is is an effort to find an adequate substitute for collateral. Which is in this case, peer pressure and peer support."

IV. The old-fashioned way

For all their innovations, there is a sense in which the New Bankers are a throwback to the old.

"Sometimes I think we're just old-fashioned good community bankers!" Gryzwinski told NEW OPTIONS. "Our banks were all chartered to take care of the credit needs of their local service areas. And the communities of people who've needed credit have remained essentially the same. They're the same size: neighborhoods, places like that. But the banks have become international banks. And the banks can no longer relate to the neighborhoods, because the neighborhoods' needs aren't for billions of dollars. They're for tens or hundreds of thousands of dollars per deal.

"Also, I think particularly if you look at banks inside cities you'd see that bankers have very little to do with the communities in which their banks are located. The bankers typically live in the suburbs, and are sort of 'absentee bankers.' And that wasn't true before...."

"There's a proportion of what we're doing that's much more traditional, actually, than what any of the major banks in New York are doing," Comstock told NEW OPTIONS. "They're all involved in a headlong flight into investment banking—mergers and acquisitions and all that kind of stuff—and are trying to get as far away from traditional banking as possible....

"They might still have a department that does small-business lending. But look at the amount that they do! Their focus on small-business lending has greatly declined compared to what it was 15 years ago, let alone 30 years ago.

"There's parts of the old-fashioned thing that I don't like. I mean, you know, there was racism in the old banking world, there was sexism, there was classism. . . .

"The capital flow *now* is as classist as could be. Basically, the entire collective savings of our society are being funneled into the banking system, which then funnels it out into the wealthiest sectors of the economy. . . . The savings of the people of this borough are being siphoned out and taken to Japan, and Donald Trump! I mean, how do you think Trump builds all this stuff? He didn't start out having $100 million. *It's our collective savings* that allows these people to do what they do!

"It is outrageous. And it's entirely related to why there are so many miseries within this country."

Comstock pauses, looks around. "In the Sixties, we were outraged and were trying to figure out some way to STOP IT!!—which we didn't make a whole lot of progress on. Now it's more a question of, you know, how to get our hands on some of these economic tools.

"We've gotten our hands on an immensely powerful tool compared to what used to be available to us as community organizers and fledgling co-op managers. To me it's the same kind of excitement I suppose as the day I first got my hands on a really good power saw as compared to working with a hand saw. Boy, this is, you know, having the ability to put together an institution where you've got $100 million in assets, $100 million in loans and investments—that to me is really exciting, to have that kind of tool to work with. And not just work with, but *use* to create something beautiful."

Another pause. And a grin. "Who could ever think of using the word 'beautiful' in connection with a bank, right? I mean, it's a contradiction in terms. . . ."

9 It's Overdue!—An Income Tax That's Simple and Fair

April 1990

By April 16 most of us had had it up to here with our outrageously complex and unfair tax system. But we didn't riot, like they did in Britain this year. We simply sat on our anger, not knowing quite what to do with it—for now.

Fear of our anger had, after all, prompted the politicians to pass the much ballyhooed Tax Reform Act of 1986. And what good did that do, really? According to the Gallup poll, Americans by lopsided margins feel that the tax system is *more* complicated and *less* fair now.

Our tax laws certainly aren't fair. Thanks to all the deductions, exemptions, "adjustments" and "credits," the system still taxes many high-income Americans at lower rates than the less well-off. For example, you can deduct up to $100,000 for home mortgage interest payments, but try deducting anything for rent. If you work in an office or factory, you can't deduct the cost of a peanut butter sandwich, but your boss can write off 80% of the cost of his or her "power lunch."

The system has become complicated beyond belief. In 1913 the personal income tax return had two pages of accompanying instructions. This year it had 48. (And try reading them!) In the 1950s only 10-15% of us sought professional help to complete our tax returns. This year it was nearly 60%.

The Tax Reform Act was supposed to simplify things, but two tax experts—Jerome Ellig of Citizens for a Sound Economy and Alvin Rabushka of the Hoover Institution—separately lamented to NEW OPTIONS that the new tax law only made things worse. "In principle" the Tax Reform Act looks more fair, says Daniel Nagin of Carnegie Mellon University, but in practice it doesn't work out that way "because mortals cannot administer it."

The monumental unfairness and complexity of the tax laws creates a monumental amount of resentment; partly as a result, we lose $50 to $100 billion a year from cheating and outright noncompliance. In addition, the tax laws contribute mightily to our alienation from government and public life. It's as clear as day: If we don't trust or understand the tax collection process, we're not going to think kindly about what government does or can do.

I. Three voices

The tax laws are the product of two voices, neither of them functional as we enter the 21st century.

One voice is that of selfishness and greed—or, more politely, shortsightedness. It was epitomized for me earlier this month by a top corporate lobbyist, Mark Bloomfield. In an appearance before the Congressional Study Group, Bloomfield—"Mr. Capital Gains," as he's known on the Hill—argued forcefully that lowering the capital gains tax rate would immediately increase investment in the U.S. economy. But when he walked up to a group of us afterwards, and one of us asked him whether lowering the capital gains rate would increase investment *in the long run,* he smiled and said he really didn't know. He thought so, he said. He certainly hoped so.

The second voice is that of the demagogue—or, sometimes, that of the old New Deal liberal. Unlike the first voice, it is concerned with fairness. But it defines "fairness" as steeply progressive tax rates, even though we've learned by now that relatively high rates simply mean that rich (and even not-so-rich) people will pay lawyers and accountants to find "tax shelters" for them, leaving everybody worse off.

A third voice, faint but distinct, is beginning to emerge. It completely crosses ideological lines, taking in some of the work of neo-libertarian economists like Ellig and Rabushka, mainstream economists like Harvard's Lawrence Lindsey (author of *The Growth Experiment,* 1990), and Greenish scholars like Herman Daly and John Cobb Jr. (authors of *The Common Good,* 1989).

These thinkers don't have a unified program. But you can derive one from their work. Put their ideas together and you can envision: a flat tax that would apply only after you'd earned enough to meet your basic needs; a postcard-sized tax return that would be the epitome of simplicity; an end to the regressive corporate and social security taxes; and a series of estate and excise taxes that would put social responsibility firmly into the tax system.

It all hinges on a redefinition of fairness.

Until now, "fairness" in the tax system has been synonymous with steeply progressive rates. The assumption is that the more equal we can make everybody's incomes, the fairer things will be.

Daly used to think that way. In the 1970s he was a prominent advocate of maximum and minimum levels of income. But in his new book, he and Cobb stress not levelling but community. Fairness no longer means cutting the prosperous down to size, but making sure everyone's basic needs are met.

"In a true community," they write, "the basic needs of all are met so far as the community can do so. This...has been characteristic of traditional village life."

For Lindsey, too, fairness means that "low-and moderate-income taxpayers must be allowed to obtain the necessities of life, by modern American standards, before we treat any significant portion of their income as discretionary and tax it away."

These reflections on fairness represent something genuinely new under the sun.

For many decades, the U.S. has been polarized between those who believe in an "egalitarian" society and those who believe that inequality is a necessary source of productivity and individual striving for excellence. In the 1960s, the pendulum swung in the direction of the egalitarians; currently it's swinging (some might say, flying) in the opposite direction.

Daly, Lindsey and others are early exponents of what is, in effect, a third position: Inequality is okay and even socially useful so long as everyone is able to meet their basic needs. This position is significant and exciting because it appears to incorporate the legitimate concerns of both sides in the traditional debate.

II. Flat tax

If the centerpiece of a Great Society type tax plan would be steeply graduated tax rates, and the centerpiece of a conservative plan would be making the poor pay relatively more and the rich pay relatively less, then the centerpiece of a post-liberal, post-conservative plan might be...the flat tax.

Under the flat tax, everyone would be taxed at exactly the same rate. Under a post-liberal, post-conservative flat tax, there'd be a personal exemption high enough to permit everyone to meet their basic needs *before contributing a cent* in taxes.

Rabushka proposed a widely-discussed flat tax plan in the early 1980s. One big problem with it, for our purposes, is that the personal exemption is very small: $3,800 for singles. Lindsey recently proposed a flat tax plan with a personal exemption of $6,000 for each adult, $3,000 for each child, and $2,000 for each child under four years of age.

We would drop Lindsey's exemptions for children. (This country isn't exactly suffering from underpopulation.) But we would raise the personal exemption to *$15,000*—our sense of what a person needs (in this country today) to meet their basic needs without the help of further tax breaks. Note that a family of four with two young children would pay no tax on its first $22,000 under Lindsey's plan; on its first $30,000, under ours.

Lindsey's plan taxes income at a single rate of 19%. He claims we'd raise just as much in personal income taxes as we do today. But he'd *preserve* the corporate and social security taxes (both notoriously regressive). And his personal exemptions are still so small that many working-and middle-class people would pay *more,* under his scheme, than they do today.

That's not the case with our plan. We'd *eliminate* the corporate and social security taxes (see below), give every adult a personal exemption of $15,000, and tax all income over $15,000 at a single rate of 38%—not too different from the marginal rate most of us pay now (28% + 7.5% social security + whatever part of the corporate tax gets passed on to us as a sales tax). The tax would be "flat," but its impact would be progressive thanks to the big personal exemption.

Just consider: A single person making $15,000 would pay no taxes. Someone making $20,000 would have a taxable income of $5,000 and would pay $1,900—9.5%—in taxes. Someone making $30,000 would pay 19% in taxes. Someone making $50,000 would pay 27%. Someone making $100,000, 32%.

The reason we'd be able to accomplish all this at such a reasonable tax rate is we'd eliminate personal deductions.

In other words: Our tax system would be *simple* as well as flat and fair.

As it is today, the income tax exempts *over half of personal income from taxation,* thanks to the crazy-quilt of deductions, exemptions, tax "benefits" and tax "credits" that are permitted under the tax code.

Our tax plan would also exempt a great deal of this nation's collective personal income from taxation: 43%, to be exact. But only because that's what we collectively earn *under $15,000.*

Apart from the personal exemption, Ellig would permit three deductions: for charitable contributions, contributions to IRAs, and interest on home mortgages.

Lindsey would permit the same three, but with friendly amendments. The charitable deduction would double for contributions over 5% of income, "establishing a new social standard—the half-tithe—for all Americans to strive for." IRAs would become Individual *Savings* Accounts, helping us pay for education and health as well as retirement. And the home ownership deduction would be limited to $5,000 of real interest payments per adult taxpayer.

Daly and Cobb would retain or adopt deductions for: taxes and repairs on the home, charitable gifts and activities, "expenses necessary for earning a living," and "small gifts to politicians, since these at least somewhat decrease their dependence on large donors."

Even *with* the deductions above, our tax return could—as Rabushka likes to say—fit on a postcard, and the instruction manual would be two pages long.

But we think the very generous personal exemption built into our plan should substitute for *all* deductions. Once you start giving them out, you can never really stop.

III. Demagogue's tax

A simple flat tax of 38%, coupled with increases in some other taxes (see below), would permit us to eliminate the corporate and social security taxes.

We think both taxes are extremely regressive and are useful mainly to demagogic politicians.

The corporate income tax has critics now across the spectrum— including liberals like Lester Thurow and Greens like Daly.

"Many people, including the man on the street, think [the corporate tax] is a way to tax the rich," says. Thurow. "This is simply a mistaken perception. . . . There is no such thing as taxing corporations as opposed to individuals. They simply collect money from someone—their shareholders, customers or employees—and transfer it to government.

"This immediately raises the issue of who ultimately pays the corporate income tax. Depending on the exact assumptions used it could be a tax on shareholders, a sales tax on consumers, or a tax on employees. Personally, I believe it is a . . . sales tax in the long run.

"While there may be a certain perverse political virtue in collecting a tax where no one is sure whether he pays it, simple economic efficiency and equity would seem to call for the elimination of taxes where incidence is uncertain."

Thurow would have corporations send each stockholder the equivalent of a W-2 form at the end of each year, telling them how much income they'd earned and how much tax had been withheld on it.

Daly—more concerned about social responsibility than economic growth per se—would handle things differently. He would have corporate profits be actually distributed to each stockholder at the end of each year. His rationale: This would shift corporations "away from internal financing of new investment [and into] competition in the capital market for investment funds. This is a more arms-length transaction in which harder questions are likely to be asked about the . . . proposed expansion."

IV. Social insecurity

The public hardly realizes it, but social security taxes are now responsible for 37% of federal revenues—nearly as much as personal income taxes (44%). In 1970, by contrast, social security brought in only 23% of our revenues.

Social security is even more regressive than a sales tax. Not only does *everyone* have to pay the 7.65% tax on even the first *dollar* of their salaries; the tax disappears on every dollar you make over $51,300!

And everyone knows there's trouble ahead. As Nat Mills wrote in *In These Times,* "Social security deductions are not [set aside] for future benefits to the payrollee, nor are they accruing earnings as is expected for any normally retained wealth. Instead, it all drops into the general tax-revenue pot today."

Daly and Cobb advocate a negative income tax, which they'd substitute for social security benefit payments, aid to dependent children, public housing, and much else besides. In their scheme, if you made nothing the government would pay you $9,000 a year; if you made $8,000 the government would still pay you $5,000 (a "positive incentive to work," they say); if you made $12,000 you'd still get $3,000; and so on up to $18,000.

We are not sure about a guaranteed income without qualifications (see Chapter 6). However, we think negative income tax payments can and should replace payments to all *social security* recipients, now and in the future.

As Daly and Cobb remark, "There is an inherent confusion in the [social security] program between its welfare aspects and its role as a retirement plan." In the spirit of community, the negative income tax—along with the national *holistic* health care plan we advocate in Chapter 13 (a plan that would cost us *less* than medical care today)—would ensure that social security recipients could meet their basic needs. Anything more would be up to them.

V. Other sources

The personal income tax won't have to take up *all* the slack from the corporate and social security taxes. Currently the government derives 1% of its revenues from the estate tax (a tax on all possessions left after death) and 3% of its revenues from the excise tax (all taxes on the production, sale or consumption of commodities). Daly and Cobb, Lester Brown of the Worldwatch Institute, Patricia Taylor of the Center for Science in the Public Interest, and many other innovative thinkers, have proposed increasing some of these taxes dramatically—partly to raise revenues, but partly also to introduce more social responsibility into the workings of the American economy.

We believe that $200 billion—over 20% of the government's current revenues—could and *should* be raised through these taxes:

• Lindsey advocates *sumptuary taxes* on "luxury cars, boats, household servants, second homes, and the like."

• In Chapter 10, we discuss concrete plans for increasing the *inheritance tax,* the *alcohol tax,* the *tobacco tax* and the *gasoline tax;* as well as plans for introducing a *stock exchange tax* and a *corporate merger tax.*

• In Chapter 14, we make the case for legalization of drugs, and for a stiff *tax on drugs.*

• Daly and Cobb advocate a substantial *severance tax,* i.e. a tax on the use of all our renewable and nonrenewable resources: "The incentive will be toward more resource-saving, labor-using patterns of production and consumption."

• In addition, Daly and Cobb advocate a *pollution tax:* "[It will] promote equity in that consumers will then pay the real costs of what they buy rather than passing much of it to society at large."

•   •   •

Beyond left and right—beyond levelling and "looking out for #1"—is community: respecting and even encouraging human diversity while, at the same time, making sure that everybody's basic needs are met.

The simple flat tax with a generous personal exemption is a primary example of a proposal that responds not to the raucous drummings of the left and right, but to the contemporary longing for personal *and* social responsibility, autonomy *and* commitment. In a word, community.

But it is not enough to be at the forefront of the Zeitgeist. A political proposal—unlike a cultural trend—needs to be propagated by an organized movement. And we do not yet have a political movement with the breadth, savvy and self-confidence to go "beyond left and right."

But we will. And it will make the flat tax a topic of passionate national debate.

10 To Balance the Budget, Build a Sustainable Society

May 1988

When Ronald Reagan submitted his eighth consecutive unbalanced budget earlier this year—calling for a "deficit target" of approx. $130 billion—virtually no one objected. The entire traditional political spectrum from far right to far left seems to have reconciled itself to the permanently expanding national debt as a fact of life. Politicians and analysts no longer speak of balancing the budget, merely of "holding down" the deficit.

Everyone seems to believe we can be fiscally responsible OR socially constructive, but not both at once. It is NEW OPTIONS's contention—and the contention of a growing number of visionary economists and economic thinkers—that just the opposite is the case. The way to balance the budget is to build a sustainable society.

I. Deficits are not inevitable

Many politicians are trying to convince us that—through the Balanced Budget Reaffirmation Act—the deficit will be brought down to $23 billion by 1993. Even the Congressional Budget Office (CBO) laughs at the politicians' arithmetic.

In its respected *1988 Annual Report* the CBO states, "Under current budget policies...[and w]ith continued real economic growth [!!], the baseline deficit is projected to decline to $167 billion in 1990 and $134 billion"—not $23 billion—in 1993.

The CBO's figures are sobering. But even they underestimate the problem. "The budget deficit is going to be *going up again*," Robert Hamrin, author of *A Renewable Resource Economy* (1983) and former economics advisor to Gary Hart, told NEW OPTIONS.

"This past year it went down substantially. But that was just a temporary aberration in the trend of rising deficits. We're probably going to see the deficit rising to $180-190 billion over the next couple of years. If we get a recession in the next year or two—which is likely—then we're going to see the deficit climb well over $200 billion. . . .

"And the deficit problem is even worse than that. The Social Security system is starting to build up huge [albeit temporary] surpluses—and these surpluses are included in the overall 'unified budget,' as it's called. With the Social Security surpluses excluded from the budget, the real deficit soars above the $220 billion level in the early 1990s."

A $220-plus billion deficit even *with* the Balanced Budget Reaffirmation Act? It's no wonder that Democrats and Republicans have virtually stopped addressing the issue. (The left's position was perfectly expressed in the cover story in this month's *Mother Jones:* "This is not a time to chop mindlessly at government spending, but to launch an economic strategy of high growth.")

But for those of us who are committed to building a sustainable society—a society characterized by human growth rather than material growth—there can be no avoiding the issue.

Fortunately, many innovative economists and economic thinkers are rising to the challenge. All across America, in small state universities and feisty non-profit organizations, little-known thinkers are generating proposals for raising revenues or reducing expenditures that would—at the *same time*—succeed in fostering a sustainable society.

Over the last month, we interviewed 20 of these new-style economists and economic thinkers. They don't represent a distinct economic "school" or "tradition"—unless there's such a thing as an E.F. Schumacherian tradition. But you can find a good number of them in two organizations that are seeking to go "beyond left and right": the Human Economy Center and The Other Economic Summit.

Through these organizations, the New Economists are just now beginning to discover each other. Most of them don't yet realize how potent their collective message is. For example, most of them will be stunned to discover that, when we put 11 of their best suggestions together, we were able to *completely eliminate* Hamrin's projected $220-plus billion deficit. We were able to increase revenues and decrease expenditures by $250 billion a year—$127 billion more than *Time* (29 Feb. 1988), $175 billion more than *The New Republic* (30 Nov. 1987).

Come see for yourself.

The first five suggestions below would increase federal revenues by $150 billion in 1993 (we're allowing four years to implement our suggestions). The next six would decrease federal expenditures by $100 billion.

II. How to increase revenues

Merger tax ($25b). "We might want to consider taxing mergers," James Brock, professor of economics at Miami University (Ohio) and co-author of *The Bigness Complex* (1986), told NEW OPTIONS.

"The merger fever that's going around builds in all kinds of speculative value in stocks completely divorced from any kind of underlying economic reality. Mergers also add to the problem of bigness—the power that goes with sheer corporate size. . . .

"The old rationale for taxing liquor and cigarettes was as a 'sin tax,' right? Well, why not tax economic sin? Why not institute an economic sin tax?

"You could have a progressive tax scheme like we do for income: Small mergers less, giant mergers more—because they're more destructive.

"Another thing you can do to discourage mergers is eliminate a lot of the deductions associated with mergers. The legal fees and the investment banking fees and so forth can all be written off now. And a lot of the deals are being financed with extremely large amounts of junk bonds and debt on which the interest is all deductible. . . .

"Suppose we take $200 billion a year as a rough figure for the size of all mergers and acquisitions. Figure a 10% tax on that, you're talking $20 billion." If we also eliminated many of the deductions associated with mergers we could raise a total of at least $25 billion in 1993.

Inheritance tax ($20b). "I think we should have a high inheritance tax," Lon Smith, professor of economics at Mankato (Minn.) State University, told NEW OPTIONS. "We should all sort of start equal in this country.

"Some people earn a lot of income, and I'm willing to let them keep most of it. But when you see the second or third generation with its inherited millions—well, I don't see them deserving it.

"I think a high inheritance tax has some Biblical foundations; I think it's tied to at least the purpose of the Jubilee year. Also, in the pennant races they go for a year and the next year they start all over, don't they? They don't continue with the last team 15 games behind and just keep going and going.

"You'd want to allow people to pass on their family farms; you wouldn't want people to have to sell them. A certain amount of acreage could be exempt. Also, you'd have to allow people to pass on a family home. You don't have to pass on a mansion, or second or third homes, but I would say you have to treat homes the way you'd treat farms.

"But basically everything besides your home and your land should be subject to the inheritance tax.

"Ideally, I'd set a limit rather than a tax. I'd go up to $100,000 and that's all. I'm not tied to that figure. But I think $100,000 is enough to get a person going."

The CBO estimates that, if we taxed capital gains at death (under the income tax), we'd raise approx. $6 billion in 1993. So it is safe to say that if we adopted even the mildest, most watered-down version of Smith's scheme, we could raise $20 billion in 1993.

Stock market tax ($15b). "I think we have to consider a transfer tax on stock purchases," Don Cole, professor of economics at Drew University (Madison, N.J.), told NEW OPTIONS.

"We need a federal tax on stocks and bonds traded on the U.S. stock exchanges," echoed Mark Lutz, professor of economics at the University of Maine (Orono) and co-author of *The Challenge of Humanistic Economics* (1979).

"The tax would apply to the purchase or sale of securities," says Cole. "It's basically aimed at taxing financial speculation. I mean, financial speculation in my view contributes absolutely nothing to real economic activity. So why not simply tax those transfers?"

"The tax would discourage short-term buying and selling," Lutz told NEW OPTIONS. "It would boost the cost of speculative transfers and therefore make them less attractive and discourage them. But it wouldn't discourage the long-term serious investor."

Lutz suggests a tax of up to 1% on exchange of stocks and up to 3/4% on exchange of bonds ("speculation in bonds is much less harmful"). Lawrence Summers of Harvard recently calculated that a tax of 1/2% on exchange of financial securities would raise

more than $10 billion a year (*The New Republic,* Nov. 30, 1987).
So we can assume Lutz's tax would raise a minimum of $15 billion
a year.

"Health tax" ($25b). "We have a concrete proposal," Patricia
Taylor, director of the Alcohol Policies Project at the Washington,
D.C.-based Center for Science in the Public Interest, told NEW
OPTIONS. "What it would do is raise the beer and wine tax to
the present liquor rate—and then double all taxes on alcohol.

"The excise tax on beer and wine has not been increased since
1951! And the liquor excise tax was only raised nominally in 1985.
Right now in many parts of the country it's cheaper to go out and
buy a six-pack of beer than a six-pack of soda. . . .

"We like to talk about it as a 'health tax' rather than as a 'sin
tax.' Research indicates that raising excise taxes on alcohol reduces
alcohol problems, reduces the purchasing of alcoholic beverages
by underage kids, and even has an impact on the purchases of
people with alcohol problems—which is quite a startling finding!
A number of researchers have suggested that raising alcohol excise
taxes is one of the most effective ways we can deal with drinking
and driving problems."

Taylor's proposal would raise $12 billion in new revenues. But
that's only part of the story. Public policy analysts like Charles
Phelps, professor of economics at the University of Rochester
(N.Y.), argue that "the declines in alcohol-related illness and injury
would reduce federal outlays (Medicaid, Veterans Administration,
military health care) *by comparable amounts,* a desirable double
dip" (*The Wall Street Journal,* 17 Nov. 1987). Let's err on the
conservative side and estimate that increasing the alcohol "health
tax" as Taylor suggests would improve things by $20 billion in
1993.

There could also be a cigarette "health tax." "Cigarette
smoking costs the American economy $65 billion annually in lost
health care and productivity costs," Clifford Douglas, assistant
director of the Washington, D.C.-based Coalition on Smoking OR
Health, told NEW OPTIONS. "A 16 cent increase to the cigarette
excise tax [i.e., doubling the current tax] would in one year deter
almost one million teenagers from smoking—and would prevent
860,000 premature deaths from smoking-related causes 30 to 50
years from now."

The Coalition estimates that doubling the cigarette tax would raise $3.5 billion a year in new revenues. Assuming that a decline in smoking-related illnesses would follow, let's estimate that increasing the cigarette "health tax" as the Coalition suggests would improve things by $5 billion in 1993.

Gas tax ($45b). "We could increase the gasoline tax by 50 cents [a gallon]," Lester Brown, president of the Worldwatch Institute, told NEW OPTIONS.

"The idea of increasing the gasoline tax by 50 cents over current levels may sound somewhat far-reaching in U.S. terms. But that would probably take us up to only about half the level of the average gasoline tax in Italy or West Germany or the U.K.

"And it would do several things for us. It would make a major contribution to reducing the federal deficit—it would probably raise about $45 billion. And it would reduce oil imports, which would have the effect of strengthening our balance of payments.

"From an environmental point of view, it would help reduce urban air pollution, acid rain, and the carbon dioxide buildup. So we would gain on three major fronts.

"It would also encourage the use of public transportation, which would increase the revenues there and make it easier to develop first-class public transport systems."

III. How to decrease expenditures

Health incentive ($10b). According to Tom Ferguson, M.D., editor of *Medical Self-Care,* we can lower federal expenditures on medical care by paying people to stay healthy.

"You could have a medical plan that had cash bonuses built right into the rate structure," Ferguson told NEW OPTIONS from his office at the Center for Self-Care Studies in Austin, Texas.

"The government could give you a bonus if you scored well on some health measure. Or you could get a bonus if you didn't use doctor services much.

"When people know they're going to get a bonus if they don't use doctor services, they go to the doctor much less. This has already been proved in some school districts.

"If all the people under federally-funded health insurance were to get, you know, $10 for every month they didn't use any medical services, it would cut down unnecessary visits to doctors—and it would give people an immediate economic incentive to keep *themselves* healthy.''

Let's assume that by 1993 Medicare, Medicaid, Federal Employees Health Benefits and the Veterans Administration all offered economic incentives for "wellness." Federal outlays for medical care are estimated to be $130 billion in 1989 and are projected to increase by an average of 10% a year between 1989 and 1993. Even if incentives for wellness were to decrease medical care outlays by only 5% in 1993, that would still save nearly $10 billion.

Energy efficiency ($10b). According to Richard Heede, research associate at Amory Lovins's Rocky Mountain Institute, we can lower federal expenditures on energy in three ways.

"One way," Heede told NEW OPTIONS, "is by reducing the program obligations that are spent on behalf of the energy industries or consumers of energy. I have a list of *60 programs* that are energy-related. I totalled them up a few years ago and got over $8 billion.

"Most of that money is devoted to increasing our *supply* of energy. Not very much at all is spent on how to use that supply more efficiently. [Doing] the latter would be far more cost-effective. . . . I'm pretty confident we could cut the $8 billion in half.

"The second way to reduce energy expenditures is by eliminating energy-related tax breaks, [now approx. $10-15 billion a year]. It's my position that almost all tax breaks skew the market and skew rational investment.'' Not incidentally, it's also Heede's position that a "level playing field" in energy would doom nuclear power and permit conservation and renewables to attract a far higher percentage of the private money now spent on energy.

The third way Heede would reduce federal energy expenditures is by reducing the amount the government spends on its *own* energy costs—its own utilities, buildings, vehicles, etc. Simply by increasing "energy efficiency" (conservation), Heede is convinced the government could cut its annual $7-8 billion energy bill by at least a quarter.

So: If we reduced energy program outlays by $4 billion, eliminated most energy subsidies, and reduced the government's own energy costs by $2 billion, it seems safe to say we could save $10 billion in 1993.

Sustainable farms ($10b). According to Jeff Bercuvitz, director of Community Regeneration, we can lower federal expenditures on agriculture by moving to a system of sustainable or "regenerative" agriculture.

"The solutions that are needed do not require large-scale federal dollars," Bercuvitz told NEW OPTIONS.

"For the most part, today's huge agricultural subsidies are part of the problem. They're perpetuating a mode of agriculture that is bad for farms and farmers in that they're encouraging overuse of chemicals. And the subsidies are skewed to larger farms.

"Provided we had a plan in place to help farmers make the transition from conventional farming techniques to regenerative farming practices, over the next five years or so we could get to the point where we could eliminate the *entire subsidy program.*"

Expenditures on farm subsidy programs are estimated to be $20 billion in 1989. Let's assume that, by 1993, a "regenerative" approach to farming will have permitted the elimination of half the subsidies. That means a savings of approx. $10 billion in 1993.

Worker democracy ($10b). According to Jon Wisman, professor of economics at American University in Washington, D.C., we can lower federal expenditures by moving to a system of workplace democracy.

"Workplace democracy would, itself, reduce the deficit," Wisman told NEW OPTIONS. "Workplace democracy is America's only way of competing in an increasingly competitive world.

"We are locked into capital-labor strife, and the only way we can overcome all the impediments to productivity that result from that strife is by 'marrying' capital and labor: that is, encouraging ownership and control of capital by workers themselves.

"That move would greatly enhance productivity—and that alone would increase the tax base dramatically."

How greatly would it enhance productivity? The National Center for Employee Ownership recently conducted some studies. Among its findings:

• A sample of 43 "majority employee owned" firms grew at about 3.9% per year compared to a weighted rate of about 1.1%.

• A sample of 13 "publicly traded firms that were at least 10% employee owned" outperformed their rivals 62-75% on such measures as sales growth and return to equity.

• A sample of 13 failing firms that were "bought out" by their employees had an employment growth rate twice that of comparable conventional firms.

Four years into a concerted move to workplace democracy, it does not seem unreasonable to expect that enhanced productivity would generate an additional $10 billion in federal revenues.

Military spending ($45b). According to many of our visionary economists and economic thinkers, we can—and should—lower federal expenditures by cutting military spending.

"It is just ridiculous that in 1987 55% of federal expenditures went to various different things related to the military," Susan Meeker-Lowry, author of *Economics as If the Earth Really Mattered,* told NEW OPTIONS. "Knowing what I know about the way major corporations work and the way defense contractors work, I am convinced we could cut the defense budget considerably."

Let's assume a 15% cut in the official military budget, and let's permit military spending to keep pace with inflation. (Let's put further cuts on hold until we come up with an alternative defense *strategy*). Since the official military budget is approx. $300 billion, that means we'd save $45 billion in 1993.

Interest payments ($35b). *Time* magazine (29 Feb. 1988) estimates that if we raised taxes and cut outlays by $110 billion, interest payments on the national debt would fall by $18 billion in 1992. Assuming we raised taxes and cut outlays by $215 billion (as suggested above), interest payments should fall by approx. $35 billion in 1993.

IV. C'mon. $250 billion?

Last year, Congress sweated for weeks to cut the deficit by $76 billion over two years (and the effort did Congress in; nothing like that was even contemplated this year). And yet, NEW OPTIONS has just managed to suggest new taxes and savings amounting to $250 billion a year by 1993. What's going on here? What's the NEW OPTIONS difference?

The main difference, we suspect, is that Congress—*every member* of Congress, from the farthest left to the farthest right— is intent on preserving the Old System: the growth-oriented economy, mammoth wealth and income differentials, giant corporations, a medical care system that rewards illness not wellness, and all the rest of it. And there's just not that much slack in the system (unless you go after the income of middle-class Americans). In fact, as Congress' own budget projections show, just keeping the Old System afloat is an increasingly expensive proposition.

NEW OPTIONS's budget suggestions—and the visionary economists and economic thinkers who helped us to them—would set in place a different system. A New System favoring human growth, economic equity, small community-based businesses, a medical care system that rewards wellness, and all the rest of it.

One of the reasons people may have shied away from contemplating such a system in the real world is that they suspect it would be prohibitively expensive. The moral of this article is that the opposite is the case: When implemented fully, decentralist/globally responsible proposals can be expected to raise revenues or cut costs. Or both.

Jeff Bercuvitz, cited above, put it well and made the essential political point when he told us, "There are a lot of people who assume that if you are concerned about farming in America, then you need to vote more money for federal subsidy programs. You have slogans like 'More farms—less arms.' Whereas the fact of the matter is that the more innovative solutions require *fewer* subsidies."

Under the Old System, some of us get to play the role of the Compassionate Ones, others of us the role of the Hard-Headed Ones. It's at the heart of the old left-right political game (and also, of course, the old sexual division of labor).

As our economic thinkers' proposals demonstrate, however, the New System would collapse that basal dualism. For the humane and sustainable choices are also the economically rational ones. To balance the budget, we *have* to build a human growth-oriented society. To become fiscally responsible, we have to risk feeling and dreaming.

PART THREE

BEYOND THE WELFARE STATE

Today the traditional left is trying to pump more money into the welfare state; the traditional right is trying to "hold the line" on spending. But does anyone really believe that money is the heart of the issue?

The Second American Experiment is not about spending more money on people, but about changing our *patterns* of government assistance in order to reduce government bureaucracy and help people take charge of their own lives.

In this sense, the Second Experiment is part of the larger "freedom movement" that is sweeping the globe—and that was in part inspired, as African-American historian and NEW OPTIONS Advisor Vincent Harding likes to point out, by the *militantly* decentralist, *militantly* pro-empowerment thrust of our own civil rights movement.

The pieces in this section all show, concretely, how we can move away from bureaucracy and toward decentralization and empowerment—*and* how we can save money in the process!

The first piece, "Our Schools Need Imagination More Than They Need Money," makes the important point that this decentralizing-and-empowering process may be a lot more complex (delicate, many-sided and values-based) than some of its enthusiasts suggest.

The next two pieces, on transportation and health care, make the related point that government cannot just "wither away." We'll need public policies that *actively move us* toward trolleys and bikes, and toward preventive health care, for example.

The fourth piece, "Drugs Are Not the Enemy," makes the complementary point that sometimes the best the government can do is say "No" to its own natural tendency to want to control every aspect of our behavior...meanwhile providing all the resources we'll need to cope with the consequences of that behavior.

The final piece, a searching investigation of "multiculturalism," implies that it is not enough to decentralize government and empower people. If we want to go beyond the depersonalized "caring" of the welfare state, we must also make sure that people care deeply about *who* they are, and about the *quality of their relations* with others...all others. We must make sure that on the far side of the welfare state is a caring society.

11 Our Schools Need Imagination More Than They Need Money

May 1989

Typically, "progressives" and change agents have demanded *more money* for social programs. But today it's clear that the *way we do things* needs to change—and that if things were done more appropriately, more humanely, more intelligently, we might end up spending *less* on social programs than we do now.

Take education. Over the last 25 years, the number of students enrolled in our elementary and secondary schools has varied very little (from a high of 51 million in 1970 to a low of 44 million in 1985). But we spent $30 billion on elementary and secondary education in 1966; $72 billion in 1975; and *$159 billion* in 1986.

That means spending on education has increased *more than one and one-half times as fast as inflation* since 1965. And what have we gotten in return?A generation's worth of declining test scores. A report by the educational establishment itself that concludes, "The educational foundations of our society are presently being eroded by a rising tide of mediocrity that threatens our very future as a nation and a people" (*A Nation at Risk,* 1983).

The Democratic party thinks it knows how to turn things around. In its 1988 platform it calls for (surprise, surprise) spending even more on education—the same kind of education we have now. There isn't even a *hint* that the *ways we educate* our children might be part of the problem!

According to the Democrats' logic, the problem isn't with the educational system but with us. We're so damn greedy. We're just not willing to spend what it takes.

Over the last 10 years or so, a handful of education reformers have operated by a different sort of logic. They've come up with exciting new ideas for changing the ways our schools are administered, the ways our children are taught, and the kinds of things they're taught.

And *nearly all their ideas would cost no more than our current practices cost.* Some would actually save us money!

Despite their concern that their proposals be cost-effective, the new education reformers can hardly be characterized as conservative. They tend to borrow equally from the moods and movements of the 1960s, 70s and 80s. Their key words and phrases transcend left and right: choice, diversity, empowerment, learning styles, children helping children, education with production, learning to learn.

We talked with many of these reformers over the last few months, including directors of the two most exciting education-reform organizations in the country: the Center for Collaborative Education in New York City and New Horizons for Learning in Seattle. Among them they stressed 12 key proposals. What follows is an attempt to pull those proposals together, the first such attempt we've seen.

Do we have an education reform *program* here, one that can take us beyond the structurelessness of 60s-style efforts and the "new traditionalism" of today?

I. Re-inventing the teaching profession

Deregulate teaching. One of the first things the new reformers would do is deregulate the teaching profession...making it possible for people to teach in our schools without teaching certificates.

"There are not many teachers in the public schools whom I think of as knowledgeable people," John McKnight told NEW OPTIONS. McKnight is director of community studies at the Center for Urban Affairs and co-author of *Disabling Professions* (1977).

"If you asked, Does the average physician know some significant medical procedures and methods?, I'd have to say yes. If you asked, Does the average electrician know something methodologically significant?, I'd have to say yes.

"But the professional qualifications of the teacher are the least significant around. The teachers' degree has more hokum associated with it than that of any other profession, and teachers' schools are looked down upon at every college of education. Why? Because what they have to offer, methodologically, is so insignificant.

"Training in pedagogy should not be a requirement for someone to be associated with young people. Instead I'd have us ask a wonderful question: Whom do we want our children to be learning from?"

Empower teachers. Another idea the new reformers are talking about would shake the profession up just as much: Give teachers a lot more control over *what* and *how* they teach.

"One of the reasons I think teachers are frustrated and dissatisfied is they feel powerless," Mary Ellen Sweeney, co-editor of *Holistic Education Review,* told NEW OPTIONS.

Teachers know best, and it's teachers who should be making decisions about kids, about the curriculum, about the goals of the school. State mandates should be waived—what works in one town doesn't necessarily work in another....

"If teachers become decision-makers, they'll experience fewer discipline problems with kids, because they'll be able to engage them in interesting and worthwhile work.

"And teachers will have the potential to grow more as individuals. They'll be able to develop and expand upon their areas of interest. And that will attract a different sort of person into public school teaching.''

Peer tutoring. Frank Riessman, director of the Peer Research Lab in New York City, thinks kids can often be their own best teachers. ''Kids talk to kids much more readily than they talk to adults,'' he told NEW OPTIONS. ''So what we do in our work is try to set up approaches in school systems where everybody has a chance to play the tutor role.

''That breaks away from the remedial, I'm-helping-you kind of approach. In most cases today the 'more advanced' kids tutor the 'less advanced' kids. That makes the receiver feel 'I need help!' rather than, 'I need help for the moment but I can give somebody else help tomorrow.'

''But if I'm in the sixth grade I can be tutoring fourth grade; if I'm in the fourth grade I can be tutoring second grade; and so on down to kindergarten. Even within a grade you can train half the class to tutor the other half part of the time, then reverse it.

''One recent study compared peer tutoring with computer-assisted learning. It found that peer tutoring was far more cost-effective. There's also evidence for massive increases in feelings of empowerment and democratic and cooperative attitudes.''

Co-teaching. Many new reformers would have *other adults* help out, as well. Andy LePage, author of *Transforming Education* (1987), is one of our most persistent and effective advocates of volunteer teacher programs.

''If teachers are willing to share their power,'' LePage told NEW OPTIONS, ''and to recognize they can be so much more effective when someone else puts another angle to something— then they are going to welcome the idea of *co-teaching*. This is where a non-teacher shares in the teaching of a subject they both care about.

''For example, suppose someone in my town has spent 30 years putting together a Civil War collection and really understands that period well and has maybe been a curator at a museum or something. For me to say, Gee, I'm gonna teach this whole section on the Civil War—when I have that extraordinary person right nearby—is kind of ludicrous.

''Now, who are these potential co-teachers? I believe they're all around us.

"There are all kinds of *experts* who'd be glad to volunteer their time. A broadcaster can come in and do a section on communications. A psychologist can come in and do a section on listening skills.... There are *senior citizens*. There are *former teachers, clergypersons, business folks*. Then there are the *hands-on people*. Cooks. Forest rangers. People from the symphony...."

II. Re-inventing school structures

Open enrollment. Nearly all the new reformers believe parents should be able to decide where they'll send their kids to school. That's why they favor open enrollment. But they're also sensitive to the racial issue, so their support for open enrollment hinges on certain other conditions being met.

One of the most sophisticated documents on this whole subject was recently produced at Oakland University (OU) in suburban Detroit. Called "Schools of Choice," it was written by OU's Project to Access Choice in Education (PACE) and published by Detroit's non-profit Metropolitan Affairs Council. James Clatworthy, an associate dean at OU, was the gray eminence behind the document.

"The term 'open enrollment' dates back to the late 60s," Clatworthy told NEW OPTIONS. "It can be defined as the freedom for families to choose the full-time public school of attendance....

"Early open enrollment plans appear to have been motivated by the desire to counteract mandated school desegregation orders. This type of open enrollment is not based on sound educational motives.... PACE was an attempt to define choice in a socially responsible way. And the PACE team defined it as not *just* open enrollment, but as teacher empowerment and [school and program] diversity.

"Where all three exist, there's significant choice—and better learning outcomes for students."

Diverse schools. All the new reformers celebrate the increasing ethnic, racial and cultural diversity in America's public schools. And all would endorse the PACE report when it says, "Student diversity, however, is often unmatched by programmatic diversity....

"Students are better and more enthusiastic learners when they are able to choose schools and programs compatible with their interest areas and learning styles. Open classrooms, cooperative learning, cross-age grouping, block time, Montessori, and gifted-talented are some examples of strategies that meet the needs of different students."

"The real key to choice, I think, is programmatic diversity," Clatworthy told NEW OPTIONS. "That means encouraging schools to offer special programs that all students in the district can select if they meet the requirements. Encouraging schools if they want to create an arts school or a school where the bulk of the curriculum is related to environmental awareness. Allowing schools to have different mission statements....

"We're even talking now about allowing each school to develop its programmatic diversity through a special charter. First off, the charter would have students, parents and teachers get together and *define* what they'd like the school to be...."

Smaller schools. "I think schools work well when the people in them can all sit around a table together," Heather Lewis, director of the Center for Collaborative Education, told NEW OPTIONS. "The advantage of a small unit is that you can talk to kids as people you know, listen to them, respond to their fears and confusions, help them understand that ideas matter.

"Another reason we favor small schools is I don't think you can disconnect size from autonomy. And a school that's small is *able* to make decisions about curriculum, organization, students, etc., without being told from the top down what to do....

"Finally, when you have a smaller school you often have a real school *community.*"

Democratic classrooms. All the new reformers would introduce democracy into the classroom—as revolutionary a concept there as it is in China, unfortunately.

Linda MacRae-Campbell is an enthusiastic proponent of classroom democracy. She makes her living as an international consultant on "holistic teaching methods" and is developing a new model of teacher education at Antioch University West based on such methods.

"We are living in a democratic society," she told us from her home near Seattle. "And we expect our students to grow up and function in it as informed citizens. And yet, in most classrooms, the democratic process is not enacted!

"This is something we need to look at. We need to give students an opportunity for some self-determination in their learning activities. And we need to let them work as a group and make some group decisions.

"The school climate breeds competition and isolation among students. We need to move more into working with cooperative and collaborative processes, so students become better used to working together as a team."

III. Re-inventing the curriculum

Learning styles. Dee Dickinson, founder and president of New Horizons for Learning, feels there's a gap between traditional teaching methods and the needs of kids in school today.

"It is no longer possible to teach 'down the middle of the road' and expect that everybody's going to get it," Dickinson told NEW OPTIONS. "Most teachers teach the way *they* best learn—which does not necessarily reach the majority of kids in the classroom."

Worse, most teachers teach passively, "which means kids in their seats listening to information being poured in a funnel through the top of their heads, right?" The most destructive result of the passive-"intellectual" teaching style: the growing conviction, on the part of many in our society, that many kids just can't learn very well.

One of the key tenets of the new education reformers is that, in Dickinson's words, "there isn't anybody who can't learn." All that's needed is to develop different teaching styles for different learners.

Much of the groundwork has already been laid, Dickinson told NEW OPTIONS. "For example, Howard Gardner of Harvard talks about seven kinds of intelligence.

"He talks about verbal and mathematical-logical intelligence, okay? But he also talks about visual-spatial; bodily-kinesthetic; musical; interpersonal (i.e., able to work cooperatively with other people); and intrapersonal (understanding more about our inner world)."

For the new reformers, the implications of Gardner's theory are both obvious and profound. "We never tap into most intelligences," Dickinson told us, and *that's* why most students fail to learn. "We give kids athletic scholarships in college, kids with high kinesthetic intelligence, and then we force them to learn in the classroom by sitting and listening to lectures!...

"In the future teachers will have to be innovative and utilize art and music and dance and drama throughout the curriculum as ways to reach these other kinds of intelligence...."

Peace education. A number of new reformers have written books or articles or "curricula" on peace or global education. But Ruth Fletcher's book *Teaching Peace: Skills for Living in a Global Society* (1986) is special.

Talk about holism, its 64 chapters—written for teachers of elementary and junior high school kids—cover not just "the threat of nuclear war," but conflict resolution (mediation, "active listening," etc.); "structural violence" (racism, sexism, poverty, etc.); "whole earth system" (basic human needs, scarce resources, "responsible consumerism," etc.); and much, much more.

We tracked Fletcher down—she turns out to be a regional minister for the Northwest Regional Christian Church, based in Seattle—and asked her why she cast her net so broadly. "A lot of the Educators for Social Responsibility stuff has to do with just the nuclear issue," she replied. "But the central issue for me is violence.

"Now, most people will define violence as only physical violence. I like to use a broader definition. Anytime you do harm, you know, that's an act of violence. So poverty can be considered violence; racism and sexism can be considered violence...."

There a sense in which Fletcher feels even her own book falls short. "All the peace curricula I've seen seem to focus on content; you know, let's teach kids how to solve conflicts in the classroom, or let's teach multicultural education. Kids don't really get it that violence is *everywhere:* it's on TV, it's in their textbooks, it's in the culture.

"So if we're going to teach peace, we have to make it more than book-learnin'. Peace has to be embedded in all the processes that are used in the classroom—like, are the students included in the processes?"

Education with production. Chris Hennin is, among other things, a young turk at the World Bank, an expert on Third World self-help, and an integral part of an international network pushing for something called "education with production" (EWP).

"There are lots of different kinds of EWP programs," Hennin told NEW OPTIONS. "But basically, they all incorporate productive activities into the academic program. They all link learning with productive work."

In elementary and secondary schools in North America, that basically means getting kids to grow their own food; getting them to prepare and market it; and getting them to clean and maintain their school buildings.

"I think there's nothing more educational than growing things," Hennin told us, "simply because kids have an opportunity to see life transform itself. And they become aware of the fragility of life. . . .

"I think disagreeable tasks like carrying the garbage or cleaning toilets should be done by all the kids. So they'll learn to be more conscious and responsible. . . .

"All the time I hear the argument that, if kids work, it takes away from their academic concentration. But what I've found is that, if you give kids the opportunity to work at real things, it *stimulates* their intellect.

"Animals are self-sustaining at maturity, and I think humans have the same inherent need."

Learning to learn. For the new reformers, the goal of schooling is *not* the inculcation of "information" or even "knowledge," but what they call "learning to learn." It's a slippery concept, but you know it when it's happened.

"For me, learning to learn is learning to *sustain the act* of learning," Ruben Nelson of the Post-Industrial Future Project told NEW OPTIONS.

"Ideally, learning to learn becomes an exercise that is self-generating. . . . One of the critical requirements is that you ask yourself rude questions. And that you ask the world rude questions. But always from the point of view of psychological security. . . .

"When you're at the stage of learning to learn, you can learn in any situation. You can read a thoroughly bad book and learn an immense amount from it! You can listen to bad lectures and learn as much from them as good ones. . . . Learning to learn is an attitudinal set that pervades everything."

IV. Overcoming the resistance

To some of you, what we've written above may seem as "controversial" as mom and apple pie. So it's important to remember how the real world sees it. Virtually every interest group in the education profession is opposed to most of what we've written. So is much of American culture.

"The resistance is systemic," Linda MacRae-Campbell told NEW OPTIONS. Just consider:

• "Our major *teacher training institutions* are 25 years behind the times," MacRae-Campbell said. "They don't teach teachers how to deal with the different kinds of intelligence in the classroom. They don't teach teachers how to deal with emotional issues in the classroom. . . ."

• "The *school boards* don't want to give teachers more power," James Clatworthy said. "They don't want teachers telling administrations what's good for students. And they don't want teachers entering policy areas that they feel is 'their' responsibility."

• "The resistance comes from the *principals*, who have a hard time giving up control," Heather Lewis said. "They are used to running their schools a certain way and are unwilling to grant any kind of autonomy to teachers."

• "Most *teachers* are unwilling to share their power with students and with adult co-teachers," Andy LePage said. "They're going to have to recognize that they have that need."

In response to these barriers, the new education reformers have plenty of bright ideas—but few organizations that can take those ideas into the mainstream.

Probably the most competent idea-dissemination organization is Dee Dickinson's New Horizons for Learning, based in Seattle. A non-profit membership organization, it sponsors talks, workshops, seminars, conferences, and a 16-page quarterly newsletter that can keep you up to date on the new reformers— and on how their ideas are faring in the profession.

The most promising organization of new-reform schools is Heather Lewis's Center for Collaborative Education in New York City. "We've organized a network of [innovative] public schools," Lewis told us, "and we're constantly adding schools as well as providing assistance to administrators, teachers and parents who are interested in either starting such schools or in starting programs *within* schools that share a similar philosophy to ours."

Despite these organizations and some others, the gap between potential and reality is very, very wide now. Before we see substantial movement in the direction of teacher empowerment, smaller schools, education with production, etc., we may first have to see a change in the values and goals of the larger society. Which is to say: We may have to foster a political movement. One that doesn't blame most of our social problems on lack of money.

12 Bigger Roads—or Trolleys, Bikes and Urban Redesign?

October 1988

A little more than a year ago, my friend Tobi Sanders called up to chat. A NEW OPTIONS Advisor, she was full of advice that day—and so was I. We laughed and laughed.

A couple of hours later, another call. A dull-gray voice. While driving home, Tobi's car had been hit by a truck, killing her instantly.

Since that day I've tried to do something that I think we were all trained not to do. I've begun to notice—I mean, really *take notice of*—the toll the automobile has taken on my friends' lives. One friend's legs are brutally scarred; another was hospitalized for months and still suffers dizzy spells; another was awarded $50,000 in damages, which doesn't help her constant spinal pain.

Last week I called the National Safety Council and got hold of the figures. Every year, approx. 48,000 Americans die in automobile accidents. Another 150,000 are "permanently impaired" (love this bureaucratese). Another 1,600,000 suffer "temporary disabling injuries." It's as if we fought the Vietnam war on our highways *every 14 months.*

There's another parallel with Vietnam: It's an undeclared war. Did any elected official ever ask you if you thought we should kill off half a million Americans every 10 years, rather than think seriously about alternatives to the automobile?

Some other telling statistics:

• Car ownership is *not* levelling off. Americans operate 27% more motor vehicles today than they did ten years ago.

• "Today's average motorist will spend an estimated six months of his [or her] lifetime waiting for red lights to change" (Priority Management Pittsburgh, quoted in *Time*).

• Over 60,000 square miles of land in the U.S. have been paved over—10% of all arable land!

Consider, too, some of the less quantifiable costs of the auto system—how it's degraded the environment, how it's reinforced our obsession with efficiency and speed, how it subjects us to constant background noise. . . .

Neither liberals nor conservatives are addressing any of this. (Occasionally you'll find some "progressive" willing to stand up for stultifyingly expensive subway systems.) But if you know where to look, you can find other voices, proposing real solutions to our transportation problems.

I. Train power

The National Association of Railroad Passengers (NARP) is located just around the corner from the Amtrak station in Washington, D.C., and a couple of flights above an ice-cream store. Its cramped offices are stacked to bursting with books and papers—among them, the back issues of one of the most affecting newsletters in the social change movement, *NARP News*.

NARP's executive director and guiding spirit, Ross Capon, is white bearded and extremely articulate, and equally at home with railroad industry executives and federal administrators,

Congresspeople and environmentalists and "just plain passengers." He has to be: he's constantly in touch with all of them.

When we visited, a *Time* magazine story on transportation had just come out, and he was steaming: "They completely ignore the success stories of rapid transit! They ignore the San Diego light rail line, which is expanding, which is covering almost 90% of its operating costs from the fare box and which is widely regarded as a tremendous success. Everybody loves the trolleys...."

How does Capon's vision differ from *Time*'s? "The vision I'd offer is heavily influenced by the fact that people *like* to ride rail transit. And they tend *not* to like to ride buses. And they don't like to sit in traffic jams all day—although far too many people have been given no other choice....

"There has to be a lot more attention paid in most U.S. cities to what's going on in California in terms of the new light rail systems. In a place like L.A., it may well be that subway construction is justified. But, in general, I think that most of the cities that do not currently have rail transit are going to find light rail a much more effective technology than subways—simply because it's so much more flexible. You can stick the tracks wherever you want to put them, in a road, in a private right-of-way, elevated, whatever....

"There are an awful lot of places where travel demands are dense enough to justify rail transit but where there's no right-of-way other than your basic highway. We have to go and wrench that right-of-way out of the hands of the state highway administrators—or change their thinking—and put trolley tracks down...."

Capon is just as enthusiastic about Amtrak. "Amtrak is already the Number One carrier in the New York-to-Washington market. Can it become that in other corridors? The answer is yes—it's a matter of making the investment."

We were mystified. If trolleys and Amtrak made so much sense, what was the problem? Capon had a ready answer: "We've created these monstrous money-machines that spew out oodles of federal bucks for highways and airports.

"When you earmark all the gas taxes for highway building, and all the airplane ticket taxes for airport building, you've created a system that guarantees that the transportation systems you have today are going to get bigger—and the other transportation systems are going to get squeezed out.''

II. Pedal power

When we visited Marcia Lowe, in her tiny white research assistant's office at the Worldwatch Institute, her article "Pedaling Into the Future" had just come out in *World Watch Magazine,* and she was getting calls from *The New York Times* and invitations to talk shows. She couldn't have been more pleased—or surprised!

The article pulls no punches. "Bicycles are the transportation alternative,'' it begins, "that can relieve the congestion and pollution brought on by automobiles.''

She didn't pull any punches with us, either. "There are some things you can accomplish with a car that you can't with a bicycle,'' she said. "But I believe the reverse is also true, especially in the bigger cities—where the over-reliance on cars has created a situation where the bicycle is actually more effective in downtown traffic!

"And bikes don't require the same space for parking. . . .

"Consider the sheer aggression that comes out in people when they're behind the wheel! They honk at each other, they rush each other, cut in front of each other. Whereas the same people, if they met each other on the sidewalk, would probably say 'Excuse me,' move out of the way, maybe even smile! It's just *different* when you have the power of the steering wheel, when you have a couple of tons of metal at your disposal.

"So I think bicycle commutes would be much more relaxing. With bicycle paths, you wouldn't get to work all stressed out by rush-hour traffic. And there'd be green spaces. . . .''

We asked Lowe how she'd have us get from here to there. "The number of bicycle commuters in the U.S. has quadrupled in the last decade,'' she replied. "This happened with virtually no public policy push, suggesting that official encouragement could inspire a more dramatic changeover. . . .

"Commuters are not likely to choose bicycling when it means taking their lives into their hands on busy city streets. Effective bicycle promotion calls for bike paths separate from roads, and space on regular roadways dedicated to bicycles.

"Free parking provided by many employers in effect pays the gasoline costs of commuting. The Environmental Protection Agency has concluded that if employees were directly handed this subsidy, public transit ridership and bicycle use would go way up."

III. Redesign power

In another tiny white office at the Worldwatch Institute sits Michael Renner, author of an ambitious Worldwatch booklet, "Rethinking the Role of the Automobile." Unlike Capon, and Lowe, Renner doesn't have a favorite transportation alternative.

"Looking at the alternatives people have come up with, all of them are sort of technofixes," Renner told us. "They don't really deal with the underlying problem. In my view, that problem is the land use policies that have been adopted and have made us *dependent on* using cars, whether we 'want' to rely on cars or not.

"We have to try to adopt land use policies, regulatory policies, zoning policies, that get away from the sprawling pattern we've seen throughout the postwar period. . . .

"We need to move toward a more diverse suburban setting. Not go back to the traditional city structure, but move toward something that's sort of in between—where there's some sort of suburban 'core' where people can go shopping and take the children to school, go see a play, go to work, whatever, all either on foot or by bicycle or, if need be, by public transportation."

Three thousand miles away from Renner, in Berkeley Calif., is Richard Register, president of Urban Ecology, Inc., and author of a visionary book, *Ecocity Berkeley* (1987). If Renner is mild-mannered to a fault, Register is, well, blunt.

"What I think about," he told us, "is not just the automobile but its relationship to sprawl, which I call 'Auto Sprawl Syndrome'—the acronym is ASS, 'cause we're always sitting on our ass in the automobile and at the office and in front of the television. The whole society *sits*. It's a vicarious society, and I don't know how people can feel alive. . . .

"Transportation is supposed to deliver access to whatever you want to have in your life: your job, your living place, your friends, a movie or whatever. But the fact of the matter is we've let transportation give us access, when we could have been getting access by designing our cities differently. Then we'd have what I call 'Access by Proximity' instead of 'Access by Transportation.' 'Access by Proximity' means you're closer to things....''

Register is less tolerant of suburbia, even a modified suburbia, than Renner. "Ecological development *requires* proximity. If you put a solar collector on suburbia, it's just bulls—. Because you're going to spend 12 times the energy you can gather in your solar collector, driving around! People would do less damage if they simply moved to town and did without solar.

"Now, if you start having mixed-use zoning, if you have people living close to where they work, if you have the little compact European-style towns and cities, instead of these sprawled, scattered ones, *then* you'd have a context in which you could start talking about really good transportation policies, and energy policies, and all the rest of it. And you'd get exactly the opposite kind of hierarchy from the one that's common in America today.

"At the top of the existing hierarchy is the automobile; second on down is buses; then trains; then bikes; and finally shoes. A healthy city would be one in which most people would walk most places; then they would bicycle (note that at this point there'd be no pollution, no fossil-fuel use at all); the next one down would be trains and streetcars; then buses (still public); and then, finally, the worst of all would be cars."

13 National *Holistic* Health Care Program: Too Sensible?

February 1987

Nearly everyone agrees that medical spending in the U.S. is (1) wildly out of control, and (2) increasingly ineffective in terms of actually providing us with good care.

In 1965, we spent approx. $40 billion on medical care; in 1986 we spent approx. $450 billion. But we still have an infant mortality rate lower than that of 14 other countries. Twenty percent of us are still grossly overweight. Twenty-five percent of us are still uninsured or underinsured.

The amount of time we spend actually talking with our physicians is way down. The amount of time we spend in surgery is way up—we are now *twice* as likely to be operated on as are the British. . . .

The conventional political responses to these appalling facts are boringly predictable. The Reagan administration recently proposed reducing Medicare and Medicaid outlays by $90 billion over five years—brilliant, brilliant. Meanwhile, liberals and socialists are coming up with all kinds of schemes for national health insurance and a National Health Service—schemes that often have poor cost controls and always lock in the high-tech, curative-but-not-preventive approach of current medical practice.

The point of view of holistic health care providers has generally been missing from the national health debate.

There is no great mystery about that point of view. Holistic health care providers claim that the body cannot be (properly) treated apart from considerations of mind-environment-spirit. They claim that promoting wellness is just as important as curing illness.

Thoughtful conservatives are not unattracted to holistic providers' emphasis on self-care and personal responsibility. Thoughtful liberals and socialists are not unattracted to holistic providers' emphasis on environmental factors in disease. But neither left nor right has ever acknowledged that the holistic health movement carries within it the seeds of a whole new approach to a national health care *program* for this country, with its own coherent ideas about finance, delivery, research and education.

Partly that's human nature: the left and right would *rather* co-opt the movement than acknowledge and accept its implicit challenge. But partly that's because the challenge has remained implicit. Caught up in achieving and maintaining a certain professional status, and in various licensing disputes, holistic health providers have had little time or energy left over to systematically spell out the implications of their views for national health care policy.

To begin to discern such a policy is not difficult, however. All you have to do is talk with holistic providers and spokespeople and you'll get plenty of clues. Last week we spoke with four of the most distinguished of them:

— Tom Ferguson, M.D. (Yale Medical School, 1978), editor of *Medical Self-Care* magazine;

— James S. Gordon, M.D. (Harvard Medical School, 1967), co-editor of *Health for the Whole Person* (1980);

— Craig Salins, executive director of the American Holistic Medical Association; and

— J. Warren Salmon, professor of health policy at the University of Illinois-Chicago and editor of *Alternative Medicines* (1984).

Among them, they give us a glimpse of a health care program that is almost too sensible to contemplate.

I. Financing

• **Persuade insurance companies to pay for holistic techniques.** We can move toward greater reliance on holistic care *now,* Craig Salins told NEW OPTIONS, if we could just "persuade insurance companies to cover holistic techniques.

"There are some studies that have already been done that show that, when you provide preventive holistically-oriented care, people stay healthy—and there are fewer medical claims. Now we need to find one or two or three insurance companies that are willing to cover holistic techniques and methods: acupuncture, nutritional therapies, biofeedback, lay midwifery.... Working with the insurance companies on a pilot basis, we think we can demonstrate to them that it'll save them money."

• **Pay people to stay healthy.** "I'll tell you one way to have an impact within 20 years," Tom Ferguson told NEW OPTIONS from his office in Austin, Texas. "The government could simply pay people to stay healthy.

"The government could offer health insurance that gives you a bonus if you *don't* use health services. Or if you score well on some kind of health measure.

"Another way the government could pay people to stay healthy is to make it so everyone can have, say, their cholesterol tested for free. Then set up a policy so that the city or state or feds of whomever would pay $100 to anyone who comes to get tested and has a cholesterol of under 175.''

• **Decentralized national health insurance.** The holistic health movement is less than enthusiastic about the left's favorite health insurance schemes. However, many holistic providers *are* enthusiastic about some of the more decentralized schemes that have recently been proposed—e.g., by Rashi Fein, professor of medical economics at Harvard Medical School, in his book *Medical Care, Medical Costs* (1986).

The best recent proposals, writes Fein, ''have shifted from enrollment through a universal social insurance program to a mandated approach embodying the continuation of [private] insurance and the coverage of [all] other individuals through [government insurance]. . . .

''Over the last half-century most proposals have called for a federal program and federal controls. Yet arguments for state control (with federal standards and oversight) are not without merit. The individual patterns [in the organization and delivery of care] are best understood and best addressed at a locus of control that is closer to those [patterns] and to the people they serve. . . .''

• **High deductibles.** Ferguson doesn't want to make access to care *so* easy that people will turn all responsibility for their care over to health professionals. Thus, he'd insist that all federally-mandated insurance policies have high deductibles.

''In our own family's case,'' he told NEW OPTIONS, ''We have a $15,000 deductible health policy—in other words, we pay the first $15,000 of all medical expenses, the insurance pays the rest. It's a very inexpensive policy. . . .'' The fact that the first $15,000 comes out of Ferguson's pocket serves to encourage him to take good care of himself and his family.

A $15,000 deductible may be a bit steep for most. Professor Fein suggests a way out: in any decentralized national health insurance scheme, tie the size of the deductible to the person's annual income.

II. Delivery

• **Mandate less intrusive procedures.** "Some insurance companies are now saying you have to have a second opinion before surgery, and that's fine as far as it goes," James Gordon told us from his office in Washington, D.C. "But I think if they were to require that—for all except life-threatening conditions—before we went to pharmacotherapy, say, we had to have a trial of something else, something you could do for yourself—that would change things markedly!

"The government could mandate that that be done through Medicare and Medicaid, and the insurance companies would then follow."

• **Holistic HMOs.** "Basically, Health Maintenance Organizations are disease-treatment organizations," Gordon told us. "They have large agglomerations of doctors who for the most part treat the illness in isolation and use the high-technology model. So they have not lived up to their name.

"I think it's time to start getting practitioners together to set up according to the regulations that govern HMOs, and then to create within that framework a system in which you bring to bear the techniques that are part of holistic medicine. The bulk of the time would be spent in teaching people how to take care of themselves. The emphasis would be on low-cost techniques that people could do for themselves, like using exercise to deal with anxiety, rather than medication...."

• **Lay health networking.** "Some significant portion of doctors visits are simply to get information," Ferguson told NEW OPTIONS. "There have got to be better ways to make that information available.

"I'm amazed that there's not more government funding of lay health networking. For example, it would be incredibly valuable for people with the same diseases to be able to talk with each other. If people with, say, a certain kind of debilitating arthritis were able to meet and become part of some group, they'd be able to find new ways of coping...and at relatively little cost."

• **Community-based care.** Warren Salmon is convinced that the traditional public health approach to social problems—screening and health education—is woefully inadequate. In order to combat AIDS, drug abuse, alcoholism, infant mortality, and many other social problems, he sees no alternative to "mobilizing communities for action."

He points to some community-based approaches to the AIDS epidemic in San Francisco. The most effective groups did not seek to "institutionalize the problem—put it in hospitals," Salmon told NEW OPTIONS. "Instead, they used a lot of volunteers, used a lot of family members and allied health professionals, and came up with a program emphasizing social support for the victims of AIDS. . . .

"It made a lot of use of home-care agencies. It trained volunteers to promote public awareness, using a lot of different kinds of media. It introduced many people in the community to people with AIDS, and many got involved in the care of these people."

III. Research and education

• **Fight to change research priorities.** "The money in the research establishment does not go to studying the kinds of techniques or approaches that we're talking about," Gordon told NEW OPTIONS. "It goes for the most part to very specific biomedical research and to research on new technologies and new drugs. One thing that will have to be done to make holistic health respectable and viable is to change around the allocation of research dollars. There has to be some push to open up the vision of what important research is. . . ."

According to Salins, AHMA intends to sponsor some research itself, and along with other groups is considering setting up a "national clearinghouse for information on scientific studies related to holistic medicine."

• **Educate the kids.** "Our dependency on the medical profession is largely a product of training by the culture," says Ferguson. "So if you want to make the biggest impact in a 20-40 year period, probably the most cost-effective thing you could do would be to arrange the first graders to be in charge of a 'health program' that would allow them to study whatever they wanted, and that would put people who knew something about health— nurses, doctors, health educators—at their disposal. They would learn that *they* could initiate and control and be in charge of health care—which is just the opposite of what we learn now.

"I ran a model program myself, while I was a student at Yale. We went in and worked with a group of first-graders. We spent the first couple of sessions just giving them a chance to use the tools in the doctor's black bag. . . ."

• **Educate the physicians.** "I think there has to be some federal mandate to emphasize prevention and health promotion in medical school," Gordon told NEW OPTIONS. "There has to be some insistence that medical schools teach some of these things."

• **Holistic Health Service Corps.** Gordon would have all young physicians "perform community service for a couple of years, in return for whatever subsidy there was for their education from the federal government." Their community service work would consist of "teaching people self-care techniques." Not least of all, says Gordon, a holistic-health-service obligation would virtually *force* medical schools to teach holistic care to their students.

•　　　•　　　•

Next month, the American Holistic Medical Association will be holding its annual meeting, and many of the topics raised above are going to be discussed. We find it scandalous that scarcely *any* national politicians or political movements are helping the AHMA channel its perspectives into the public debate. We appear to have reached a point where the political left and right would rather ring down the curtains than share center stage.

14　Drugs Are Not the Enemy

November 1989

A couple of blocks from where I live in Washington, D.C., the drug trade flourishes. Twelve year old "lookouts" hang out near the crack houses. Dealers stand on the street corners waiting for customers.

It is so tempting to blame drugs for this scene—some outside "enemy" that can be combatted and destroyed—and virtually everyone does, of course. Not just Drug Czar Bennett but the liberals and "progressives," as well. "Drugs are poison," Jesse Jackson said in a recent interview. "Taking drugs is a sin. Drug use is morally debased and sick. . . . A commitment to life means a commitment to avoid the short-term pleasure and long-term pain of drugs."

If only things were so simple! If only drugs were the enemy! But if the Sixties taught us anything, it is this: Drugs are neither good nor bad. When abused, they can cause great harm. When used properly, they can help us expand our consciousness and enjoy our world.

Quite a few people do remember that lesson—though they tend to be scientists and scholars rather than politicians, and they tend to be overlooked by the mass media. We've spent the last two months contacting some of them. Put their ideas together and you've got an innovative new approach to the drug crisis.

Because it sees drug use as natural and inevitable, rather than as a "sin," I call it the "New Honesty."

The political right and left are united in assuming that drugs are "bad." The right asks, How do you get rid of drugs? The left asks, How do you discourage drug use? The New Honesty begins with an entirely different assumption: Getting high, getting intoxicated, changing one's consciousness, is a universal human need. Therefore, the New Honesty asks an entirely different question: How do you encourage people to use drugs wisely?

Instead of launching a drug war, the New Honesty would launch a campaign to re-define the problem. Once the problem was defined not as drugs or drug use but as drug *abuse,* further steps might include: decriminalizing all drugs, taxing drug revenues (including alcohol and tobacco revenues) to cover drug users' costs to society, designing safe drugs, and promoting a variety of ways of changing consciousness of which drug use is but one.

The New Honesty is politically risky. But unlike Bennett's and Jackson's approaches, it might work. It might even help us grow as human beings.

I. The "New Honesty"

Andrew Weil may be the best-known proponent of the New Honesty. His first book, *The Natural Mind,* was published in 1972, just a couple of years after he graduated from Harvard Medical School; currently he's an adjunct professor of "addiction studies" at the University of Arizona. Last month he had his publisher send us a copy of his most recent book, *Chocolate to Morphine* (1983), in which he and his co-author, Winifred Rosen, make a powerful case for the naturalness—even inevitability—of drug use.

"The basic reason people take drugs is to vary their conscious experience," say Weil and Rosen. "Many drug users talk about getting high.... Having high experiences from time to time may be necessary to our physical and mental health, just as dreaming at night seems to be vital to our well-being."

Another semi-prominent proponent of the New Honesty is Ronald Siegel, associate professor of psychopharmacology at UCLA and consultant to the innovative World Health Organization. "Throughout our entire history as a species," Siegel says in his new book, *Intoxication* (1989), "intoxication has functioned like the basic drives of hunger, thirst or sex, sometimes overshadowing all other activities in life. *Intoxication is the fourth drive....* The solution to the drug problems of our species begins when we acknowledge the legitimate place of intoxication in our behavior."

Not only is drug use natural, these analysts claim, it is universal. It's found at all times, at all places, and even in many species.

"With the possible exception of the Eskimos," Weil said in a recent speech, "I know of no human society which has not been heavily involved with the use of psychoactive substances. Nor do I know of any period in history when that's [not been true]."

"The pursuit of intoxication with drugs is a primary motivational force in the behavior of organisms," Siegel says. "Birds gorge themselves on inebriating berries, then fly with reckless abandon. Cats eagerly sniff aromatic 'pleasure' plants, then play with imaginary objects. Cows that browse special range weeds will twitch, shake, and stumble back to the plants for more. Elephants purposely get drunk on fermented fruit...."

If drug use is natural and universal, then it is kind of ridiculous for us to think of drugs as the "enemy" and of drug use as a "sin."

But according to the New Honesty, we're no different from anyone else in this regard; all societies accept some drugs and reject others.

Weil made this point very forcefully in his speech. "In every society," he said, "the use of one or a small number of drugs is not only tolerated, but actively encouraged and promoted. And that goes hand in hand with defining all *other* drugs as 'bad' and trying to keep them out, make them go away.

"But there's no agreement from culture to culture as to which are good drugs and which are bad drugs!

"If you are a mainstream American today, alcohol, tobacco and the various forms of caffeine are the 'good' drugs. And all the rest are Other People's drugs, and we wage war on them.

"[But] if you're a Muslim, alcohol is the Big Bad Drug, the worst thing you could put in your body. In India today, there are certain religious sects that consider marijuana as a religious sacrament, and are very upset if you try to call it a drug."

According to the New Honesty, it follows from this that drugs are neither "good" nor "bad," and that all drugs can be used positively or negatively.

"From years of looking at other cultures," says Weil, "I feel very strongly that in fact there are no good drugs or bad drugs. That drugs are just drugs. And all of them have the potential to be used creatively or positively, and all have the potential to be used negatively or destructively.

"There are some factors, like the dose and the purity and the manner of administration, that influence these things. But there is no goodness or badness inherent in any drug.

"Goodness or badness come into the picture only in looking at how individuals relate to these substances. How they think about them; how they use them; how whole societies think about them and use them. . . .

"The AMA some years ago defined 'drug abuse' as any use of a 'drug of abuse' without the supervision of a physician. What is a 'drug of abuse'? That's a fancy way of saying 'a bad drug'!

"There is no such thing as a drug of abuse. *Any* drug can be abused. And any drug can be used. . . ."

One implication of this view is that there's no good reason why we tolerate and even promote some drugs (alcohol, tobacco) and declare "zero tolerance" of others. Weil goes so far as to speak of the "irrationality" of our drug choices, and the "emotionalism behind maintaining" them.

"People in this culture are never funded to look for beneficial effects of marijuana," he says. "We only look for negative effects. That's just the way it is. We don't get money, generally, to look for negative effects of coffee. . . .

"I still very commonly hear the phrase 'drugs and alcohol,' as if alcohol is something else, as if it's in some other category. But not only is it a drug, it's the hardest drug—in terms of its physical effects, its mental effects, its toxicity. . . .

"There is no drug I know that is so tightly correlated with crime and violence. There is no drug that causes such devastation to the body if it is abused over time. . . .

"[And look at tobacco.] Tobacco, in the form of cigarettes, is the most addictive substance known. . . .

"Nicotine is the most powerful stimulant you can put into your body without causing convulsions—more powerful than cocaine. . . . [And] smoking is a much more direct way of putting a drug into the system [than] intravenous injection. . . ."

II. Toward decriminalization

If drug use is natural and normal, and all drugs are open to abuse, and today's legal drugs are just as hazardous as the illegal drugs, then it makes no sense to criminalize some drugs and not others. In fact, the more you listen to the New Honesty, the more you realize that criminalization of drugs is part of the problem.

Luis Zapata is a former civil rights and farmworker activist who runs a national organization called RAPID (for "Rational Alternative Policy to the Interdiction of Drugs"), and when we visited him last week at RAPID'S headquarters he gave the lie to all those white and black liberals who say that continued criminalization of drugs is the best way to protect poor and minority communities.

"We've had community watches," he told us, looking out at one of Washington's most drug-ridden neighborhoods. "We've tried to organize. Over in the next neighborhood they have community residents stand on the street corner. And it really doesn't stop either the flow of drugs into our communities or the murders and robberies that take place as a result of the trafficking. . . .

"We're turning our neighborhoods into war zones! And as long as there's profit to be made in drug trafficking, *big* bucks to be made, there's going to be killing.

"I don't see any quick answers to the problem of drug abuse. I do see a need to do something about the number of people who are dying."

Weil put criminalization in telling historical perspective when he said in his speech, "If you look back to America of 100 years ago, before we had any drug laws, everything was better.

"I think the [proportion] of people using drugs was probably about the same. It was probably very high—and I think it will always be high. But I think *abuse* of drugs was much less.

"There was no crime associated with drugs, no crime associated with the distribution and use of psychoactive substances. That is entirely a creation of our social policy.

"Young people generally did not take psychoactive drugs in 1888. That's something else we made happen—by making the drugs we don't like, look attractive. By trying to exaggerate their dangers in ways that don't correspond to people's experience of them, while being hypocritical about the dangers of the drugs that we promote.

"People did not generally take drugs to drop out of society in 1888. It was not seen as an anti-social process. We made that happen through our policies and prohibitions."

Logic, history and compassion all point, then, to decriminalization of all drugs as *part* of the solution to this nation's spiralling drug crisis.

"The only answer I see is for communities to work on pressuring our elected officials to legalize drugs," Zapata told NEW OPTIONS. "Just like alcohol during prohibition, you're not going to be able to stop drugs from coming into communities. But you can stop the violence."

We asked Zapata whether he thought drug abuse would skyrocket after legalization (as Harlem Congressman Charles Rangel never tires of saying). "I don't see how the number of users *could* increase," Zapata replied. "Any drug you want is available as per request.

"The price will go down somewhat after legalization. But price doesn't seem to be a problem now."

Zapata tugged at his hair, which was braided in the traditional manner of Mexico's Indian peoples. "I can't see that the rate of addiction will go up much more. What you will have, though, is you'll get rid of that seller—the local kid who's driving the fancy car, the kid with all the gold chains who is the peer group leader. He's the one who's hooking his younger brothers and sisters on dope—'cause that's how he makes his money.

"And he's a good salesman! He uses his flashiness just like the pimps do—to say, This is an admirable lifestyle, do these drugs, that's how you get into it. . . .

"So I think the enticement will go after legalization."

It's easy to talk about decriminalization, much harder (and braver!) to propose a specific plan. Almost alone among elected officials, Joseph Galiber—a black New York State senator from the Bronx—has introduced a bill outlining just such a plan, and last month we obtained reams of documents from Galiber explaining his bill and defending it against its numerous critics.

"My bill would fully decriminalize drugs," Galiber wrote in a 1988 memo to all New York State senators. "The possession, distribution, sale and use would become legal.

"[At the same time], a State Controlled Substances Authority, similar to the State Liquor Authority, would be set up. This Authority would issue licenses to doctors, pharmacists and chemists to sell these drugs.

"Thereby any adult desiring these drugs would simply go to his or her local doctor or pharmacist; a prescription would no longer be necessary. Isn't this better than going to [the] local street-corner pusher? . . .

"The Authority would regulate the prices of these drugs [and exercise] quality control."

In a more recent memo, Galiber spells out some rules for drug sales: "It will be illegal to sell any controlled substance to a person under 21, and it will continue to be illegal to sell or distribute drugs in or near school grounds."

III. "Harmfulness tax"

Even if decriminalization eliminates drug trafficking and violence, there will still be a need to design—and pay for—massive drug education and rehabilitation programs. Decriminalization would make it possible for us to pay for these programs by taxing all drug sales (since all drug sales would be part of the formal economy).

Lester Grinspoon, an associate professor of psychiatry at Harvard Medical School, is the author of the only tax plan we've seen that is consistent with the New Honesty, i.e. that totally integrates alcohol and cigarette sales in with those of the other drugs. Last month he sent us an advance copy of a speech in which he outlines his plan.

"Let currently controlled substances be legalized and taxed," he says in his speech.

"The taxes would be used for drug education and for paying the medical and social costs of drug abuse. A commission would be established to determine these costs separately for each drug. . . . The drugs that are now legal, alcohol and tobacco, would not be distinguished from the others. . . .

"Present prices might be maintained at the start. Then, as the commission collected more information, pricing could change to reflect social costs. . . .

"In [the present drug] war a kind of self-reinforcing cycle is developing, as drug enforcement operations begin to pay for themselves by funds confiscated from the drug traffickers whose operations they make enormously profitable. The taxing system suggested here would establish a different kind of revenue cycle, in which society would pay for the costs of drug abuse by extracting them from the drug users in proportion to the amount they contribute to the problem."

One obvious implication of Grinspoon's plan is absent from his speech—perhaps for political reasons. If the cost of each drug begins to reflect the costs its users inflict upon society, then marijuana will almost certainly become the cheapest drug, and the most popular.

Would that be a good thing? Could America handle it? To shed some light on these questions, we attended the annual meeting of the National Organization for the Reform of Marijuana Laws (NORML), which took place this fall just two blocks from our offices.

It was a colorful affair, with men in tie-dyed T-shirts talking happily to women in business suits, and women in short skirts and fishnet stockings talking happily to lawyerlike men with beards, all amidst the quiet elegance of the Dupont Plaza Hotel. Here are the kinds of things we heard from NORML's attorneys and board members:

• "Marijuana is known as a drug which induces serenity rather than violence."

• "Americans who use marijuana are generally productive members of our society."

• "In [recent] litigation, [one federal judge], after reviewing extensive medical research, stated, 'Marijuana is far safer than many foods we commonly consume.'"

Jack Herer, director of Help Eliminate Marijuana Prohibition (HEMP), was a featured speaker at the NORML conference. According to Herer, "The continued prohibition of hemp/marijuana cultivation prevents our society from utilizing nature's premier renewable resource—hemp—for paper, fiber, fuels, food, paint and medicine. . . . Today we have the technology to use hemp biomass to produce much of the clean and renewable fuel we need to reverse the Greenhouse Effect. . . ."

Sounds good to me.

IV. Two further strategies

As Weil and Rosen say, all drugs *can* do harm if used improperly. So we might not want to stop at decriminalizing drugs and funding honest education and effective treatment programs. We might also want to pursue two further strategies: developing improved drugs and promoting alternative ways of changing consciousness.

Ronald Siegel, author of *Intoxication* (cited above), is the leading spokesperson for the "improved drugs" strategy. "We [must] acknowledge the legitimate place of intoxication in our behavior," he says. "[But] we must [also] ensure that the pursuit of intoxication with drugs will not be dangerous.

"How can we do that? The answer is to make drugs perfectly safe. . . .

"Scientists and futurists predict that we could do it by early in the next century. We could do it with molecular chemistry, twisting and bending already known psychoactive molecules. It seems equally likely that we could find new and more suitable molecules in nature's own botanical laboratory. . . .

"The ideal intoxicants would balance optimal positive effects, such as stimulation or pleasure, with minimal or nonexistent toxic consequences. The drugs would be ingested as fast-acting pills or liquids or breathed in the form of gases. They would have fixed durations of action and built-in antagonists to prevent excessive use or overdoses. [They] could even be engineered to provide brief but safe surges of intense effects, thus appearing more dangerous and thrilling than they really are."

The other "perfectly safe" strategy is using advertising and the school system to teach us to recognize—and celebrate—other ways of changing consciousness.

Weil and Rosen make a good case for this strategy when they say, "Is it any better to get high without drugs than with them? The main advantage of drugs over other techniques is that they can work powerfully and immediately. *Their main disadvantage is that they reinforce the notion that the state we desire comes from something outside us.*

"Not only can this idea lead to trouble with drugs, but it can also make people feel inadequate and incomplete. . . . Meditation, chanting, prayer, communing with nature, playing music, and artistic expression of all sorts are especially attractive ways of changing consciousness because they require little outside oneself. . . .

"Ways of getting high without drugs often do not work as fast or as powerfully as popping a pill. To master them you may have to invest some time and effort. Many people may have little motivation to acquire these skills, especially since society does not stress the value of being high or teach us practical ways to get there."

•　　　　•　　　　•

If you think of drugs and drug use as the problem, then a "war on drugs" is a sufficient solution. But if you think of people's *relationship with* drugs as the problem, then even the measures outlined above will not suffice.

The New Honesty goes beyond drug policy to ask: How do you foster the psychological "set" and economic "setting" in which people might use drugs to affirm themselves and celebrate the universe?

The answer, of course, is that the economy, the political structure, social services... all are going to have to change to reflect egalitarian, multi-cultural and human-growth-oriented values.

Until that day, people are going to continue to abuse drugs, each other, and nature. Which is to say: Until that day, people are going to continue to abuse *themselves*.

15   Multiculturalism Will Make Us Whole

June 1990

Like most of us, I grew up in white America. All my playmates were white. One of my high schools was legally segregated, the other might as well have been. When I first heard the song "California Girls," there was no question in my mind what they looked like.

That America is fast disappearing. Already 25% of us are nonwhite. Over the next 30 years, the number of nonwhite U.S. residents will more than double (to 115 million), while the number of whites will stay the same or even decline. In 65 years most of us will trace our descent to Africa, Asia or Latin America— not to Europe.

Our most important states will become nonwhite even sooner. In New York State today, 40% of schoolchildren are minorities. White high-school-age "California Girls" are already a minority.

The press does not often give these facts the attention they deserve. When it does, it comes up with basically three kinds of stories:

• Some, like the recent story in *Time,* "Beyond the Melting Pot" (April 9), stress that the "browning of America" is **inevitable.**

• Others, like one recent story in *The New York Times,* "California Is Proving Ground for Multiracial Vision in U.S." (June 16), stress that it's in white people's **economic self-interest** to adjust to the new realities. For example, in a less than inclusive America, will a majority-nonwhite workforce happily agree to pay Social Security for retired whites?

• Finally, some stories, such as "Whose America Is This, Anyway?," in *The Village Voice* (April 24), stress that multiculturalism is **simple justice,** since it would give The Oppressed their richly deserved seats at the table.

All three kinds of stories make valid points. But none of them stresses what is surely the most important point of all.

Multiculturalism is not only inevitable, necessary and just. If it's done right, it will expand our mental horizons. It will enrich our interpersonal lives. It will make us whole.

Many traditional activists have a hard time understanding why that's the most important point. So let me spell it out:

Multiculturalism will never be fully or happily embraced in this country if we choose it because we feel we "have to" or "should." It will only really flourish if we choose it with fullness of heart.

•   •   •

What *is* multiculturalism, exactly? How can it be "done right"? How would it affect our common culture? Why would it make us whole?

Those are some of the questions we ask in this special "theme" issue of NEW OPTIONS.

The answers we've come up with draw on many people's expertise. Over the last month, we interviewed 20 prominent advocates of a multiracial, multiethnic, multisexual America. They ranged from corporate consultants to gay poets, from Hispanic politicians to professors of African-American studies. All the quotations below are from those interviews.

As you'll see, our "experts" disagree about many things. But on one thing they are in full accord. Multiculturalism will make this country better, and each of us better. Listen to them long enough and you'll begin to suspect that multiculturalism may be the next great social movement of our time.

I. Great monocultural melting pot

Maybe the best way to approach multiculturalism is by looking critically at its opposite, namely, the cultural style we have now— "monoculturalism," aka the great American melting pot.

"Monoculturalism is when each person feels unworthy unless they fit into the dominant culture," says Sarah Pirtle, author of an award-winning children's book that features an African-American and an Asian-American as its two principal role models (*An Outbreak of Peace,* 1987).

"Monoculturalism has given us just such a narrow, restrictive view of how everything should be done," adds Joan Lester, director of the Equity Institute, which conducts "interrupting racism" workshops at many of our colleges and corporations.

Many of the people we spoke with have thought critically about monoculturalism. They make three major points. In the *society at large,* monoculturalism is responsible for the loss of ethnic richness and vitality. Among *immigrants and minorities,* monoculturalism has taken a terrible personal toll. And among so-called *white people,* in some ways it's done even greater damage.

Losing that flavor. "You can't force people to be Northern Europeans," says Molefi Kete Asante, chair of African-American Studies at Temple University and author of *The Afrocentric Idea* (1987). "But that is what we have done since the beginning of this country! Even Eastern Europeans have been psychologically forced to be Northern Europeans."

Because we've tried to do what Asante says we "can't" do— because we've tried to force people into a monocultural straitjacket—we've drained our citizens of much of their cultural identity. And it's our whole society's loss, says Rodolfo Acuña, founder of the largest Chicano Studies department in the country (at Cal. State University-Northridge) and author of *Occupied America: A History of Chicanos* (1981).

"I was brought up in old Los Angeles," Acuña told us. "The ethnic groups all fought each other. Somebody may have called me a 'spic,' and I may have called somebody a name, you know. But still, there was a *flavor* here.

"Once you got beyond the group level, you'd get to know people. So you went down to the Rossi's house and you saw the way the grandmother made homemade noodles, you know; or the way they made the wine. The Jews at that time were different Jews. They spoke Yiddish, you know; their houses smelled like garlic, like my house.

"I mean, there was a *flavor,* a strong flavor, and I think we're losing that. And I think we're not the better for it."

Too big a price. Our whole society may have paid the price for "monoculturalism," but minorities and immigrants have been paying it most directly. And they do so every day.

"Most Americans wear or watch or do something 'foreign' in origin every day," says James Zogby, director of the Arab American Institute. "The problem is we deny it. And in the process of denying it we create psychological hurt for those who are denied.

"I mean, my bread—the bread that my forefathers invented, right?—is eaten every day. But no one will call it Arabic bread. It's got some diluted name—'pocket bread,' or 'pita bread.'. . .

"I think all of us remember the pain of being 'foreign.' I never quite understood how it was that Italian kids made me feel like I wasn't quite American, when they'd just barely gotten off the boat themselves.

"You know, there's a sense that we projected that people caught on with right quick, of who was in and who was out—and what it *meant* to be in and out. And it's the source, it's the continuing source, of a whole lot of tension. In Detroit you've got Polish and Italian autoworkers beating up on Koreans for being 'foreigners.'. . .

"On one level we've done well at integrating [everybody]. But each group had to pay too much of a price. And we are exacting too big a price from the new groups."

The bell tolls for thee. Ironically, it's possible that mono-culturalism has harmed straight, middle-class, white people most of all.

"The white heterosexual middle-class model is so huge that how can you find yourself in it, really?" asks Judy Grahn, well-known poet and author of a popular history of gay people, *Another Mother Tongue* (1984). "What you find is your ambitions. And that's not enough—this career-oriented, spiritless wandering that happens in the model...."

"I think the emptiness of white culture is very painful to people," says Shea Howell, Detroit activist and co-author of a widely-read pamphlet, *The Subjective Side of Politics* (1989). "And as a result, they try to find ways to answer that spiritual emptiness. One glaring example is the people who go wholesale to Native American practices. Often they just sort of take the practices that are comfortable, as a way of filling that void....

"In the U.S. we don't see people as having a living ethnic identity, or being connected to a particular geographic place, or existing in relation to various social and political struggles. We don't have any real sense of *who a person is*. In the U.S. we never use the word character, we always use the word personality, because what we judge people by is their personality. Our basis for judging one another is just very superficial."

II. Visions of multiculturalism

As a welcome alternative to monoculturalism, many innovative thinkers have begun to promote what they call multiculturalism. For better or worse, there are almost as many multiculturalisms as there are multiculturalists. But nearly all multiculturalists seem to agree on three things.

First, multiculturalism would be characterized by a tremendous cultural diversity. Second, it would—must—include a commitment to economic justice. And, third, it would encourage white people to define themselves as something other than just "white."

Embrace diversity. "I think we should embrace the partially hidden diversity of this culture, and see that diversity as a tremendous natural resource," says Scott Walker, co-editor of the first book about multiculturalism in America, *Multi-Cultural Literacy* (1988).

"I would like a world that offers an opportunity for balance between the public and the private, the rational and the intuitive, economics and values," says Magaly Rodriguez Mossman, Cuban-American "diversity consultant" to the Du Pont corporation. "And if we were to honor and pay attention to other cultures, we'd get this kind of diversity, this kind of richness.''

"My vision,'' says the Equity Institute's Joan Lester, ''Is of a world and a society in which there will be more variation than there is now.

"Standards of scholarship, for example, have basically been 'normed' on one population, primarily white middle-class to upper-class males: And, you know, that's a nice, very interesting, reasonable method of scholarship. *And* there's just so many other ways out there of thinking about things that have been excluded from the academy and its derivatives!''

The justice connection. For many multicultural advocates, cultural diversity and economic justice are inseparable. In a multicultural society, ''human beings would be committed to each other's well-being in a very strong way,'' says Cherie Brown, director of the National Coalition Building Institute (which does training in ''prejudice reduction'' in schools, churches, corporations and even police departments).

"You can't separate multiculturalism from class and economic issues. There's a parallel between how things are going economically and group antagonisms.

"I think it's real important that we're not just talking about a society where everybody kind of likes each other and the real injustices don't change.''

"White" is not enough. Probably a majority of multicultural advocates would agree with Detroit's Shea Howell when she says, ''We must rid ourselves of 'white' identity and embrace our true cultural identities. For many of us, this will be an opportunity to come to terms with the fact that we are the children of many different and distinct cultures—Irish, Jewish, Spanish, Armenian, Syrian, Hungarian. . . .

"The only way we are able to maintain a majority status in this country is by calling ourselves 'white.' The South Africans use 'white' as an umbrella word too, which should give us pause.''

Suppose we just *can't identify* with our ethnic ancestors? According to Howell, we might take a page from Jesse Jackson's book and identify with a social struggle that touches our lives: ''In all his speeches, Jackson appeals to people as workers, women, poor, dispossessed. He uses those categories for giving us a sense of *who we are.*''

III. But what about our central culture?

If we really do begin to value diversity more than uniformity, and even the notion of "white people" begins to fall apart, what will happen to our central culture? Will we still have one?

Multicultural theorists have come up with basically four views on this.

One view is that our common culture will remain predominantly Anglo. Another view is that it will become an exciting new mix of all the cultures.

A third view is that it will become not so much a mix as a mosaic, with soft boundaries. A fourth view is that it will become a mosaic with hard boundaries.

Anglos still on top. "The American culture does dominate," says historian Rodolfo Acuña. "There's always going to be [that] central culture.

"You go back to de Tocqueville, you realize this is a nation without traditions. And that's why they're so f—in' insecure about their culture. It'll exist irregardless. . . . Those English Only groups running around, they're a bunch of kooks."

Other spokespeople think the Anglo culture will remain dominant, but over an ever shrinking terrain. "There is a kind of two-tiered culture in America," says Mark Thompson, senior editor of *The Advocate,* the biggest gay periodical in the U.S. "There's the official culture, and then there's the culture that's developing."

The coming synthesis. Many observers think we're on the verge of merging all our cultures—and look forward to that with an almost missionary enthusiasm.

We're in the process of adopting a "different approach to life," says Senator Art Torres of the California Assembly (who's often touted as a future governor or U.S. Senator). "The best way to look at that is through food. Even Dodger Stadium food has become multi-ethnic! . . .

"Food begins the interactive process among cultures. The next step—which is also occurring—is the intermarriage of cultures literally, to form new families."

Sylvia Wynter, director of Afro-American Studies at Stanford University, is a critic of (some kinds of) multiculturalism. But she is no defender of what she calls "Allan Bloom's high culture," either. She is as wary of the notion that white, Western culture is "best" as she is of what she calls "multicultural bantustans."

What she insists upon is the honest recognition that we are *currently* "integrated in the nation-states of the Americas on the basis of a single culture. That culture is the culture of Western Europe—the Judeo-Christian cultural model. . . . Whether we like it or not, there was a dominant civilization! That is the way history happened!"

What she wants to see now is what she calls a "vernacular synthesis" of all the major cultures of the Americas. In fact, she thinks it's happening already.

"The vernacular culture of the Americas is now emerging," she claims, "after having absorbed everything that it needed from the high culture, the European culture. It is carrying the high culture over—not negating it—into a new synthesis" made up of European *and* African *and* Latino *and* Native American elements.

"The different cultural traditions of the Americas. . . have entered into an 'Americanizing' process to constitute something genuinely new."

Thomas Bender, University Professor of the Humanities at New York University and author of *Community and Social Change in America* (1978), shares Wynter's belief that our central culture should remain dominant—and her faith that it is changing.

"The dominant culture is not fixed," Bender says. "It is historically constructed. . . . The culture keeps remaking itself, historically, as time goes on.

"There's a public culture made in America. And that public culture is not, as some people on both the left and the right are saying now, a WASP culture or an Anglo-Saxon culture. It has been in the making since the beginning of the 17th century. A person of Anglo-American descent would today have to establish *their relationship to* this public culture, just like anyone else."

The coming mosaic. Probably more multicultural thinkers would like to see a *mosaic* than a synthesis.

"I don't want to be forced to become part of some mush that is 'everybody's' culture," says Arab-American Institute's James Zogby. "Instead, we should all be able to look at the American mosaic and recognize the chip we place. And recognize the marvelous contribution that everyone's made to it."

"What I advocate is pluralism without hierarchy," says Temple

University's Molefi Asante. "Pluralism without hierarchy means the appreciation of individual cultures in terms of their legacies and their contributions to American society without having some notion of dominance on the part of any particular cultural group.

"For example, my idea of Afrocentrism does not assume that that worldview is universal, but that it is the expression of a *particular* heritage. Eurocentrism has often assumed that the European experience was universal and, as they would say, 'classical.' That of course is where the problem lies."

Most advocates of a mosaic want the boundaries of the mosaic to be soft, permeable. "Each person has to own and control their culture, and be able to define it the way they want," says Ethelbert Miller, director of the Afro-American Resource Center at Howard University. "But they shouldn't be limited to their one square. They must see the whole picture. If you just see that little square, then you're not going to go anywhere, see; that's the whole thing where racism starts breeding in that little square...."

Mosaic with walls. Some multicultural advocates don't think the "soft" mosaic goes far enough.

Harry Hay, a founder of the Mattachine Society (the first gay political group) and, much later, of the Radical Faeries, thinks that multiculturalism today would be premature. "The important first step between what we have now and the multi-ethnic, multi-cultural, multi-sexual community of the future should be a *plural community*....

"We're beginning to see it here in L.A. We have Koreatown, we have Japantown, we have the Mexican barrios, we have the Black community, and we're going to be having the gay community. All of these are separate communities.

"They live side-by-side. And they have to learn to work together and with each other. But for the moment it's right that they remain separate societies. First of all we have to be self-respecting, plural people.

"A plural society may need a century at minimum before it is ready to entertain visions of multiple integrations."

Mike Myers, a Seneca Indian, is program director of the Seventh Generation Fund, which assists Native American self-help projects. His preferred vision of the U.S. includes "whole areas of cities where English is not heard," and full recognition of Native

Americans' "rights to land, and our ways of life, and our ability to govern ourselves."

He has no desire for a common culture. "It's impossible! The Communists tried to blend everything together in Eastern Europe and the Soviet Union, and as soon as the iron hand that held it all together relaxed its grip, nationalism sprang back up—you know, the demands of people for their cultural rights, their linguistic rights, etc.

"When you see anyplace that does have a common culture, it's forced, and it's very heavily controlled. You look at Japan. Japan really demands that everybody who goes there act like a Japanese. It's very strictly enforced."

IV. What they have that we need

So—how would multiculturalism make us whole?

I asked many of my so-called minority-group interviewees to try to say what it is, exactly, that heterosexual, white, middle-class Americans have to gain by opening up their hearts to people from their group. What is the special "chord" that your group strikes, I asked, that we need to hear for our own happiness and well-being?

It was an awkward question, awkwardly asked, and was met with some hesitation.

"Well, Mark, I don't think that the issue is what black people *can* offer," said Vincent Harding, author of the much-acclaimed *There Is a River: The Black Struggle for Freedom in America* (1981). "The issue is the recognition of what black people *have* offered."

Nevertheless, nearly everyone I talked with went on to answer that question. They knew their answers mattered.

The gay chord. "I think we can give an enormous sense of fun and joy back to heterosexual people," says *Advocate* editor Mark Thompson. "I mean, I think we live in a fairly joyless culture. Don't you? [laughs]. There's a sense of joy and a sense of celebration in gay culture, even in the little things of daily life."

"By my clothes and bearing I model a certain freedom for women," says lesbian poet Judy Grahn. "By parenting a child my lover and I present an obvious example of alternate family structure. All of this puts ideas into people's minds.''

"We live in an extremely sex-phobic, or I guess I should say erotophobic, culture," says Thompson. "And I think one of the primary reasons gay people seem to threaten people is that we seem so in tune with our sexuality. I'm not talking about the promiscuity of the 70s, but just that we seem more at ease, more with a sense of fun and creativity about our sexuality."

"The first thing we have to teach is that sex doesn't have to be about reproduction," says gay writer Toby Johnson. "One of the reasons we're having all the problems in the world today is overpopulation. And the example of gay people makes it very clear that one can live a very fulfilled life without having children or focusing one's life on children."

The Latino chord. "What Hispanic people contribute to a full life is passion, spice, imagination, dreaming," says Du Pont's Magaly Rodriguez Mossman.

"A Hispanic bureaucrat recently received a memo from a woman requisitioning supplies. His response: Ay, madre, your letter, it has no soul. Give me some flowers, madre. Give me some poetry, a little bit of life.... So she re-wrote the letter and got everything she asked for.

"The point is that, for him, life is not this curt, to-the-point thing. It *needs* flowers. And I think Hispanic people bring that kind of spice, a little mischievousness, a spark."

Hispanics also bring "very basic values," says Senator Torres. "Values about the importance of work and family. Our immigrant families are bringing the Protestant work ethic back to America."

The Native American chord. "One of the things that disturbs us the most," says Seventh Generation's Mike Myers, "is the *lack of roots* that non-Native peoples have to a specific geographic area, a specific bioregion.

"They're not *anchored*. They can pick up and, you know, just wander wherever they want. They can mess up one place and move on. And leave their mess behind them.

"Some people are beginning to talk about the feelings they have for the places they've chosen to live in. I think that needs to get more rooted in the American psyche. Because then you will have a certain attitude and spirit and *soul* to what is called the environmental movement, that'll move it to the next level.

"People will really want to fight for their place if they have a really solid commitment to it, and can really see their future generations growing up there and being a part of it."

The Black chord. "The African-American culture certainly doesn't take itself so seriously as I think the European culture does," says Temple University's Molefi Asante. "And that will probably help us in terms of just learning to relax."

"I think Black culture in America has within it the groundwork and possibility for true maturity," adds historian Vincent Harding.

"From my perspective, true maturity comes only through the process of loss and suffering and difficulty and up-against-the-wall-ness and knowing what it is to be refused the things that one feels she or he needs desperately. And only as people go through that kind of experience can they come to any true maturity.

"My sense is that that has been the experience of the African-American people of this society from the beginning.

"And coming out of that experience, I think in a sense, when we are at our best, we are able to offer a grounding that is much more in keeping with human reality. A grounding that is not a, quote, success story, but a story of people enduring, of people's willingness to continue suffering, of a people's ability to overcome fantastic odds.

"That kind of history being built into the ground of our nation's history is, I think, of great importance. Not only does it provide us the kind of maturity that a very powerful society needs to balance its power. It provides us with a hook into the experience of the majority of the world."

V. The next great social movement?

I believe that the multicultural vision is such an attractive one that, sooner rather than later, multiculturalism will follow environmentalism as our next great social movement. More than any large idea I know now, multiculturalism has the capacity to inspire vision and idealism.

Sarah Pirtle sees multiculturalism as a kind of restoration.

"I think people are born curious about differences," she says. "And they unabashedly ask questions about the people that they meet. But what happens is that this unbridled curiosity begins to be stopped—people find that the doors start closing for them as children, or they get a message that you 'should' stick to people like yourself.

"So when I think of a multicultural society, I think of restoring that basic sense of interconnection between all people."

Joan Lester sees it as the logical next stage for the civil rights movement. "It's amazing to remember that we had legal segregation until 1964," she says "So we're only one generation removed from that.

"But now that we've had those barriers removed for a generation, we're seeing that there are other barriers. Those other barriers are our monocultural norms, and they're going to have to be removed in order to have full participation by everyone."

Toby Johnson sees it as a way to build a certain modesty into our national psyche. "There's a way in which all sides are right," he says. "No side has got the corner on the Truth. We need to understand that to practice multiculturalism."

Thomas Bender sees it as a chance for us to model the first world civilization. "Henry James thought there was a chance of a kind of 'world culture' being born in the U.S.," he says. "And I think that's still true. The U.S. has already gone through a lot of the steps the whole world is going to have to learn to go through.

"The notion of national and cultural purities is being annihilated! And I, at least, find the possibility of much more complicated conversations about our national culture more interesting rather than less."

Vincent Harding sees it as an opportunity for national rebirth. "For me," he says, "what we're saying essentially is that we are now a nation that is coming into being again.

"We are saying that we are now people who have come from many directions, many cultures, many backgrounds. Some of us have occupied this land for a long, long time; some for a shorter but still long time; and some only very recently. But all of us are now together, trying to understand how you create a nation out of such tremendous diversity.

"It's a marvelous opportunity for going far, far beyond any of the old definitions of what America is and who Americans are."

Count on it happening. Already, in the summer of 1990, it seems vaguely un-American that I grew up in white America.

PART FOUR

BEYOND BEING THE WORLD'S POLICEMAN

There is no question that it is sometimes important to take up arms in defense of our national interests, and I am proud that NEW OPTIONS has never succumbed to the siren songs of the pacifists or the obsessive self-blame of the far left. As a former Vietnam war resister who spent 11 years in Canada (and founded the largest emigrant aid group, the Toronto Anti-Draft Programme), I am well acquainted with both kinds of temptations.

But if it's one thing to want to be strong—all right, strong*est*— it's quite another thing to base your foreign policy on being the toughest kid on the block. Participants in the Second American Experiment don't just prefer peace to war, they are convinced that war and its corollary, military threat, are among the *least effective ways* of spreading post-liberal, post-socialist values.

The first piece in this section, "How to Do Good in the World," is a veritable catalogue of non-military approaches this country can use to foster social justice, human rights, ecological responsibility, etc. Some people might confine their use to places like South Africa; others, to places like Cuba. I say use them everywhere. Few of my subscribers liked my term for this: "Neo-Interventionism."

My next piece looks more closely at how we in the U.S. can improve the lives of the world's poor, surely Political Priority #1 for the 21st century. The approaches I suggest are pure Second Experiment—they focus on consciousness-raising and community-building and popular empowerment, and they'd cost us *less* in "foreign assistance" than what we're paying now!

The U.S. cannot—and should not—go it alone, and many Second Experimenters have been asking how the United Nations could be empowered to play a larger role. In "Reforming the U.N." I give some of their best answers.

All these suggestions are predicated on one larger suggestion: that we learn to listen, really *listen,* to everyone in the circle of humankind. In "Twenty-eight Ways of Looking at Terrorism" I try to show what that means in practice, and indicate how our consciousness would have to stretch as a result.

Of all the pieces I've written for NEW OPTIONS, this is my favorite. Even now I have a hard time stretching my own consciousness to "dare to take it all in," as that last headline proclaims. One thing is sure: If you can take it all in, you have definitely achieved a global consciousness!

16 How to Do Good in the World

September 1985

Last month South African Bishop Desmond Tutu startled the sensibilities of the "Vietnam generation" when he called for U.S. "intervention" in South African affairs. Later he said, "We are intend on dismantling [apartheid] peacefully. *Our last hope is the intervention of the international community.*"

Meanwhile, South Korean opposition leader Kim Dae Jung was saying, "The U.S. should pressure the South Korean military for change. . . . There are democratic elements in [our] military which would be greatly encouraged by such a move."

How *can* the U.S. apply responsible pressure for change in the world? Under what circumstances should we seek to use our power and influence? Until recently, many of us had stopped even asking such questions—in part because the public debate had grown so stale.

In one corner is the political right, which would have us intervene with force in other countries' affairs whenever we felt it was in our short-term interest to do so. In the other corner is the political left, which takes a strongly anti-interventionist position. According to *The Nation,* the "real" struggle in Central America is between the far left and far right, and the only role for the U.S. is to get out of the way. Moreover, "to insinuate a concern for human rights into that setting is, as conservatives insist, ridiculous" ("Colonialism by Modern Means," 16 June 1984).

Fortunately, this "debate" has begun to lose some of its rigidity, thanks to a number of recent developments:

• Some of the most militant anti-interventionists have discovered that they can be among the most militant *pro-*interventionists on South Africa. This has made a lot of them—and a lot of us!—think twice about their neo-isolationist rhetoric.

• There is a growing realization that there *are* viable, democratic alternatives to the far left and far right in the Third World. In El Salvador and Peru, key factions of the ruling parties preach "cooperativismo"—decentralized self-government. In South Korea and the Philippines, democratic reform movements are well underway. In Cambodia an armed, democratic resistance movement has sprung up in opposition to Pol Pot's Khmer Rouge *and* the Vietnamese puppet regime.

• Many activists have been discovering, or re-discovering, that the so-called "American" values, such as freedom of speech, freedom of press, freedom of assembly, freedom of religion, are not just *relative* values. They are, instead, *absolutely necessary preconditions* for a democratic society.

It's easy to scoff when comfortable American politicians say this. But listen to South Korea's Kim Dae Jung: "The biggest obstacle supporters of democracy in my country face is there is no freedom of public meeting." Listen to Green spokesperson Petra Kelly: "The progressive left has left the issue of human freedom and the issue of human rights too long to the right-wing forces."

I. The new interventionism

These kinds of considerations have caused many of us to re-assess our aversion to the projection of American power in the world. Out of this re-assessment is coming a philosophy that might well be termed "neo-interventionism."

By "neo-interventionism" we mean a willingness to consider any kind of action, short of military intervention, that is intended to nudge a country in the direction of social justice, economic equity, ecological responsibility, human rights or genuine democracy.

Thus, neo-interventionism does not include military intervention; and it is aimed not at protecting American power and privilege in the short-term, but at encouraging humane and democratic values.

The neo-interventionist impulse is coming from many quarters—from baby boomers in Congress like Rep. Steve Solarz (D-NY), from social change groups like TransAfrica, from post-liberal theorists and activists like the ones joined together in The Other Economic Summit. They disagree profoundly on issues. But they share one core conviction: the rights of individual people are more fundamental than the right of undemocratic nation-states to non-intervention.

Of course, many good people are opposed to the idea of American intervention.

• Some of the opposition comes from a too narrow, and rather too innocent, understanding of the word "intervention." For example, Archibald Gillies, president of the World Policy Institute, calls for a "policy of nonintervention" but at the same time says we should "end our military support of dictators and promote international programs of economic assistance." Gillies's suggested "alternatives" to intervention would, of course, affect the internal dynamics of countries just as much as gun-running and probably more!

• Some of the opposition comes from a desire to have us act solely through international institutions. In the best of all worlds, this *would* be preferable. But we must recognize that, as it is now, even genuinely constructive, minimally bureaucratic institutions like UNICEF have neither the responsibility nor the capacity to democratize undemocratic regimes.

132

• *The New Republic* argues that "to intervene solely for reasons of democratic morality is to confuse foreign policy with philanthropy.... Intervention must be both morally justified and strategically necessary" (6 May 1985). But it is not only for philanthropic reasons that we want democratic governments and an empowered world citizenry. It is also, and primarily, because without them we cannot have world peace! Kim Dae Jung puts it crudely but accurately when he says, "Only when there is democracy—only when a democratic government may enjoy people's voluntary and strong support—will there be stability and security enough to force North Korea to abandon its long-lasting vision to communize South Korea."

II. A typology of interventions

Recently, many people and groups have been suggesting "positive interventions" that the U.S. could and should—under the right circumstances—carry out. This is a mere sampling:

1. Citizen diplomacy. Each of us can take steps that will affect the internal processes of countries for the better.

We can hold *demonstrations and protests* against other countries' practices. After hundreds of Americans had been arrested at the South African embassy, Senator Lugar demanded release of black labor leaders who had been jailed. The next day, most were set free.

We can take part in *diplomatic encounters.* Earlier this year, 20 American professors, human rights advocates and media personnel escorted exiled opposition leader Kim Dae Jung back to Seoul, South Korea. Purpose of the entourage: to protect Kim from possible harm by the governing regime.

We can commit *civil disobedience* abroad. John Runnings, a Seattle pacifist, is organizing a "political invasion of the Soviet Union by balloon and on foot"—the idea being "to play-act the desired relationship between the two countries until the relationship becomes a political fact."

2. "Strong" or "moral" diplomacy. U.S. government officials can constantly encourage the process of democratization abroad.

We can lend *moral support* to movements for democracy and human rights.

We can make *symbolic gestures* indicative of our support. If Benigno Aquino of the Philippines had been invited to the White House before his return to his home country—would he have been assassinated?

We can engage in *public displays of displeasure.* Harden Smith, a retired foreign service officer, feels this approach would work well in undemocratic countries that think of us as their ally ("Exporting Idealism," *Washington Monthly,* April 1985).

We can have our embassies *confront authorities in the host government* with evidence of all the official abuses that we know about. Smith feels this approach would work well in Africa.

3. The corporate connection. We can take advantage of—rather than lament—the presence of our banks and corporations.

We can force our banks to *make new loans* to Third World countries. "With new loans," says Smith, "should come new strings: not the recessionary strings the bankers have imposed, but requirements that debtor nations promote democratic institutions and practices."

We can *postpone business-as-usual* in order to apply political pressure. Currently under discussion with regard to South Africa: barring new private investment.

4. Conditional aid and trade. We can use our aid to induce other governments to move toward empowerment and democracy.

We can *withhold aid* unless certain measures are taken by the host government. The House Subcommitee on Asian and Pacific Affairs—Rep. Solarz's subcommittee—recently refused to approve an increase in aid to the Philippines "in light of the failure of [that] government to make a number of essential reforms."

We can make *military assistance conditional on domestic reform.* The House Subcommittee on Africa recently recommended that security assistance to Liberia be based upon "successful completion of free and fair elections."

We can use *access to American markets* as leverage to encourage democracy. Some research associates at the Overseas Development Council, a D.C. think-tank, would have us create a one-way free trade area for designated countries.

We can *refuse imports* from countries that are exploiting their own people. The Other Economic Summit would have us refuse to import food or other agricultural produce from countries that were not satisfying their own internal food needs.

5. Targetted aid. We can spend our aid on projects that would directly foster humane values.

We can finance *Human Rights Funds,* which could be used to pay for legal and other assistance to legal and political detainees and their families, and for support of action by community organizations. (We've already established two such funds—in South Africa and Indonesia.)

We can funnel our aid *through the Catholic church and private voluntary organizations,* not through corrupt regimes. Solarz favors this approach.

We can give aid *directly to indigenous self-help organizations,* bypassing governments and intermediaries alike. Two small U.S. government agencies—African Development Foundation and Inter-American Foundation—give aid in just this way.

6. Tightening the screws. Even without military intervention, we can bring physical pressure to bear.

We can impose *airline embargoes,* as Atlanta Mayor Andrew Young has proposed for South Africa. "It's possible to implement," he says, "it's effective, and it doesn't hurt any poor people. It doesn't really destroy the economy, it just puts an added burden on South Africa's ability to function."

We can have the *CIA work with the "good guys,"* with the democratic opposition. Smith explains: "The CIA has a valid and useful function [not in] helping local security services ferret out opponents of the regime, but rather [in] establishing contact and working with the opposition [and in countering] extreme groups such as the 'death squads' in El Salvador."

•   •   •

It is possible to project American power for good or for ill. However, all too often the foreign policy debate is between those who'd like to see American power used for selfish and tragically short-sighted ends, and those who'd rather not see *any* projection of American power abroad.

Very fortunately, a third point of view is now arising. It recognizes that—because of its military might, because of its cultural prestige, because of its vast wealth—the United States has an obligation to foster the democratization and empowerment of the world's people.

Perhaps, in the process of advocating this course of action, we can also awaken in the American people a much greater desire for their *own* empowerment and for the creation of global institutions committed to democratization.

One thing is sure: political activists will never awaken these positive qualities if they continue promoting a neo-isolationist foreign policy that assumes the U.S. is the bad guy in the world.

17 Siding With the World's Poor

May 1986

It is astonishing how quickly we've begun to accept terrorism as a permanent part of the international landscape. Astonishing because there is a fairly painless (and fairly obvious) alternative.

The U.S. could seek to acquire the moral authority to act as a healing presence in the world. Our role could be to adjudicate disputes, support "all-win" solutions to international problems, and make our resources available to people, groups and governments that were willing to help themselves.

Easily the most practical way to begin moving in this direction is for us to change our foreign aid policies.

We could seek to play a catalytic, rather than a dominant, role in the Third World. We could pay more attention to what the poor themselves want. We could concentrate less on funding massive projects, and more on building up the capacity of indigenous institutions to do for themselves. We could pay more attention to the *context in which* our aid is given.

This may be a highly unconventional approach to foreign aid. But it could also be a highly popular one. It combines the traditional left's emphasis on equity and the traditional right's emphasis on self-help. Moreover, in each of the major aid agencies, and in certain cutting-edge organizations in Washington D.C., people are already quietly working to change our aid program in just these ways. In this article, three of them come out of the closet, so to speak:

• **Steve Hellinger** is co-director of The Development Group for Alternative Policies, better known as The Development GAP. "Maybe it's a bit presumptuous," Hellinger told us from GAP's cozy office trimmed with rough-hewn wood in downtown Washington, "but we try to represent the perspective of the Third World poor, and translate it into policy."

• **Tom Stoel,** an early dropout from the Nixon Administration, is president of the Global Tomorrow Coalition and director of international programs for the Natural Resources Defense Council, easily the most effective environmental lobbying organization in Washington.

• **David Korten** is Asia Regional Advisor on development management to U.S. A.I.D.—the major U.S. aid organization.

I. Doing more with less

Probably most of us associate "doing good" in the Third World with "spending more." In the early 1970s, the U.N. General Assembly urged the industrialized countries to expand their aid to 0.7% of the Gross National Product—more than twice what we're spending now. In their 1983 election platform, the West German Greens went even further, calling for the diversion of a "far higher share" of the industrialized countries' GNP to the Third World.

Hellinger, Stoel and Korten fundamentally disagree with the "more is better" approach.

"Development is not something that you buy with money," Korten told NEW OPTIONS flatly. "The basic premise of most of the aid agencies is that it is a product of money. My own philosophy is that development is a product of people; it's a people-intensive process."

"There has been too much emphasis on the quantity as opposed to the quality of aid," says Stoel. "In some of the world's poorest nations, and especially in sub-Saharan Africa, there are crises which threaten the very foundations of sustainable development. In these areas, the needs which can be properly met by aid appear so great as to justify considerably greater expenditures. But in general, the kind of decentralized development I advocate is not very costly, and I do not perceive a need for massive increases in foreign aid.... There are times, particularly in the non-governmental sector, when too much money can smother an organization.''

"The amount of money is not the crucial issue,'' Hellinger told NEW OPTIONS. ''What's crucial is the type of development it's meant to support, the people who receive it, and the channels through which it's provided.

"We have given an *enormous* amount of aid over the last generation. And it's wound up in places like the pockets of Marcos and Swiss banks and projects that have had the effect of *undermining* the position of the poor in the Third World— principally because we have channeled our aid through elite structures, private and governmental alike.

"What happens with very well-meaning groups like the Greens, and church groups, and others, is that a lot of them really haven't been 'on the ground' and seen the impact of aid on the local level. So a lot of them are just thinking, hey, we've got to give more aid to the Third World in general, without thinking what that means.''

II. Helping people help themselves

Unlike many critics of U.S. aid, Hellinger, Stoel and Korten all have well-thought-out alternatives. Taken together, they constitute what can be called a post-liberal or New Age approach to foreign aid.

Catalyze, don't dominate. Stoel argues strongly that aid should play a catalytic, rather than dominant, role in the Third World. ''The non-governmental people from developing countries that I've been working with are generally of the opinion that foreign aid has to be marginal,'' Stoel told NEW OPTIONS. ''Of course, Northerners look at it and say it has to play a major role because we furnish it. But obviously these countries have to supply most of the wherewithal and in the end, all of the impetus that goes into shaping their future. And if you conceive of foreign aid as playing a major role in *that,* it's almost a contradiction in terms!

"If people are going to live decently in the Third World, then they're going to have to move to small-scale agriculture and other things that are going to meet their basic needs. And for that, again, the impetus has to come from the local people almost by definition.

"On the other hand, I think aid can do training of personnel. It can provide expert advice for fairly short periods of time. And it can, I think, be a catalyst for helping people see their future in a slightly different way.

"In other words, aid agencies can come into a country and sometimes serve a role of pulling people together and seeing needs that maybe people themselves have lost sight of—because they're so close to the problem. For example, people with foreign experience could see that two departments of government may be overlapping, or there may be a gap between them, or the non-governmental people might not be talking to the governmental. And the field representatives could, in a low-key way, if they're perceptive, build some bridges."

Respond to the poor. Hellinger makes a perfectly complementary point when he says that, in order to provide meaningful development, we simply *must* work with institutions that represent the poor.

"There are organizations in the Third World that represent the interests of the poor," Hellinger told NEW OPTIONS. "Some are governmental; many more are non-governmental. Some were created by the poor, others are truly responsive to the poor. . . .

"These institutions range from community organizations, women's groups, small co-ops and church groups to national-level organizations, many of them governmental.

"What our aid must do is be responsive to *these organizations*—to how *they* define development in their country; to what *they* see as the direction their communities, regions, countries need to take.

"That requires a very different posture on the part of aid agencies and policymakers in this country. It takes a certain amount of humility and understanding that we don't have the answers here. That's a very different mentality than has been exhibited over the last generation. . . ."

Build the base. "The most important thing of all," Hellinger told NEW OPTIONS, "is building up the institutional base in a country.

"That is what makes development happen. You've got to build up a base upon which development can progress. You've got to build up the institutional capacity at the local level, at the regional level, at the national level.

"And we're not doing that. What we're building up is elite structures that 'implement' projects. And once those projects end, they disappear—leaving nothing behind. Because the poor haven't been involved. . . ."

Create a context. Korten would agree with most of the above. But he would add another crucial point: private voluntary organizations (PVOs) can be used not only to build up the institutional base at the local level, but to create a *policy context* in Third World countries that could speed up the base-building tremendously.

"The first generation of PVO development activities," he told us, "tended to concentrate on expanding welfare and health care services and that sort of thing. Then in the late 1970s there was a major shift in many of them toward a focus on what I call 'second generation' activities. The emphasis there has tended to be on village level activities—developing co-ops and agricultural assistance organizations and self-help projects and so forth.

"That was a very positive thing to do. The problem is, it takes place within a larger institutional and policy context in the host country that really is not supportive of that kind of thing. So it's very difficult to sustain it. After the donor goes away it's often problematic whether anything is left.

"Now some of the PVOs are beginning to recognize the limitations of that exclusively local focus, and are moving toward what I call a 'third generation' strategy, where the concern is with trying to develop sustainable policies that could influence more than a single village. They can, if they position themselves properly, have even a national impact.

"Take CARE in Indonesia. For many years CARE has done village water projects in Indonesia. The CARE people are now saying, well, that's fine, but what about the support systems for maintaining these water systems over time? And what about the rest of the country? We don't have the resources to put water systems in thousands of villages. . . . So now CARE will be working with the government—and other PVOs—to ensure that all rural communities in Indonesia have water."

III. Down to Earth

How can these new approaches to foreign aid be brought "down to Earth," down to the policy level? In large part, say our three experts, by establishing new—and explicit—criteria for the dispensing of foreign aid.

Stoel recommends that our aid agencies channel *at least* 50% of their funds to international non-governmental organizations and to U.S. private and voluntary organizations. He further recommends that aid agencies adopt "stringent requirements for environmental impact assessment."

Hellinger's Development GAP has drawn up a list of 15 suggested criteria. Among them:

• **Participation.** Is the beneficiary group involved in the planning, design, implementation and evaluation of the project?

• **Decentralization.** Do outside participants disengage themselves from the project over time? Do indigenous institutions assume increasing responsibility?

• **Scale.** Is the size of the project appropriate to the stage of development of the beneficiary group?

• **Participant education.** Will participation in the project enhance the beneficiaries' understanding of their environment, their relationship to it, the causes of their poverty, and their capacity to induce change?

Korten would accept these criteria, but he stresses that certain other, more subtle kinds of criteria might be even more important. "Yeah, there are explicit project criteria that have to change," he told NEW OPTIONS. "But organizational pressures have to change, values have to change, ways of working have to change. . . ."

• • •

This month sees publication of a prestigious anthology, Benjamin Netanyahu's *Terrorism: How the West Can Win* (1986), whose underlying message is this: the root cause of terrorism lies not in grievances but in a disposition toward violence on the part of semi-civilized or poorly civilized peoples.

The message underlying the post-liberal approach to global conflict is dramatically different. It is that we cannot live with one another if we are not willing to listen to each other, and learn from each other, and respond to each other's needs.

If the U.S. is willing to begin doing these things—first and foremost, in its foreign aid policies—then it may well achieve the moral authority necessary to engage the world in a search for constructive alternatives to terrorism.

18   Reforming the U.N.

December 1986

Right-wing journalists are painting the Iran-contra scandal as the Reagan Administration's first major tactical blunder; left-wing journalists, as a sign of its perfidy. But Iran-contra is about more than Reagan's presidency. Its deeper lesson may be that it is impossible for the U.S. to run the world, any more, in a way that benefits even U.S. citizens. . . and that we had better begin thinking about ways we can build a world political community that can help each nation get what it wants and needs. It is time to turn to a new approach to guaranteeing our national interests: military power, yes; economic power, yes; but also—and primarily—strengthening global institutions: making them at once more powerful and more democratic.

In the U.S., three kinds of groups have been supportive of global institutions:

• *System-maintainers.* These groups support the U.N. and publicize its positive achievements. The most prominent of them, the United Nations Association of the USA (UNA-USA), has 175 chapters from coast to coast and an annual budget of $2.7 million, thanks largely to contributors like The Ford Foundation, Atlantic Richfield Company and United States-Japan Corporation.

• *System-transcenders.* A group like the World Constitution and Parliament Association has little patience for the U.N. Based in Lakewood, Colorado, it has already divided the world into 1000

"Electoral and Administrative Districts" and convened a provisional world parliament.

• *System-transformers*. Ranging from the World Federalist Association to the World Policy Institute, the Center for War/Peace Studies to Americans for the Universality of UNESCO, these groups would make the U.N. more representative, more competent and more powerful. They are perfectly situated to take center stage, politically, in the wake of the Iran-contra scandal, and they have lately been discussing a proposal for U.N. reform, the "Binding Triad" proposal, that is perfectly designed to spark a national debate over how we should restructure the U.N.—and, more broadly, over what kind of international political community we want to live in...now that we know we can't run things on our own....

The Binding Triad proposal comes from Richard Hudson at the Center for War/Peace Studies. He is no starry-eyed young idealist. He was a rather cynical young reporter when, in 1949, he was asked to cover a Rotary Club meeting where the speaker was from the United World Federalists. The experience changed his life. For 15 years he edited and published *War/Peace Report,* a magazine that was read by many anti-Vietnam War activists, and now here he is in his early 60s, running a small think tank and promoting the Binding Triad as hard as he possibly can.

I. "Binding Triad"

Most system-maintainers—such as Elliott Richardson of UNA-USA—contend that the U.N. would work well if only its member states had sufficient political will. "There is some truth in this view," Hudson told NEW OPTIONS from the Center for War/Peace Studies's office in downtown Manhattan. "But I hold that lack of will is only part of the problem. I contend that the U.N. was structurally flawed from the beginning, and that as the years have gone by two flaws in particular have kept the U.N. system from working out fair solutions to problems:

• *It's not representative.* "In the U.N. General Assembly, small states have a voting strength vastly disproportionate to their populations and economic/military strength. Botswana has the same vote as the U.S.! Vanuatu has the same vote as the Soviet Union!

• *It's not potent.* "Moreover, Assembly decisions are only recommendations. They can be—and often are—flouted with impunity. In the U.N. Security Council, no action can be taken without the approval of all five 'permanent members'—Britain, China, France, the Soviet Union and the U.S. The veto has crippled the Security Council."

"In order to deal with these structural flaws," says Hudson, "the Center for War/Peace Studies has developed a proposal to introduce a rational decision-making process into the U.N. This proposal is called the 'Binding Triad' and it is deceptively simple, requiring amendments to only two articles of the U.N. Charter. But make no mistake: it would transform the General Assembly from a powerless town meeting of the world into a global legislature whose laws could be carried out by the Secretariat [that is, the Secretary-General and the U.N. bureaucracy–ed.] and interpreted by the World Court.

"One of the Binding Triad amendments would change the voting system in the General Assembly from its present 'one nation-one vote' basis to a weighted voting arrangement. There would still be only one 'house,' one chamber, one decision-making body. But each member-state's vote would be counted three ways according to the following three factors or 'legs': (1) one nation-one vote; (2) population; and (3) contributions to the U.N. budget.

"In order for a resolution to pass, it would have to win two-thirds majorities on all three legs.

"The second amendment to the U.N. Charter provides that resolutions adopted on all three legs would become binding on all member-states.

"There you [have it in a nutshell]—the Binding Triad."

"The basic purpose of the Binding Triad," says Hudson, "is to provide a means for the global body politic to make decisions that will be in the overall interest of the planet and that will be accepted and implemented by the nations and the peoples of the world.

"It is an attempt to make a substantial forward movement toward effective governance of the Earth, while at the same time keeping the degree of change within the realm of political practicability so it can actually be achieved within the remaining years of the 20th century.

"Just think! For a resolution to pass the Triad, it would have to have the support of most nations of the world, most of the people of the world, and most of the economic and military power of the world."

"This is all well and good," we interrupted. "But even if a resolution passed all three legs of the triad, how could it possibly be made binding? Sure, you've amended the Charter to *say* it would be binding. But how could you enforce it?"

"If the General Assembly wished," Hudson replied, "it could use peacekeeping forces [that is, police forces–ed.] or economic sanctions to ensure that its resolution is implemented. However, it would be barred from employing military forces such as tanks, fighter planes, warships or rockets.

"Also, the Assembly would be bound by the Charter provision that says it cannot 'intervene in matters which are essentially within the jurisdiction of any state.' If the jurisdiction were in doubt, the issue would be referred to the World Court, and if the Court ruled the question were essentially domestic, the Assembly could not act."

Recently, the Binding Triad proposal has begun to receive some attention outside the circle of U.N. reformers:

• The Center's 28-minute videotape, "The Case for the Binding Triad," has been shown in Congressional offices and on college campuses.

• A bill in the last session of Congress called for giving "special attention" to certain proposals for improving the effectiveness of the U.N.—among them, the Binding Triad. It gathered 89 co-sponsors in the House.

• Hudson and others have been lobbying for the proposal at the U.N. "There is talk," Hudson says, "of getting it formally on the agenda."

Still, the Binding Triad is by no means everybody's favorite U.N. reform. It may be supported by most U.N. "system-transformers," but not many of them support it with the same enthusiasm or give it the same priority as Hudson. Some feel it goes too far too fast, others feel it doesn't go far enough.

II. Not so fast

Walter Hoffmann leans back at his spacious desk at the national office of the World Federalist Association, of which he is executive director, and looks at us from under his bushy eyebrows. An intern had taken us to the second floor of the old townhouse past a maze of ancient and modern stacks of Federalist literature.

Like Hudson, Hoffmann is short and stocky, with vivid streaks of white in his hair, and like Hudson his involvement with world federation organizations goes back to before we were born. "During my first year in college," he says, "I wrote a book entitled *World Union by 1950.* That looks a little humorous at this stage— however, I've never really wavered from that goal." In the 1960s he held political office; in the 1970s he founded the Campaign for U.N. Reform, basically the lobbying arm of the federalist movement.

Last fall, the World Federalist Association adopted a resolution urging all U.N. member-states to support a "serious and balanced study" of the Binding Triad proposal. But it is not pushing for immediate adoption of the Binding Triad, and talking with Hoffmann reveals at least three reasons why:

• He thinks other reforms should be given a higher priority. Among them: improving the U.N.'s dispute settlement capacity, and improving the U.N.'s capacity for verifying arms control agreements.

• He thinks it's poor tactics to start out calling for an amendment to the U.N. Charter. "Hudson is pushing for a Charter amendment and it may come to that. But there are steps in between...."

• He thinks the U.N. is moving, less than fully consciously, in the direction of weighted voting and modification of the veto *already*—and that that spontaneous movement must not be thrown off course for a song. "In the budgetary area, I think it is very possible that we could get weighted voting in committees. They're going a little bit in this direction right now.... A majority of the Security Council—*even if there's a veto*—can refer something to the General Assembly. And the General Assembly can then act...."

III. Not so slow

John Fobes, a former deputy director of UNESCO, is another long-time world order advocate for whom the word "retirement" is meaningless (currently he is chair of the U.S. Association for the Club of Rome, and president of Americans for the Universality of UNESCO). Like Hoffmann, he gives qualified support to the Binding Triad proposal. But his qualifiers are very different from Hoffmann's.

"I think it's a very constructive way of getting people to think of other voting procedures than one nation-one vote," Fobes told NEW OPTIONS from his home in Asheville, N.C. "But Hudson is a traditionalist, and the Binding Triad is a traditionally-minded approach to improving the present structure and procedures of the U.N. without addressing what I think will be the changes that are going to occur over the next decade.

"Right now too many things come up in the General Assembly and other plenary conferences and more things ought to be settled below the level of the plenary.... The nation-state is going to become less and less important because of the U.N.'s specialized agencies [World Health Organization, Food and Agriculture Organization, etc.]. Even the specialized agencies are too centralized and I think they are going to be creating more and more semi-autonomous bodies and councils in which governments sit *but other actors can also sit*. There will be more and more representation of non-governmental groups....

"At some of these agencies, it's already begun. UNCTAD recently introduced a 'people's assembly' on certain issues of trade and development. In UNESCO, in the Man and Biosphere Council, you don't have a formal representation of scientific bodies, but representatives of those bodies are sitting right there, right next to the government delegates. And some of the government delegates to the Council are more representative of their national academies of science than they are of their governments...."

IV. Not so timid

Nearly 20 years ago Saul Mendlovitz convened the first meeting of the World Order Models Project—an international consortium of scholar-activists that's still going strong. His perspective on the Binding Triad proposal has an activist, grassroots, "struggle" quality to it that sets it apart from Hoffmann and Fobes's more evolutionary perspectives.

"I would give Hudson a very high grade on the conceptual thinking that's gone into his proposal," Mendlovitz told NEW OPTIONS. "But I don't see that it has much appeal for ordinary people. What it misses is that people don't find themselves involved in U.N. operations.

"What you have at these U.N. meetings, by and large, are people appointed by executives. Even citizens in Western-style 'democracies' never have anything to say in any real sense about who gets appointed. They don't vote for them, there's no running for those offices.

"So what Hudson has to do—if he wants to make his proposal into a real Political Project—is think of an alternative chamber for the U.N. What we need is some kind of chamber of people's organizations. As it stands now, the Binding Triad proposal is perpetuating a system which most people in the world find remote from themselves."

We asked Mendlovitz to say more about the alternative chamber. "Unfortunately," he replied, "the people who've been dealing with 'alternative chambers' so far have been amateurist and worse. There are a couple of things around now called 'people's assemblies.' They've met a couple of times and are really quite pathetic. . . .

"One might take a look at the European parliament, which is elected by the members of their own societies. Western societies might begin to say, Why don't we elect our representatives to the U.N.? That's one possibility.

"Some alternative-chamber people are trying to figure out a way to decide which people's organizations should have representation in the chamber. Would they be certified by the U.N. itself? The U.N. was set up by the nation-states. It's a complicated problem!

"But I'll say this: We would do as well to study the alternative-chamber kind of thing as we would to study the Binding Triad. Even if you didn't come up with an acceptable chamber proposal, you might come up with some participatory mechanism that would allow and encourage people to feel they were part of what was going on at the U.N."

• • •

As we go to press, all over Washington reporters are competing with each other to get the latest, deepest "scoop" on the Iran-contra affair. Meanwhile, the larger story—that Iran-contra is definitive proof (if any more proof were needed) that we can no longer run the world in ways that benefit us and we had better, therefore, join it in a meaningful way—goes unremarked and unrecorded.

It is nothing short of a tragedy that the debate over how we can best join the world—a debate involving four of our most senior and experienced U.N. reformers—and hopefully, soon, involving some of you—is being conducted in the pages of NEW OPTIONS. . . while the pages of *Time* and *Newsweek, The Nation* and *The New Republic,* are preoccupied with hot Iran-contra rumor and innuendo. . . .

19 Twenty-eight Ways of Looking at Terrorism

January 1986

Dec. 27, 1985: *in nearly simultaneous attacks, terrorists kill 14 innocent people at airports in Rome and Vienna.* Nov. 23, 1985: *an EgyptAir plane is hijacked after leaving Athens, and in a rescue attempt the next day, 57 people perish.* Oct. 7, 1985: *Palestinian gunmen seize the Italian ship Achille Lauro and murder a handicapped Jewish-American passenger.*

How to make sense of these incidents? In our eyes, one of the most frightening things about the recent wave of terrorism is the narrowness of the public debate. The moral poverty of the killings is matched by the poverty of the discussion about how we should respond. Terrorism might not yet be "banal," as a recent Rand

Corp. report suggests, but the conventional responses to terrorism—from the left, the right, and in between—have become just that.

It is for this reason that this issue of NEW OPTIONS is entirely devoted to one theme: alternative and perhaps more healing ways of looking at the New Terrorism.

But first, a look at the three traditional views. . . .

I. Predictable views

We good, they bad. On the political right, there is nothing particularly Earth-shaking about the terrorist threat. It is just the latest strategy of predominantly Marxist revolutionary groups and their allies. It is the latest tactic of the cold war aimed at the vulnerabilities of Western democracies and aspiring Third World democracies. It is, above all, a *coordinated* effort among groups and across borders fueled by Cuba, Libya and the Soviet Union.

The right-wing solution to this situation is to seek to put diplomatic, economic and military pressure on Cuba, Libya and the Soviet Union and on all who deal with them. Robert McFarlane, until recently President Reagan's national security advisor, perfectly captured this perspective when he remarked that we ought to "focus our power on dealing with the root causes of terrorism— where people are trained, where they are housed, fed, sustained."

We normal, they crazy. The liberal response to terrorism typically downplays the degree of coordination among terrorist groups and among the nations that fund these groups. It focuses not on bad nations but on bad people—in fact, mad people, crazy people. A spate of articles in liberal newspapers and magazines has dwelt at length on the alleged personality characteristics of terrorists. Richard Cohen, columnist for the *Washington Post,* laments, "We wait on the actions of Palestinian crazies (sincere or not, what does it matter?) and, sometimes, Israeli zealots such as Ariel Sharon." Then he adds the inevitable Tragic Note: "History laughs at Big Powers and their deluded belief that they can control events. Once again, the sane think they can control the mad!"

Beyond this, liberals are just not comfortable with the subject. The 1984 Democratic National Platform devotes four paragraphs to the "legitimate rights of self-determination of the peoples of Namibia," not one word to terrorism. But there is a liberal solution to terrorism-as-the-product-of-insane-and-irrational-forces. It is a combination of short-term policies aimed at deterrence coupled with even shorter-term policies meant to deal out quick and effective punishment when deterrence fails.

Newsweek's widely-noted article, "Ten Ways to Fight Terrorism" (July 1, 1985), is the most ambitious attempt to date to articulate this approach in the popular media. Among the deterrence measures suggested: tighten airport security, expand intelligence gathering, improve international antiterrorist cooperation. Among the punitive measures: don't rule out rescues, lean on terrorist allies, order selective reprisals.

They bad, we worse. The radical-left response to the latest wave of terrorism is just as boringly predictable as the right-wing and liberal responses. It is that ultimately, "in the final analysis," the terrorism we are subjected to is our own fault. Or more precisely, Ronald Reagan's fault.

An editorial in the newspaper *In These Times,* probably the most intelligent social-democratic publication in the U.S. today, captures this perspective well when it says, "Ultimately, the blame [for terrorism] rests with [the Reagan] administration's policies, and those that preceded [it], rather than with the desperate people striking out in reaction to events over which they have little or no control" (June 26, 1985). As if to convince readers that this was no mere emotional outburst, the point was repeated two issues later: "The problem is not the terrorists but the policies of the Reagan administration" (July 10, 1985). *The Progressive* apparently agrees: "It was this country's foreign meddling, after all, that triggered the current wave of lawlessness" (August 1985).

•   •   •

The problem with the conservative, liberal and radical-left views is not that they are "wrong," but that they are narrow—too narrow to explain terror in its full dimensions and too narrow, therefore, to permit us to come up with effective and appropriate solutions.

Each of the traditional views embodies *part* of the truth. Terrorist groups *are* cooperating across international borders. Some terrorists *are* unbalanced, even irrational. Some U.S. policies *are* deeply resented, often for good reason, in many parts of the world. But even taken together, these views do not add up to a convincing explanation of the New Terrorism.

Fortunately, some U.S. scholars and activists are coming up with innovative post-liberal/post-conservative/post-socialist perspectives on terrorism—perspectives that, when *added* to the three above, might well enable us to come up with life-serving understandings and strategies.

II. Emerging views

The new terrorism. George Lopez, 35, co-editor of a recent anthology on terrorism, occasionally gives briefings for State Dept. officials, but is happier in his role as convenor of the Peace and Global Studies Program at tiny Earlham College in Richmond, Ind. He is convinced that the new terrorism is qualitatively different from the old.

"By the mid-1970s," he told NEW OPTIONS from his Earlham College office, "there'd been a conscious decision by most world governments to work together to try to prevent terrorism; and many states did take coordinated action. After 1978 we witnessed a downturn of terrorist incidents, in part at least because the coordinated measures had some effect, in part because the political climate changed.

"But terrorism took off again after about 1983. And it is very different from before. For one thing, it is not meant to 'wake the masses.' And it is not meant to make political demands or to assert political rights. It is basically just for punishment—for example, to punish the Israelis.

"In the 1970s, there came to be quasi-rules for terrorist events: negotiations were possible, sandwiches were sent in, etc. The new terrorists aren't setting up that kind of deal. On the Achille Lauro, they were just going to take passenger after passenger and shoot them. Today the terrorists aren't playing fair.

"Now no politician is going to say that in public: 'It's not fair.' But in private they do distinguish politically motivated activists who are terrorists, from those who have no purpose but anarchy, horror, punishment, and striking out at civilization in general."

Before we hung up, we asked Lopez how he could spend his entire professional life dwelling on the subject of terrorism. He said living in Indiana helped keep him grounded.

Their terror—and ours. One thing many news stories fail to mention is that, even today, "private" terror pales in comparison to state terror. Saul Mendlovitz, vice president of the World Policy Institute, puts it well when he says, "It is important not to exaggerate the scope of the problem of terror, especially when compared to the systematic terror wielded by 'legitimate' governments or official leaders ranging from Stalin to Pol Pot and from Hitler to Amin, or to overlook the cold efficiency of Latin American 'death squads.'"

One recent Amnesty International publication, "Political Killings by Governments," includes detailed reports on incidents in 20 countries since 1980, as well as analyses of such preferred government techniques as "official cover-ups," "disappearances" and "mass liquidations."

"State terrorism really reared its head in the French government's sinking of the Rainbow Warrior," old G.O.W. Mueller, terrorism expert at the U.N., told us with fiery passion from his Long Island home. "It's not always them against us. It's also often us against them, or us against us!"

The new warfare. The most important long-term effect of the new terrorism may have to do with the way we make war. The new terrorism will almost certainly make our current notions of warfare and "appropriate weaponry" thoroughly obsolete.

"Terror is terrifying to the traditional military mind," energy analyst Amory Lovins told NEW OPTIONS. "After all, whom do you retaliate against? And now that you can put World War II in a little box under your bed, ox-carts, cars, UPS, briefcases, become the most likely delivery vehicles for bombs. Incidentally, if Star Wars were ever deployed—and it did everything Reagan claims it would—then it would *surely* move enemy bombs out of missiles and into car trunks...."

Lovins's claims were recently echoed by independent military analyst Bernard J. Sussman. "Reprisals are extremely difficult when the culprits cannot be precisely identified or located," Sussman wrote. "This will become worse as anonymous bombings and the use of pseudonymous proxies or mercenaries increase.... When both large and small governments adopt such methods, the weaponry of old strategies, such as MX missiles and armed satellites, becomes not only a waste of money but a hindrance to the adoption of newer strategies that are desperately needed.''

Global irresponsibility. Benjamin B. Ferencz is pessimistic about our chances for coping with terrorism—and he has earned the right to be. An independent scholar (''not an academic,'' he says proudly), he is the author of a highly-regarded trilogy on international law enforcement, written mostly at the U.N. library; as a young man he was a prosecutor for the United States at the Nuremberg war crimes trial. He has seen quite enough in his life, thank you.

''The international community doesn't want to cope with terrorism,'' Ferencz told us bluntly from his home in New Rochelle, N.Y.

''The measures taken at the U.N. regarding terrorism are deliberately laced with loopholes in order to permit every nation to pursue what it perceives as a legitimate goal. The U.N. measures are therefore inadequate. You can only combat terrorism on a cooperative, international basis, with a coherent body of international law. . . .

''People should demand a lawful regime. *We* had a terrorist society—the Wild West. We established courts, law enforcement agencies, etc., and enforced the law. If you look at the U.N.'s Terrorist Convention, you'll see that it says that if terrorism is done for self-determination or for freedom from alien domination or whatever, it is not really terrorism. This is not serious. . . . Terrorism will continue and will expand until nations are prepared to write clear and consistent international laws.''

Global progress. G.O.W. Mueller is more hopeful than Ferencz—and he's no less wordly-wise. In 1965 he published the first-ever book on international criminal law; from 1974-82 he was director of the Crime Prevention and Criminal Justice Branch of the U.N.

''When I started out at the U.N.,'' Mueller told NEW OPTIONS from his office at Rutgers University-Newark, ''we were unable to agree on even a definition of terrorism—on who are freedom fighters and who are terrorists. In Dec. 1985, there was unanimous condemnation of all terrorism as acts against civilian targets outside the framework of military action. . . .

"Recently the U.N. General Assembly has been debating the establishment of an international criminal court that would include jurisdiction over international terrorism. There is a greater willingness now to discuss these matters—now that Soviet diplomats are getting kidnapped and killed. . . ."

Dangers of counterterror. It is possible to frustrate many terrorist acts through increased intelligence and surveillance, as *Newsweek* and others suggest. But it is probably impossible to prevent them altogether. And a number of analysts have emphasized that, beyond a certain point, such "cures" might be worse than the disease.

"Intelligence and surveillance effectively rob terrorists of two of their most powerful weapons: the choice of target and the element of surprise," Saul Mendlovitz, cited above, told NEW OPTIONS. "But there are high costs associated with mounting antiterrorist campaigns. Surveillance, even if diligently carried out, poses a danger of abuse for any free society. . . . Worse still, antidemocratic elements often raise the banner of antiterrorism as a pretext for gaining public support for repressive policies and practices."

An even more skeptical view of counterterrorism comes from Irving Louis Horowitz, protege and biographer of the great sociologist, C. Wright Mills, and a U.S. representative to Amnesty International's 1982 conference on terrorism.

"A society without terrorism is quite possible to achieve," says Horowitz, all too sincerely. "Fascist systems manage quite adequately to reduce terrorism by a series of devices: mass organizations in which membership is compulsory; block-by-block spying network; mandatory police identification certificates; clear delineations of 'friends' and 'enemies' of the regime.

"With the increased sophistication of computerization techniques, such mechanisms for social and personal control are increasingly available. The question remains: does a citizenry wish to pay such a premium price for social tranquillity?"

"It is fascism." But bring up the New Terrorism—the PLO, for example—and Horowitz changes his tune. "I don't consider this to be terrorism by any traditional definition," he told NEW OPTIONS. "It is really fascism: ethnic group and religious group persecution directed at Jews. It's a concerted, fascist assault clearly directed at Jewish objects, Israeli objects, Jewish-owned shops. . . .

"It's a classic case of fascism."

The end of the world. "Terrorism is the last step in a trend toward social and cultural disintegration," says Moshe Amon, a young Israeli historian and philosopher who's taught at several North American universities. "Terrorism is tolerated by large segments of our society, as if the social body itself has declared a moratorium upon its own life in recognition that it cannot sustain itself any more."

At the core of our disintegration, according to Amon, is the "spread of personal reliance on the state." As we've become less and less responsible for our selves, the mentality that leads to the use and abuse of others—up to and including the random killing of innocents—has flourished. "The terrorist is the product, and the most perfect representative, of this trend to evade responsibility. He is not responsible for the existence of anything; he turns over the responsibility for all his actions to a group. . . ."

The hope of the world. An entirely different analysis comes from William Clark, maverick former vice president of the World Bank and chair of The Other Economic Summit. In Clark's novel *Cataclysm* (1985), a summing-up of everything Clark learned in 40-plus years as a journalist and diplomat but wasn't allowed to say in print, it is only terrorism that is going to bring Britain and the U.S. to the conference table to work out equitable economic arrangements with the Third World. But it is terrorism of a special sort.

According to Clark, this new kind of terror might reasonably be called "inconvenience terror." It will be practiced by the Third World against the countries of the North once the Third World realizes that in Europe and North America, at least, "the IRA style of assassination and gun-toting terror is totally counterproductive." In its place, the Third World countries will begin to practice a kind of terrorism meant to demonstrate "that the well-organized, computerized, automatized world of the urban North cannot run smoothly while ignoring and repressing the poor in the outside world and in their midst."

Cataclysm is full of examples of how this new "inconvenience terror" might be made to work. On one level, in fact, it's a kind of handbook for would-be Third World terrorist-activists and their supporters in the North.

Clark would have us begin by using short-burst radio transmissions to interrupt Euro-American radio programs with information on deteriorating conditions in the South. We could also manipulate television satellites to insert one-minute spots into national TV programs. These Third World-generated radio and TV programs could eventually be used to make economic and political demands on the North. If the demands weren't heeded, additional means of inconvenience terror might be used.

For example, we could use pocket-sized transmitters to disrupt electronic check-out counters—in order to remind people what it's like to live in the collapsing big cities of the Third World. We could tamper with computerized water purifiers, causing unpurified sewage to mix with purified water—in order to "bring home" what it's like to live in the Third World where literally tens of millions of people die every year for lack of purified water.

In *Cataclysm*, Clark outlines a strategy consisting of one part education, one part fear, that just might induce the North to make economic and political peace with the South. After 40-plus years on the international scene he sees no other way, in practice, to bring about such a restructuring.

III. Some causes

Arrogance vs. fanaticism. Abdul Aziz Said (pronounced "sigh-eed"), professor of international relations at American University in Washington D.C., is going to be the token "non-mainstream" speaker at an important meeting of terrorism analysts sponsored by the U.S. government this April. He is thinking of titling his speech something like, "The West and Islam: Arrogance and Fanaticism."

"Terrorism has sharpened our words, but not our understanding," Said told NEW OPTIONS from his inner-city apartment just hours before he was to leave for a peace conference in Poland. "In many ways Muslims have been saying they want respect, freedom, legitimacy. But that's not what the West sees. The West sees the Islamic revival as a threat to Western civilization.

"This Western reaction feeds into the cycle of hostility and misunderstanding and hastens the self-fulfillment of both sides' worst prophecies. Thus, Muslims react with more zeal and violence while the West becomes more sanctimonious.

"The West really is so sanctimonious. The West is outraged now because terrorists don't play by the rules. However, the rules favor the West! The deployment of the battleship New Jersey fits the rules. Car bombs and hijackings do not. The terrorists don't have a battleship New Jersey.

Twisted brothers. Even if terrorists aren't, strictly speaking, "mad," and even if the rest of us aren't altogether "sane," it may still be true that the new terrorists are unusually psychologically damaged human beings who find in terrorism a ready-made and personally appealing outlet for their frustrations. So say many analysts and—interestingly—a number of ex-radical activists from the 60s.

David Rapoport, who has taught political science at UCLA, writes of "terror as personal therapy." According to Rapoport, "One can gain therapeutic value from conflict, especially if a cause seems worthy. One who stands up for his convictions feels more like a person for doing so. Perpetually overcrowded psychiatric facilities emptied during Berkeley's revolutionary days. Never did life seem more interesting or worthwhile."

Our generation has a special relationship to terrorism, having already been both the perpetrator of terror through such groups as the Weathermen and the target of state terror, e.g. on the campuses of Jackson State and Kent State. In *Growing Up Underground* (1981), activist Jane Alpert tries to capture some of the unbalanced personality-types in and around the Weathermen. Her lover, Sam Melville, for example:

"After working until midnight on my *Rat* article, I found Sam lying in bed, listening to WBAI. Bob Fass was taking calls about the turmoil at City College. The caller on the air was condemning the strike leaders.

"'How long has this jerk been on the air?' I asked Sam as I crawled into bed next to him.

He made no answer. To my surprise, he was wearing his clothes under the sheet. Then he said in the darkness, 'I'm going to blow up WBAI.'

"I stared at his face, partially visible in the moonlight. His left eye was jumping.

"'Are you stoned?'

"'No,' he said. I didn't believe him.

"'Tell me why you want to blow up WBAI.'

"'Because they're liberal assholes. It's time they learned that things are serious.'

"'But, Sam, they're the only station in New York that gives the movement any airtime at all.'

"'That's exactly why we need to shake them up.'

"'You're crazy,' I said.

"The words came out of me before I thought of censoring them.

"'Don't you talk to me that way,' Sam said, sitting up.

"I cannot remember what I said then, but it must have been another mistake. Sam leaped from the bed, gripped the edges of the six-foot mirror mounted on our bedroom wall, and tore it from its brackets. For one terrifying moment, he held it over me while I covered my head with my hands. Then, coming to his senses, he relaxed and laid it gently against the wall."

Alpert's summing up of this incident is meant to apply to more than just her lover: "For Sam, politics was just an excuse. He was as likely to turn his violence toward me or toward Nathan or Pat or WBAI or the *Guardian* as toward the people we agreed were the enemy."

Just kids. James Shenton might well reply that all that psychologizing isn't necessary. According to Shenton, who teaches history at Columbia University, and was Mark Rudd's faculty advisor in the pre-Weatherman days, the most important single fact about terrorism is how *young* the terrorists are.

"Most terrorists are young adults or adolescents," Shenton told NEW OPTIONS late one night from his home in northern New Jersey. "The Archduke Ferdinand was assassinated by a 15-year-old; the entire conspiracy that led to that assassination took place in a high school. . . . The terrorists in Russia in the late 19th century were all college students. . . . Almost everyone involved in John Brown's band was in their late teens or early 20s. . . .

"This also holds true for the various terrorists today. The young men and women may be *guided* by older people such as Abu Nidal, but the terrorists themselves are at an impressionable age. . . .

"The ones who do the shooting are young people acting in defense of transcendent causes, which tend to appeal to the young. They're not into subtleties at that age; they tend to have an either-

or mentality. It perhaps requires youth to act 'irrationally,' without thinking deeply about the consequences of their actions.''

USA: terrorist haven? There is no question that—as the press repeatedly reminds us—the government of Libya is harboring terrorists. What James Shenton would add is this: the U.S. has also played host to many who were terrorists.

''Many terrorists have used the U.S. as a sanctuary from which they could launch assaults against established authorities,'' Shenton told NEW OPTIONS. ''Before Castro, various anti-Batista revolutionaries were here. Now many anti-Castro revolutionaries are here. The terrorist who shot the King of Italy hung out in Paterson, N.J. The Czech republic was founded in Pittsburgh! When the Russian Revolution broke out, many of the most famous Bolsheviks were in the U.S. . . . ''

As it turns out, the Sikh terrorists accused of plotting Rajiv Gandhi's murder, and suspected of having sabotaged the Air India jet that plunged into the North Atlantic with 329 people aboard, were trained in Alabama. The Sikhs took a $350, two-week course at Frank Camper's Reconnaissance Commando School, near Birmingham, in November 1984, where they studied time bombs, silent killing, and other ''relevant'' subjects.

Shenton's point: ''When a challenge to the established order comes from another country, the established order tends to see that country as sponsoring that challenge. But it's not necessarily so.''

Information ➤ terror. The conventional left-liberal interpretation of terrorism is that it is a byproduct of oppression. An alternative interpretation is offered by Amy Redlick, who's taught courses on guerrilla warfare and terrorism at Boston College. She sees terrorism as a strategy or tactic *consciously and voluntarily chosen* by rational political actors after reviewing their available options.

''There are two basic motivations for the use of terrorism as a strategy or tactic,'' says Redlick. ''First, the overwhelming balance of forces between the rebels and their opposition may offer the dissidents no other option. . . . [But] second, the transnational flow of information may provide dissidents with the inspirational and material spark that will cause them to resort to terrorism.

''For example, a variety of external factors, such as the writings of Frantz Fanon, had subtle and extensive influence on the Quebec and Palestinian terrorist movements. The information obtained from external sources provided the terrorists with tactical, strategic, and ideological knowledge about the art of bomb-making, hostage-taking, and kidnapping.

"Moreover, information concerning the Algerians, Palestinians and Tupamaros permeated the intellectual milieu of Quebec and contributed to the creation of a climate in which the use of violence appeared justifiable and necessary to a small group of Quebecois."

Nuclear terror. Amory Lovins is well-known for his expertise on renewable energy. What many people don't yet realize is that he is also one of our foremost experts on the connection between energy policy and national security. His recent books have titles like *Brittle Power, Energy/War* and *The First Nuclear World War.*

Lovins thinks that "nuclear terrorism" is a clear and present danger—far and away the most serious threat of all the terrorist threats that the world now faces. He thinks the very *existence* of the nuclear bomb and nuclear power is part of what makes the "new terrorism" qualitatively new.

"There have already been hundreds of individual threats of nuclear terror in various degrees," Lovins told NEW OPTIONS from his Rocky Mountain Institute in rural Colorado. "But there've been only a handful of threats involving bacteriological weapons, which are easier to produce and more effective! I infer from this that nuclear bombs have special, 'theatrical' value which conveys itself to terrorists. . . .

"I am sometimes impressed at how *lucky* we've been. We've had attacks on nuclear power plants in 26 states and in over 40 countries—an average of once a week at this point; and yet, most of the attacks have been incompetent or just to make a point (for example, to black out a neighborhood for an hour), not to hurt people. If people *wanted* to hurt us, they could [certainly] do it much more effectively than they have."

We asked Lovins if he saw any possible solution and he said simply, "Denuclearization." Did he mean literally ridding the world of nuclear weapons and power plants? "Exactly."

Return of the suppressed. Gordon Feller, the young editor of *East/West Report,* doesn't just see the bomb as a standing invitation to terrorists. He sees the nuclear deterrent system as—all by itself—a *cause* of the new terrorism.

"Despite Ronald Reagan's rhetoric about how Mutually Assured Destruction (MAD) is immoral, that *is* our defense strategy, and the Soviet Union's, also," Feller told us. "And with the MAD deterrent system you have to keep local conflicts off the battlefield—because any violent conflict is too dangerous; because the deterrent system is too fragile.

"The underlying conflicts in Central America, in the Middle East, in the Philippines, have never been confronted in a direct, frontal way; they've never been fully addressed or resolved. It's just too dangerous to do so. If there's a small war, it could explode.

"Because our nuclear deterrent system has made us suppress the working out of conflict (one false move and we're all dead), now—in international terrorism—we're seeing the dark side of the nuclear deterrent system. We're seeing the return, in particularly ghoulish form, of all our suppressed conflicts.

"The nuclear-defense system just doesn't permit the true resolution of international crises. So we sit on the crises—we 'manage' them, we don't resolve them. And terrorism results. It's a letting off of steam. It's the return of the suppressed."

Against modernity. In a way, says Feller, it is ironic that the new terrorists make expert use of nuclear threats, of power plants, of high-tech weaponry and jumbo jets. For they are, he says, most importantly of all, traditionalists fighting against modernity.

"The favorite targets of the Third World breed of terrorist have been airports and airlines. I would think about that. If you're trying to deal with the threat to religious and cultural tradition, the place you'd want to hit is the plexus point—what connects the Middle East, say, to the rest of the world and particularly the modern industrialized world. That would be airports and airlines. They symbolize the whole modernist technostructure. And so does Israel. Culturally, Israel is the modernist pebble on the Eastern shore....

"My guess is that as airport security gets tighter, the terrorists will move on to huge office buildings and other conspicuous parts of the technostructure."

IV. Some solutions

Revenge—or restraint? How should a nation respond to terrorist attacks? In the U.S., we are only beginning to deal with this question, but Israeli theorists have been batting it around for nearly 40 years. Yoram Peri is an Israeli Labor Party military affairs specialist who has gained the respect of the Israeli peace movement. His analysis of Israel's options—basically, revenge or restraint—is so relevant to our own situation that it deserves to be quoted at length:

"Fifty years have passed since [Mapai party theoretician] Ziama Aran spoke of the necessity for ['active response' to Arab terror, as distinct from 'self-restraint'], yet Arabs continue to murder Jews. Now there is no restraint. We set a high price in blood for Jewish lives, yet the [endless] reprisal raids fail to bring about an end to terror. If we continue with them even though they are not efficient, they, in the best case, satisfy our sense of justice. [But] in the worst and probably more accurate case, [they] generate rage and the will to seek revenge. After all, the law of blood revenge still holds sway in the part of the world where we have chosen to live.

"There is, however, no end to blood revenge. The more you satisfy the lust for revenge, the more you become hooked on it. . . .

"In 1936, Labor-Zionist mentor Berl Katznelson said that Israel's self-restraint—the adult reaction to Arab terror—stemmed not only from ethical considerations but also from political ones. In this land, he said, we knew that once we chose the path of revenge, the phenomenon of 'blood feud' would arise. . . ."

Peri's conclusion: Israel must rediscover Katznelson's strategy of self-restraint.

The world-order solution. It is important for powerful nation-states to respond to terrorist provocations "like an adult," as Peri puts it; but it is also important to understand that no nation-state, no matter how mature, can possibly cope with the terrorist phenomenon in isolation. "The problem is beyond the ability of individual nations to manage," Gerald and Patricia Mische, co-directors of Global Education Associates, told NEW OPTIONS. "There's a whole global breakdown of national security systems. There's a need for international law and international institutions. . . ."

George Lopez, cited above, is one of the few American scholars who's given serious thought to the kinds of international institutions we might want to build. Among his suggestions:

- An *international criminal court* that could hear cases brought by "non-governmental actors" against former heads of state, corporations, individuals, etc.;
- A general commitment to bringing nongovernmental political actors into *some form of dialogue* with national actors in regional and international organizations;
- An *international grievance agency* "to act as a low-level intervenor in disputes and also to provide a redress procedure for forms of state terror";
- A *United Nations Commission for Human Rights* that would provide means for citizens and groups to hold national leaders accountable for violations of the Universal Declaration of Human Rights.

The decentralist solution. Kirkpatrick Sale, author of *Human Scale* (1980), paces back and forth in stockinged feet in the study of his Greenwich Village apartment. He also feels the nation-state system has got to be radically altered. But he feels the problem is not only that states are incompetent. He feels it's also that they're too powerful, too repressive, too all-encompassing—in a word, too big.

"I don't know of any terrorists that are not fighting for some kind of homeland," Sale told NEW OPTIONS. "Think of the Basques in Spain, the Montagnards in Yugoslavia, the Palestinians. You can solve the problem that gives rise to terrorism by dividing nations so that each of the groups that feels it has to have a homeland, gets a homeland.

"Instead of trying to maintain an overlarge collection of various peoples, thus frustrating groups that are truly nations, you allow each region to de-link itself—have its autonomy—develop its territory as it wants to. . . .

"We need to take off the blinders of nationalism that insist that nations are permanent, that they cannot be dismantled. We would eliminate most of the terrorism in the world plus most of the *wars* if we agreed to divide nation-states."

V. Deeper meanings

Experiencing our fear. After we'd conducted most of our interviews for this article, we were feeling terribly depressed. So we called Joanna Macy and asked for her thoughts on the subject. Macy is a creator of the "Despairwork and Empowerment" workshops, which have been so helpful to peace activists over the years; she is also the author of an excellent book on self-reliant development strategies for the Third World, *Dharma and Development* (1983).

"Terrorism is an avenue for feeling our interconnectedness with all beings," Macy told NEW OPTIONS. "It's a vehicle for teaching Americans what it's like to feel afraid—which is how most people feel on this planet." Instantly, we relaxed. And realized that the only way to really be able to live with the New Terrorism was to explore its deeper meanings, inner meanings.

"This is a time when societies are dislocating," Macy continued. "The old is passing. Fear stalks the streets and the airports. And the refugee camps. And the people trying to slip through borders. And the people being hunted. And those who are waiting for their sons and daughters to come home—waiting to see if they'll join 'the disappeared.'

"And the fear stalks the farms. Farm families are asking, 'Can we make the payments on the debt?' Taxes are so high. There's a fear of losing everything.

"The terrorists make us afraid. And all I know to do about it, on an emotional level, is to see that this is an invitation to experience a little bit of the gut-wrenching fear that shadows the lives of our brothers and sisters at this moment in time.

"I think there's going to be fear walking all the alleyways and corridors of powers until we find ways of sharing the resources of our planet more justly. I think that's obvious. . . .

"The terrible danger of fear is that we will slip the demon mask over the faces of human beings. We have to rip the mask away so we can see the vulnerable, suffering human beings underneath."

The chickens come home. "Terrorists are a shadow side of all of us," says Corinne McLaughlin, co-author of the book *Builders of the Dawn* (1985). "Terrorists represent the side we don't like to admit—the repressed negativity in us. They sort of act it out for us."

"It's not just the terrorists who are holding people hostage when they hijack a plane," adds Joanna Macy. "We superpowers are holding the whole world hostage with our weapons, our tanks and our planes, which we use to further our 'national interests.'

"So in a very literal sense, the superpowers are holding the whole world hostage. And when the terrorists hold people hostage, they're following a tradition that we ourselves are dignifying."

The pain of homelessness. "It is important to speak to the dangers inherent in the feeling of homelessness and rootlessness," David Spangler told NEW OPTIONS. Spangler is a spiritual leader and teacher, and author of the book *Emergence: The Rebirth of the Sacred* (1984).

"People are in pain all over the world," Spangler said from his home near Seattle, Wash. "That generates a kind of psychic pain or residue that's crying out; there's a lot of pain within the collective unconscious of humanity. The existence of refugees who are in effect homeless, and have no structure or sense of belonging to a place, creates an entry point through which this psychic pain can enter the world.

"Precisely because these people don't have homes of their own, they have no investment in the concept of home. They may wish to reclaim their homeland. But in the present situation, not having a homeland they don't have a sense of a need to honor the homeland of others.

"I remember playing a board game once, and after a while one fellow got up and said, 'If I can't win, I don't want anybody else to win!' If he couldn't win, he had no investment in any aspect of the game. The homeless have no connection with the world; they have been severed from the world on account of their homelessness. They have no investment in it."

The dark side of the new. Spangler paused for a moment, then continued in a deeper, slower voice: "Terrorism represents the shadow side of the kind of global consciousness that many good folks are trying to develop.

"A major thrust in our current economic and political life is toward a kind of globalness as represented, say, in a multinational corporation. We are such a mobile society—so many of the traditional bonds of place, home, geography, family, all the things that helped define us in the past, don't define us in the same way any more. We are creating a whole culture of psychic refugees—of people who are uprooted in a very basic way.

"Under that imperfectly formed, or malformed global consciousness, it becomes so much easier to move people around, and to undervalue the values of home and connectedness with other people. I begin to develop a consciousness that does not view the Earth as a home, but only as a resource. There is a breaking of the bonds of love and caring for the Earth and the things of the Earth—including human community.

"The frightening thing about a terrorist is that he or she seems to have no regard for life—whether his or her own life or anybody else's. Terrorists seek to extend insecurity and risk and devaluing of life willy-nilly into society. But at a deeper level, this could be seen as an externalization or personification of the new global culture's own devaluation of life. . . . In that sense, terrorism would seem to be almost a disease of the transition into a global age. It's the shadow side of that transition.

"Ultimately, I feel that what the terrorist phenomenon is calling out for is a return to a deeper valuing of home and place; and on the other hand, a deeper valuing of the Earth as our home. And global institutions that can act out of that perspective!"

VI. Dare to struggle, dare to take it all in

You may feel tempted to pick and choose among the perspectives described above. You should try to avoid that temptation.

One of the severest problems with the traditional political spectrum is precisely that it is a spectrum, a "straight line" of opinion. Those who cling to it—to any part of it, left, right or center—soon acquire a vested interest in seeing the world *one way* and no other. They become adept at excluding or distorting information if it doesn't fit neatly onto their preferred part of the straight line.

This article was written for those who believe that the spectrum of opinion is more like a circle than a straight line. It was written for those who believe that each of the different perspectives on terrorism has something to add to the whole.

In this view, coming up with a solution to terrorism is not a matter of adopting "correct" political beliefs. It is, rather, a matter of learning to listen—really *listen*—to everyone in the circle of humankind. And to take their insights into account. For everyone has a true and unique perspective on the whole.

167

Fifteen years ago the burning question was, How radical are you? Hopefully someday soon the question will be, How much can you synthesize? How much do you dare to take in?

PART FIVE

IDEALS ARE NOT ENOUGH

One of the most painful things I've learned is how difficult it is to take the ideas in NEW OPTIONS and inject them into the mainstream political debate.

In the 1970s I helped found an extremely idealistic political organization, the New World Alliance. It lasted all of three years.

The 80s began my love affair with another idealistic political organization, the U.S. Greens, in whom I saw the very soul of what a caring, decentralized, globally responsible society should be. But as the curtain rose on the 90s that love affair was modified into an understanding as I came to realize that a movement with greater potential outreach was needed to transform these ideals into action.

"You Don't Have to Be a Baby to Cry," enormously painful to write, recounts the story. It generated more mail than any other piece in NEW OPTIONS... most of it from Second Experimenters who'd gone through the same kind of experience.

As the simon-Pure approach of the Greens began to make less sense to me, I began to look again at the larger culture—warily at first—to see if there was anything I'd been missing. Indeed there was.

I discovered that beneath my very eyes, the archetype of the "caring individual" was breaking into the mainstream. In science, movies, rock music, business, in virtually every area of modern life, the caring individual was conducting a thousand different Second Experiments. "The 1980s Were Better Than We Thought," probably my most ambitious piece, tells his and her story.

169

The next piece has me scouring Congress for caring individuals (as defined by their voting records). I actually manage to find some, and tell you a little bit about them and about the bills they rather bravely sponsored.

It's nice to have friends at the top. But the Second American Experiment cannot possibly be conducted primarily by Congresspeople, and in my next piece I focus on four social change organizations that are making a difference in the world.

They are very different from one another. The Listening Project is helping Appalachians become articulate about politics; the Social Investment Forum is helping brokers steer rich people's money into "socially responsible" businesses. But they are all competent and focused and less-than-fully-Pure. And it is through the work of such organizations, staffed and supported by "caring individuals," that the Second Experiment is, I submit, being forged.

In that respect, at least, it is very much like the First Experiment.

My last piece steps back from the political fray and suggests that all of us—even Second Experimenters—might do well to concentrate on changing the often bitter and divisive way we talk *about* politics. I am not "making nice" here, I am being pragmatic. The Second Experiment will go nowhere if it can't be led by listeners and healers.

20 You Don't Have to Be a Baby to Cry

September 1990

This country is more than ready for a post-liberal, post-socialist, Greenish political party. Nearly everybody now knows (on some level of their being) that we can't go on this way: we can't keep piling up debt, we can't keep destroying the environment, we can't keep ignoring the Third World, we can't keep relying on growth to solve our problems and technology to shape our future.

For the last seven years, this newsletter has paid special attention to the U.S. Green movement (see Chapter 3). I thought that it would be out of this scruffy but idealistic grouping that a powerful new party—counterpart to the successful Green parties of Europe—would come.

I guess you could say my political choices reflected my life choices. When I was growing up lonely and unhappy in a small Minnesota town, I made a sacred commitment to myself. My life would not be about chasing power and privilege (like I imagined my father had done), but would be about discovering life-giving new ways of doing things—on every level.

This month I attended the third national Green Gathering, at a YMCA camp in the Colorado Rockies, and what I saw shook my confidence in the U.S. Greens as a credible, competent vehicle for change. It also made me reassess my life choices. Did I really mean to exchange power for powerlessness, privilege for marginality?

I. Sincerity is not enough

When Matthew Gilbert was in seventh grade, he had what may have been the prototypical Green experience. He suddenly realized how different he was from most of his classmates—and it made him very sad.

Now, many years later, he looked out from the podium at nearly 200 Green delegates and felt stretched out, exhausted. As head of the site committee he was the person who'd done most to pull off the Gathering, and for months he'd been looking forward to making inspiring remarks at the opening session. But now that he was up there, his words betrayed a kind of foreboding: "Try to find the space inside of you that's calm.... We may have differences of opinion, but let's remember, we are really all friends here...."

Gilbert was followed to the podium by an intense, wiry redhead from Auburn, Ala., whose bearing contrasted sharply with the laid-back image cultivated by most Green women and nearly all

Green men. There is such an avoidance of hierarchy in the Greens, and such an avoidance of information that might suggest a hierarchy, that few of them knew that the speaker, Christa Slaton, was an accomplished political scientist with a book on 21st century democracy, *The Televote Experiments,* about to be published.

What they did know was that Slaton was head of the Greens' platform-writing committee, and that she'd performed heroically in that role for over a year, coordinating input from dozens of chapters nationwide. Since one of the three main tasks of this Green Gathering was to re-write the platform and set up a process for ratifying it, they listened to her intently.

The most memorable speaker after Slaton was Danny Moses, an editor at Sierra Club Books whose inspirational speeches and calm, centered presence had helped keep the Greens on track through their previous national Gatherings.

This time his inspirational speech contained a few new twists. He characterized our national leaders as vicious, greedy fools. And he claimed that—because of their spiritual understandings and sense of solidarity—the Greens were among the "Real People" (a concept he borrowed from the Iroquois). Not surprisingly, he received a standing ovation.

I didn't stand. Despite my respect for Moses, I felt the vicious-fools-and-Real-People bit was dangerously arrogant.

I remembered telling myself how Special I was when I worked for various embattled and ineffective organizations. It helped keep me going. But it also helped keep me from being able to reach people.

Because of its rootedness in an Iroquois sensibility, Moses's speech foreshadowed the second great task of the Gathering—figuring out how to relate to Native Americans, African Americans and other "minorities."

The third great task was to restructure the organization.

Literally from the day after the Greens were founded in 1984, they had been meeting to restructure themselves. Several restructurings had already taken place. But by the summer of 1990 everyone wanted to restructure the organization again.

The Interregional Committee (IC), the Greens' vehicle for ongoing national coordination, had become a "bureaucrat's heaven and an activist's nightmare," according to one open letter signed by nine Green activists, "torturous marathons trying to reach consensus on administrative trivia while the issues of the day go unaddressed.'' In another missive, Charles Betz—co-author of one of the restructuring proposals—observed that "The [last] IC had only 10 voting representatives [present] out of a possible total of 70!''

The Greens didn't build much time for restructuring into their formal agenda. But dozens of Greens who cared deeply about the issue met several times to try to work out their differences. I attended the first of these meetings, a marathon late-night session in the lounge of one of the lodges.

When I walked in, they were debating the wisdom of having the Gathering vote on some restructuring proposals that had already been drawn up.

Dee Berry, former clearinghouse coordinator for the Greens, said she didn't feel that the proposals really came from the grassroots. She wanted a new restructuring committee.

Lauren Sargent, of the Michigan Greens, said we needed a decent structure *now.* "I'd hate for us to initiate another whole process now. Our organization is falling apart!''

Charlie Betz said he wasn't comfortable presenting his restructuring proposal to the delegates because the clearing house unaccountably failed to send it to the local chapters in advance of the Gathering.

Berry and Sargent argued over who should be on a new restructuring committee.

Nicholas Dykema, a community organizer from Ohio, said he didn't believe how difficult the Greens were making things. We should simply have the Gathering vote on the restructuring proposals that were before us. "If I described this process to any progressive group in the country,'' he added, "they'd laugh me out of the room.''

Karen Tucker, of the Maine Greens, passionately defended the process. Each local group needs to feel that they own the process, she said. And that sense of ownership will make this organization more powerful in the long run. She wanted to send the restructuring proposals back to the locals.

Round and round they went—for hours that night, and the next night, too. On the last day of the Gathering, the plenary elected a new 10-person committee to launch a new restructuring process.

I wish the new process well. But after seven years I cannot take it altogether seriously. The Greens don't even have by-laws yet, or a fund-raising capacity, or an accountable leadership structure. Something more fundamental than process or knowledge must be holding them back.

I suspect it has something to do with many Greens' mistrust of—name one—expertise/hierarchy/efficiency/rules/power/worldly success.

I've been Pure before. It's pretty satisfying. But it's more important to be effective in the world.

II. Process is not enough

The Greens began writing their platform in 1985. The effort fizzled, but took off again in earnest two years later, and now, at the Gathering, 23 sections of the platform were to be given their final re-writes before presenting them for ratification to the locals.

The Greens broke up into small groups to consider each of the sections. I spent an enjoyable afternoon drifting in and out of them.

Like most of the groups, "Life Forms and Animal Rights" met in a small log cabin. The 15 delegates began by taking turns identifying their favorite animals, personal heroes, and earliest memories. Then someone suggested they choose a spokesperson by having everyone stand up and put their hands on the shoulders of the person they preferred. Several people objected, and a long discussion about process followed.

The "Social Justice" group took up the issue of decriminalization of drugs. A couple of people spoke up for outright decriminalization. But then Kwazi Nkrumah, a black participant from California, said we needed to "transform our culture" first, and that if we just "took the lid off" things might go from bad to worse.

Nkrumah's forceful speech effectively ended people's willingness to consider decriminalization of all drugs. Nobody spoke up to explain and defend the views of such prominent Greenish advocates of decriminalization as Andrew Weil, Lester Grinspoon and Joseph Galiber (see Chapter 14).

Then someone from Santa Cruz said he felt very strongly that marijuana should be legalized. That was batted around for a while ("the public will kill us!" one woman said) and a rather timid version of legalization of marijuana—permitting it to be grown but not sold—was drafted to everyone's satisfaction.

You couldn't fault the Greens for their sincerity, or their willingness to take each other's views into account. But watching their exercise in platform-writing left me feeling both sad and angry.

For 20 years, Greenish scholars and experts have been addressing public policy issues. For the most part, their ideas have been ignored by the mainstream press—and even by the left press. They desperately need a forum, and manifestly deserve one.

The Green platform will fall far short of being that forum. Most of the Greens at the Gathering just didn't have the background to bring the best, freshest Green thinking to the table; truth be told, most of them were better versed in left-wing thought than in Green thought; and of course, Greens would never think of inviting "experts" (even their own experts) to do some of their work for them. That smacks too much of hierarchy and (gasp!) elitism.

There is something beautiful about letting anyone who wants to help write a platform, do so. It is a kind of democracy that even Jefferson never dreamed of. But it is a mistake to confuse that kind of loveliness with crafting a political movement.

•   •   •

The day after the small group sessions, all 200 Greens met in plenary session to discuss and vote on the platform.

The plenary got off to a rocky start, so Margo Adair, champion of mediation and meditation who'd been with the Greens through all three Gatherings, led them in a mass meditation: "Note that particular quality inside you where you can be true to yourself, true to your commitment. . . ."

Then each of the 23 platform planks was briefly discussed, and voted up or down (a 25% vote was sufficient to vote a plank down).

The discussions were even more superficial than those in the small groups—the severe time constraints saw to that. On the other hand, the discussions were at least as full of vim and vigor.

For example, during the discussion on the Technology plank someone got up and said, "I'd be *ashamed* of showing this to anybody—it doesn't address dozens of issues we need to address!" Someone else attacked the plank for being "too anthropocentric." Other wild haymakers were thrown. Then someone got up and cried, "We're dissipating the process of our work. All these objections could have been raised *anytime during the last two years!*"

All this enthusiasm was broken when Christa Slaton announced that every plank passed at the Gathering would go back to the locals—and Lauren Sargent rose to object. She wanted the material to go back to each of the individual members of the Greens.

Slaton was at the breaking point. Listen, she said, I've had a lot of experience here. Greens have a lousy track record meeting deadlines, and sending the material to individuals for their input is just absurd!

Every Green who'd felt manipulated or slighted by Slaton was at the edge of their seats. One young Green yelled at her to not "get so violently emotional!" Another Green stood up and rather emotionally told her he felt the group was being talked down to.

Slaton was on the verge of tears. I felt so good until two minutes ago, she said. I feel so wonderful about the overwhelming spirit that's been here. I just wish more of you would appreciate what so many of us have done to this point!

Inside her, things were churning. She'd grown up in small Southern towns. Her father was a truck driver, her mother sometimes worked in factories. She was the only person on either side of her family who'd ever attended college. Everything she'd ever achieved, she felt, was a result of extraordinary persistence and grit.

She was aware of the Greens' pattern of trashing anybody and everybody who tried to take on a leadership role. But she felt that, well, if she really worked extra hard, just like she'd always done, and sent out lots of mailings, and answered every letter and phone call—*then* every Green would feel like they were really a part of the process. And everyone would be content.

176

Now she felt overwhelmed, undone. Nothing she did was enough! By the time she'd arrived in Colorado she was sleeping four hours a night! Every day at least 10 people would come to her with their "demands"—and each of them swore that their perspective was the overwhelming view of the grassroots! And now they were implying she'd been undemocratic and elitist! It was really more than she could bear.

Inside Lauren Sargent, things were churning too. She couldn't believe Slaton was continuing to take all this so personally!

Sargent had grown up in Grosse Point, Mich., the daughter of a psychiatrist father and psychologist mother, and at night they'd sit around the dinner table and drink coffee and argue. And isn't that how you worked things out in this world? And weren't the Greens a family?

For months she'd been trying to get Slaton to adopt what her local Green group thought of as a more sustainable process—one that would keep Slaton from having to run herself into the ground. She gave her one good argument after another. And now she felt Slaton saw her as an enemy! It saddened her.

The whole scene saddened me, too.

For *seven years* the Greens had been saying they were moving so slow because they—unlike other political groups—were committed to treating their members as Human Beings. They'd introduced dozens of processes, from consensus decision-making to the hokey-pokey, to make good on that commitment.

But sitting there watching Slaton and Sargent and the others, and remembering the vast cast of characters that had passed through the Greens over the years, never to return, I could no longer believe that the Greens had any kind of special handle on sensitivity to others.

On the whole, I thought, they treated each other no better than people did in Common Cause or NARAL or the Democratic party. And sometimes they treated each other much worse.

•   •   •

After that session I felt kind of blue, the way you do when you know that a chapter in your life is ending, and I wanted to get away for a while. So I walked a friend to the YMCA swimming pool—no Greens there—and watched her swim laps, while children screamed and played all around. Someone had brought a boom-box, and it was playing all these 50s songs, including one of my favorites:

> You don't have to be a baby to cry,
> All you need is your love to go wrong.
> You don't have to be a baby to cry,
> Or to lie awake the whole night long.

III. Guilt is not enough

That night was the keynote speech, by Walter Bresette, a Chippewa activist from northern Wisconsin. Most Greens cheered it wildly and found it tremendously inspiring. I found it less than that.

Bresette argued that the Green movement, or something very much like it, is going to happen no matter what the U.S. Greens do. He reminded us that Indians don't consider that they "own" land, they're merely preserving it in trust for their grandchildren. He urged us to rediscover the importance of community, and discover what each of our contributions to it can be.

That was all fine, as far as it went. But how far did it go, really? Is it *true* that anything like a Green movement is happening spontaneously? Is it *relevant* that some Indians don't believe in private property? Is it *meaningful* to speak of "community" without defining it anew for the 21st century?

As Bresette spoke, an American flag hung from the front of the room—except a big picture of an Indian, in a headdress, had been added to it. I felt high when I saw it . . . as high as I felt when we used to paint rainbow colors on school flags in the 60s. But I also felt another 60s syndrome coming on: the syndrome of starry-eyed whites sitting at the feet of oppressed minorities.

And I had no desire to go through it again.

•   •   •

The next day about 30 Greens, including most of the informal leadership, met to discuss building coalitions with people of color. They called their group the "Rainbow Greens" (after their goal, not their composition—only three or four of them were non-white).

Danny Moses and Roberto Mendoza, a Native American activist, opened the meeting. Then John Rensenbrink said their remarks weren't very "practical." Then there was a kind of uprising—everyone wanted a woman to speak. So they called on Irene Diamond, Jewish intellectual co-editor of an anthology on ecofeminism.

She said that what Moses and Mendoza had said was very important, since it was based on the wisdom of grassroots women, peasant people and indigenous peoples. She added that she thought Rensenbrink's remarks were more mainstream, but that both perspectives were needed.

At that, Kwazi Nkrumah got very upset. He said Diamond had "condensed" everything, and defended Rensenbrink. He screamed, "I am not a peasant people!" And stormed out.

(Terri Williams, a petite Green activist from St. Louis, saw Nkrumah running. Get out of my way, he shouted, I could really hit somebody right now and I don't want to.)

People were hurt and in shock, but their discussion continued— for hours.

Linda Dallas, of the North Carolina Greens (and the only other black in the room), said she was appalled by people's inability to be "real." Why are you making an *agenda* for making contact with people of color? Why don't you all just start *doing* it—first and foremost on an individual level?

A gay Green said he was angry at the group because it didn't see him as someone who was oppressed, too.

"I think we're unbelievably constipated by talk and theory," said Mindy Lorenz, a write-in candidate for Congress in California.

An activist from Detroit said that only women and gay people seemed to be real here.

"People here have been implored to be real," said Moses. "But people are real here in different ways. We need to recognize that."

Moses's comment was one of the few I heard that wasn't riddled with blame, anger, guilt and/or self-flagellation. I figured it was a good note to leave on.

•   •   •

The next morning was the last scheduled session. Three new committees were elected with a minimum of havoc, and some people began leaving for the airport. But the Greens weren't done yet.

Christa Slaton's husband was brought on stage to read a letter from his wife. "I regret that my wounds are so deep," she wrote. "We have to change the way we treat each other. . . . While I may not see you again. . . ."

Margo Adair lamented that Slaton's heart was "too open" for us. Privately, some other Greens muttered their own conclusions.

Then Kwazi Nkrumah was given the microphone. Nearly everyone knew about the Rainbow Greens meeting the night before, and he spent almost 20 minutes lambasting the Greens because of what he felt happened there, and because of many other things.

"I was angry last night because people who know better, still can't get rid of their garbage," he announced. He never did say exactly what that "garbage" was. Perhaps that would have made things too easy on us.

"I don't want to be anybody's token! . . . I don't necessarily want to talk to you just to make you feel good! . . . I'm not afraid of making you know how angry you're making me! . . .

"We should not let Christa leave this movement! If you let her [leave], don't you dare come to me pretending to be my friend. . . ."

After he finished, nobody dared stand up to him—though privately there was some grumbling about "black macho" and "the standard black in white organizations."

Nkrumah had been an activist in the black community since the late 60s, when he was given his name by his high school classmates. It is not difficult to imagine why, in 1990, he'd feel an almost unbearable frustration and rage.

But no serious political organization can afford to recreate the 1960s dynamic of guilty whites and raging blacks. And no organization should want to. The freshest and most challenging black spokespeople today have put guilting and rage behind them (at least in their public personas). They are speaking of new paths to black self-esteem, new models for black self-help, new approaches to black-white integration.

Among them: Tony Brown (Chapter 4), Vincent Harding (15), Julius Lester (1), William Raspberry (5), Robert Woodson (21) and Sylvia Wynter (15).

The Greens could and *should* have been one of the first political groups to invite these new voices in.The constant presence, instead, of the 60s dynamic was to me a sure sign that the Greens lack the maturity and self-confidence to deal with the race issue.

IV. Restless farewell

I enjoyed myself at the Gathering. I met wonderful people, had great conversations. But after it was over I felt empty inside, for I knew—as certainly as one can know these things—that the U.S. Greens would never affect the political life of our time.

For seven years I'd been trying to convince myself that they might, just might, break out of their ghetto. (I'd been trying to convince you too, dear reader.) But I no longer believed it, even at 2 a.m. with friends.

I knew this, and yet it hurt me deeply to accept it and act on it. For whatever I may think of their internal battles and political prospects, the Greens are My People. Their life choices are my life choices; their failings mirror my own.

When I was a teen-ager and decided not to chase after power and privilege, I followed a route that took me inexorably to the Greens. To accept that the Greens are never going to make it is tantamount to accept that many of my life choices were not so smart.

I know how to deal with this on a professional level. NEW OPTIONS will not devote long stories to the U.S. Greens again until they begin to affect the American political dialogue. (I'll be rooting for them, but I won't hold my breath.) In the meantime, we'll devote more coverage to Greenish trends in effective real-world organizations like NOW, the Sierra Club and the NAACP.

I am less certain how to deal with this on a personal level. What do you do, exactly, when you realize that many times in your life you've chosen posturing over power, marginality over privilege—all in the name of some abstract political ''correctness''?

Do you have to be a baby to cry?

21 The 1980s Were Better Than We Thought

February 1990

Most "sophisticated" commentators hated the 1980s with a passion. "The My Decade," proclaimed ABC News. "The decade of glitz and greed," cried *Esquire* editor Phillip Moffitt. "The wannabe decade," "the squandered decade," "a decade of death," moaned the *Village Voice*. Now there's even a book-length trashing. *The Clothes Have No Emperor: A Chronicle of the American 80s,* by superhip political writer Paul Slansky (1989).

I guess I'm not sophisticated enough to see things correctly. I liked the 1980s. I think the 80s were a lot better than the commentators realized.

In some ways the 80s reminded me of the 50s. In the 50s many "sophisticated" commentators thought they were living through an era of bland conformity and quiescence: Uncle Ike and that sort of thing. Now we remember the 50s as the decade of the Montgomery bus boycott, the Beatniks, the beginnings of critical theory (Wright Mills), the explosion of black music into white culture through Elvis Presley...the decade that laid the groundwork for the 60s.

In the 80s we laid the groundwork for realizing the longings that were first brought to mass consciousness in the 60s. All kinds of strains are waiting to be hot-wired, now, by a new social movement. In addition, in the 80s we improved upon many of the things we ignored—or botched—in the 60s.

But the commentators didn't get it, and as a result they helped poison and mystify the decade for the rest of us. *It was a decade of death! The yuppies read books with "love" in their titles! Damn yuppies with their cuisinarts and VCRs.... The mainline churches were becoming more liberal—but people left them in droves for evangelical churches and, worse, sought instant gratification in "new age" spiritual pursuits!... The most talented rock star, Prince, was all glitz and dance beat with no message!... It was a decade of death, I tell ya....*

These media caricatures may have contained some elements of the truth. But they missed the hopeful signs that were everywhere in the 80s. They missed the new ways of approaching social change that could be found in everything from the environmental movement to Third World development theory. They missed positive themes that emerged in rock music, self-help books and other manifestations of popular culture. They missed exciting perspectives that emerged in "serious" disciplines like science, philosophy and history.

I. The caring individual has emerged

The underlying message of the 80s was one of hope. You can see this clearly if you look at the evolution of three American archetypes. During the 80s, American society and culture began to move away from a focus on the rugged individual and collective individual, and toward a focus on what I call the caring individual.

The **rugged individual** is the Republican party's model of the American citizen. Rugged individuals are ambitious and assertive, "real go-getters," leadership types. They get their primary identity from their corporation or profession. They believe strongly, even passionately, in the notion of freedom. On the down side, they don't worry much about the increasing importance of giant corporations. They figure it's an unavoidable consequence of modern life. They are not particularly introspective—they definitely prefer "doing" to "being." And they are not socially conscious— they will, if unleashed, make money at the expense of the community and the environment.

The **collective individual** is the Democratic party's model of the American citizen. Collective individuals are not particularly ambitious or entrepreneurial; they're most comfortable being followers. They get their primary identity from their labor union, ethnic, racial or religious group, gender category or sexual orientation. They believe in social justice and occasionally even fight for it. On the down side, they don't worry much about the increasing importance of bureaucracies and government. They figure it's an unavoidable consequence of modern life. And they're not particularly introspective—they think the television show *thirtysomething* portrays pointless self-absorption. In their view the "best" people are self-sacrificing.

The **caring individual** is an archetype that's emerging in the culture. Caring individuals care deeply about self *and* others; they are equally committed to self-development and social change, individual freedom and social justice. They even want their jobs to provide them with opportunities for both personal growth and social relevance. They identify with their jobs and interest groups, but also—and more profoundly—with "all humanity" or "Earth as a whole." They don't mind being leaders or followers, but they'd rather be working *with,* and they enjoy the image of society as a vast network-of-networks or web.

In the 80s mainstream American culture and public life gave us signs, portents, hints of this new way of being in the world. Part II below looks at the rise of the caring individual in social movements and institutions; Part III, in popular culture; Part IV, in the "serious" disciplines. Put them all together and you'll see why the 80s were better than we thought—in some ways even better than the 60s.

II. The caring individual and social movements

Close to home. In the 60s and 70s, we saw the environment as fundamentally separate from us. On Earth Day 1970 we chanted "Save our Earth!" as if it were being attacked by outside forces. In the 80s we began to realize that we aren't separate from the environment, and that the Earth is in trouble because of our own attitudes and values, not just because of the Bad Guys.

From New York to Nairobi, experts rushed to declare their oneness with the Earth. "We had seen the Earth as separate and colonizable.... It has been a near-fatal mistake," wrote Sri Lanka's Anuradha Vittachi, summarizing the findings of the Global Forum of Spiritual and Parliamentary Leaders on Human Survival (in *Earth Conference One,* 1989).

The old environmental movement was about legislation, lobbying, voting. The new movement included all that, but since it saw us as part of the Earth it was also about consciousness change. "To solve [our ecological] problems, humanity must begin to perceive the world in unaccustomed ways," said *New Yorker* staff writer Bill McKibben, author of the bestselling *The End of Nature* (1989). "We must invent nothing less than a new and humbler attitude toward the rest of creation. And we must do it quickly."

In the 60s and 70s, we could blame Earth's problems on a "them." In the 80s we began to realize that we couldn't pass the buck. "The [environmental] crisis exists precisely because of actions we have taken," said the brochure for Earth Day 1990. The ecology movement of the 80s was a powerful force encouraging us to re-think our attitudes and values and become caring individuals.

Money is not enough. In the 1960s and 70s, we assumed that the way to help poor blacks was by spending more money on them. "I think it's fair to say," John Kenneth Galbraith told the *New York Times* in 1975, "that no problem associated with New York City could not be solved by providing more money." By the 1980s, many responsible voices in the black community itself were arguing that money was not only not enough, it was not even the heart of the issue.

In the early 80s, the Council for a Black Economic Agenda (CBEA)—22 black leaders including Harvard's Glenn Loury and National Center for Neighborhood Enterprises' Robert Woodson— began articulating an alternative agenda to that of the major traditional civil rights organizations. What the civil rights organizations wanted was more civil rights legislation and the expansion of top-down, bureaucratic welfare programs. What the CBEA wanted was for government to help blacks help themselves and their local communities. It spoke of the need to build up feelings of self-esteem and personal responsibility among young blacks. ("Young black men can be heard to brag about the children they have fathered but need not support," Loury wrote.) It urged government to help blacks provide their own social services. It advocated tax breaks for businesses locating in black neighborhoods. It called for tenant-run housing projects, "choice" in education (i.e., voucher programs), innovative neighborhood-based adoption programs.

By the end of the 80s nearly every major civil rights organization had adopted parts or all of CBEA's self-help perspective. Without abandoning its "basic civil rights mission" of the last 80 years, NAACP president Benjamin Hooks said last year, the NAACP intends "to assign most of our future resources to programs that will enable our children to become self-sufficient citizens." Later he added, "We must begin to get our act together in our own communities."

For years we white people got to feel deliciously "anti-racist" pretending that nothing was wrong in the black community that money couldn't solve. In the 80s we started paying attention to black leaders who understood that their real task was to help more blacks become caring individuals.

The light and the dark. Dictatorships require rugged individuals and collective individuals. The former are the rulers, the later are the masses. In his well-received book *Modern Dictators* (1987), Barry Rubin described the dynamic between rulers and masses in the 80s in grisly and heartbreaking detail.

Democracy, especially grassroots democracy, requires caring individuals: personally and socially responsible individuals. While it is hardly true that the majority of the world's governments became democratic in the 1980s, I think it's fair to say we made more progress toward that goal in the 80s than we did in the 60s or 70s.

All over the planet, caring individuals were seeking to reconcile universal democratic ideals with their own particular traditions and perspectives. Edem Kodjo's *Africa Tomorrow* (1987) summed up the ideas of Africans who were moving toward a humane but "unsentimental pan-Africanism"; Ziauddin Sardar's *Islamic Futures* (1985) summed up the ideas of Muslims who were moving toward a humane and "future-oriented Islam." Some of Gorbachev's economic advisors wanted Soviet collective farms and factories to give way not to private ownership but to a leasing system that would, presumably, combine the best of capitalism and socialism.

Perhaps more than any other national leader, Czechoslovakia's new president, Vaclav Havel, spoke the language of caring individuals. In his New Year's Day address he spoke not only of his country's decayed physical environment but of its "decayed moral environment," and he added, "None of us is merely a victim of it, because all of us helped create it together." In an earlier speech he said, "We want to live as a free and dignified people who do not think only of themselves, but of the fate of generations to come."

De-massification. In the 60s and 70s, most of us thought of the people in the Third World as "the masses" or "the oppressed masses"—hapless, depersonalized victims who'd all become Marxists if given half a chance. In the 80s that began to change. The more we actually listened to Third World farmers, women and migrants to the cities, the less they sounded like proto-Marxists and the more they sounded like proto-entrepreneurs who faced two crushing practical problems: Third World bureaucracies and lack of access to credit.

Conservatives focused their attention on the bureaucracies. In his book *The Other Path* (U.S. edition 1989), a best-seller in Latin America, Peruvian economist Hernando de Soto—lionized by the U.S. right—revealed that in parts of the Third World over one-half of the work force is outside the formal economy. It's not that the "informals" (as he called them) are lazy, he said. If anything, they work unusually hard. In Lima they're responsible for 90% of the clothing business and 87% of the buses. It's that a top-heavy bureaucracy imposes crippling costs on anyone trying to go into business legally.

Liberals focused their attention on the lack of access to credit. Beginning with the Grameen Bank in Bangladesh, dozens of Third World and U.S. groups sought to give tiny ($50-100) loans to Third World farmers and vendors. By the end of the 80s Grameen alone had 250,000 borrowers. Virtually all the groups reported payback rates exceeding 95%.

De Soto's book implied that the real struggle in the Third World was between mercantilist *and* socialist bureaucrats and the entrepreneurial poor. The liberal approach implied that the struggle was between the tight-fisted rich and the enterprising poor. What both approaches had in common was the assumption that the Third World poor, far from being faceless masses, were creative and responsible individuals.

See how they run. In the 60s and 70s, most businessmen still assumed that successful companies had to be run in a top-down, quasi-authoritarian manner. In the 80s, the whole model of what constituted successful business management underwent a sea change. Instead of rugged individualist bosses and collective-individual employees, the new model stressed the need for both bosses and employees to become more personally and socially responsible: more caring.

In his best-selling book *Megatrends* (1982), John Naisbitt popularized the new business gospel. He argued that leadership-as-control was part of the problem, and leadership-to-inspire-persons was the wave of the future. He gave many examples of companies that were moving from a "hierarchical" to a "networking" style of business management.

Tom Peters and Robert Waterman's best-selling book *In Search of Excellence* (1982) took the same tack. Their "excellent companies"—which included such major players as Hewlett-Packard, Procter & Gamble and 3M—fostered "autonomy and entrepreneurship" throughout their organizations. They listened, "intently and regularly," to their customers. They treated their rank and file as "partners" and with "dignity" and "respect."

Fortune magazine started doing an annual issue on "America's Most Admired Corporations," and the criteria it used included "ability to develop and keep talented people," "quality of products or services," and "community and environmental responsibility." In the 80s, it seems, even major segments of the business community began to expect our companies to be havens and training grounds for caring individuals.

III. The caring individual and popular culture

A dose of reality. Until recently, television was not where you went to find out about the real world, or to think about real people in real relationships. It was not a medium for caring individuals.

In the 1980s, that began to change. ABC News's *Nightline,* launched in 1980, is television's best news program ever. Five nights a week, live and unrehearsed, Ted Koppel and guests discuss the burning issues of the day—sometimes even the deeper issues. Since the guests are usually blown up "bigger than life" on a large screen, you can often tell a lot about them (and their ideas) just by watching them squirm.

The guests come from a narrower ideological range than one might like. Still, they include not just politicians and former politicians, but policemen, feminists, community activists, religious leaders, union officials...a dazzling variety of American types. And they're often forced to talk *with,* not past, one another. It's as if the American family was getting to know itself well for the first time.

The 80s have also seen the best entertainment series ever. First came Steven Bochco's *Hill Street Blues,* a police drama in which the cops weren't unambiguously "good," the lawbreakers weren't necessarily bad, and some characters led three-dimensional personal lives. Next came Bochco's *L.A. Law,* which delved even more deeply into the lives of its principal characters. Suddenly we were getting "heroes" who faced some of the same dicey life situations we did.

Finally came Marshall Herskovitz and Ed Zwick's *thirtysomething,* a show about seven middle-class people who lead normal lives and take themselves seriously (when had you ever seen *that* on television?) and share their thoughts and feelings with each other...just like caring individuals do. The show raises, deftly, many of the important questions about life in the contemporary U.S. How much idealism is it safe to keep? How can we balance work and loving, independence and intimacy? For the first time on a consistent basis, television began helping us think about our real lives. For the first time, television began helping us become caring individuals.

American love trilogy. The 1960s was the so-called "love decade." But, ironically, in those days it was intellectually unacceptable for us to be seen reading self-help books about love. In the 1980s the liberal commentators still made fun of such books ("Getting Better All the Time," smirked the *Washington Post*), but they no longer had the power to define what was intellectually acceptable, and three self-help books with "love" in their titles became wildly popular.

Each saw love as a driving force in the society. Leo Buscaglia's *Living, Loving and Learning* (1982) saw love as a humanizing force. Bernie Siegel's *Love, Medicine & Miracles* (1986) saw love as a healing force. M. Scott Peck's *The Road Less Travelled: A New Psychology of Love, Traditional Values and Spiritual Growth* (published in 1978 but not a bestseller till the 80s) saw love as an evolutionary force.

On a less highfalutin' level, each contained much that was helpful. Buscaglia urged us to be ourselves, and reminded us that being ourselves has a lot to do with connecting with others. Siegel told us that the healthiest and most resilient people are—among other things—self-respecting, independent, assertive, and capable of giving and receiving unconditional love. Peck painstakingly explained the importance of discipline (and self-discipline), and reminded us how much *work* love is.

It is no accident that, among them, these books spent nearly 10 *years* on the *New York Times* best seller list. Each is a veritable handbook for the caring individual.

Sex, lies, and caring. In the 60s, you had to watch foreign films to think about the person in any kind of depthful or intelligent way. In the 80s, some of the most popular American films focused on our struggles to become caring individuals—to become self-aware and responsible to others.

Martin Scorcese's *Raging Bull* (1980) showed us what it's like to be truly without self-understanding. It told the story of Jake La Motta, a boxer who lost his career, his wife and the love of a brother because he was unable to understand or control the emotions raging inside him.

Steven Spielberg's *E.T.* (1983) did exactly the opposite. It showed us the essence of being a caring individual. The key thing was the little boy Elliott's ability to establish a heart connection with the Extra-Terrestrial. Their heart connection survived our mechanistic, depersonalized world's every attempt to drive them apart.

Some popular movies ran what I call riffs on the caring individual. Adrian Lyne's *Fatal Attraction* (1987) argued that love and caring—not feminist rhetoric in the absence of those—deserves to win out in the end. Oliver Stone's *Talk Radio* (1988) showed that the world might not be as degraded as you think, that your antennae might also be at fault. (Some of Stone's left-wing fans didn't like that message much. Writing in *Vanity Fair,* Ron Rosenbaum ridiculed what he called Stone's "need to love yourself" movie.)

Spike Lee's *Do the Right Thing* (1989) may have been the ultimate caring-individual movie. It was socially aware and talked about racism; at the same time it celebrated the variety of individual human life and was a paean to community. Moreover, it didn't tell us what to think. Every character got to speak their piece. In the end it offered us contradictory advice from Martin and Malcolm and said, Hey, you figure it out. (Caring individuals want parameters, not The One Correct Answer.) The challenge of the

90s will be to come up with solutions to the problems raised in the best works of the 80s—works like *Do the Right Thing.*

Death of the glass box. All during the 60s and 70s, the American urban landscape was being destroyed. Wonderful old buildings were demolished, and impersonal concrete-and-glass boxes went up in their place. The architects who designed them felt they owed no one an apology; they were pleased to present their brutalizations as examples of "modern" architecture.

The 80s saw the birth—and rapid critical acceptance—of a "postmodern" style in architecture. Postmodern buildings seek to be everything modern buildings are not. They're consistent with their surroundings. They respect the street. They're full of color and texture and ornaments and things (postmodern architectural theorists like to use the word "sensual"). They're full of subtle references to well-known buildings and architectural styles. They're full of not-so-subtle historic references and icons (modernized Greek columns, updated medieval turrets). Above all, they're person-friendly.

Among the best-known examples of postmodern architecture are Philip Johnson's A.T.&T. Building (1982) in New York City, whose roof looks like the top of a grandfather's clock; Michael Graves's Humana Building (1985) in Louisville, which looks like an updated medieval palace, but more fun; and Frank Gehry's Loyola Law School (1984) in Los Angeles, a sumptuously inviting collection of maroon towers, steel columns, cobblestone walkways and...hey, is that a greenhouse up there?...

Modern architecture emphasizes unity, repetition, uniformity. It is perfect for a society of collective individuals, "mass men." Postmodern architecture is diverse, complex, fully cognizant of past and present context—just like caring individuals.

Fully alive. The realistic human figure virtually disappeared from the art world in the 60s and 70s. It was as if we stopped being interesting to ourselves. The art scene in the 80s was incredibly diverse—most critics agreed it had never been more so—and one of the most striking developments was a rebirth of interest in the human form in both painting and sculpture.

Although they may never become as well-known as "pop" artists like Roy Lichtenstein, Alfred Leslie and Duane Hanson began to get some of the recognition they deserved. Leslie's paintings of people reveal so much—buried resentments, deep-seated fears, inexpressible longings—that they make you feel you're reading the most private diaries. And swear you'll do better at life! (Leslie has said he wants his paintings to "elevate" his viewers, i.e. turn them into caring individuals.) Hanson's sculptures of ordinary and mostly lonely working-class people—polyvinyl, polychromed in oil, lifesize, equipped with false hair and glass eyes—are so devastatingly accurate that at first you want to turn and run. Then you're deeply moved. Both artists managed to remind us what it means to be fully alive.

The most talked-about single art work of the 80s had an abstract design, but was as intensely human-centered as anything by Leslie or Hanson: Maya Lin's Vietnam Veterans Memorial (1982).

Yes it pronounces judgment on the war (the utter blackness of the wall), but its power comes from elsewhere. Most war memorials studiously avoid focusing on individuals. Not only does the wall contain the names of all the war dead, you are encouraged to locate the names of your dead relatives and friends with the help of a couple of big books built into the memorial. And when you go up to the shiny black wall you are shocked and appalled to see your image mirrored there. Lin is forcing us to confront our responsibility for the war dead. She is forcing us to be caring individuals whether we want to or not.

Let the day begin. By the late 1970s rock music was in crisis. The old songs were wearing thin; the new songs weren't tuneful and their lyrics were predictable and boring.

All that changed in the 80s. Melody returned to rock, yoked to a fresh drum beat. And those of us who bothered to listen to the lyrics were in for a surprise. Even our glitziest and most popular singer-songwriters were saying some important things.

Peter Gabriel's popular album *So* (1986) dwelled at length on what it takes to become a caring individual. In one song he criticized the rugged individual, the one who wants to "be a big noise with all the big boys." In another he criticized the collective individual, the one who "do[es] what we're told." In a third he suggested that an alternative was to try to become "complete."

How does one become complete? That was a key question our singer-poets sought to answer even as they sought to get people dancing and sell records. They adopted four broad strategies toward helping us become complete:

- *Practice relentlessly honest self-disclosure.* Prince did it in *Purple Rain* (1987), perhaps the most affecting rock album of the 80s; and he did it so completely, telling us about everything from his sexual fantasies to his relationship with his parents, that you couldn't listen to it without resolving to explore your own depths too. Cyndi Lauper's *She's So Unusual* (1983) mined this same rich vein and was more socially conscious to boot—one reason "Girls just want to have fun" is that "O mama dear, we're not the fortunate ones."
- *Generate an empathy so great that it passeth into understanding.* Suzanne Vega was one of the spate of socially conscious folk singers that emerged in the 80s. Her hit single about an abused child, "Luka" (1987), was as moving and convincing as anything Bob Dylan did in the 60s. She sings it in the first person, as if she herself is little Luka, and the effect is riveting—"If you hear something late at night/Some kind of trouble, some kind of fight/Just don't ask me what it was. . . ." Almost as affecting was Lisa Lisa and Cult Jam's hit single about a teenage runaway, "Little Jackie Wants to Be a Star" (1989).
- *Combine political anger at "them" with caustic criticism of "us."* Tracy Chapman does this to stunning effect on her best-selling first album *Tracy Chapman* (1988). The first song is the powerful "Talkin' Bout a Revolution." You hear it and you figure you're in for a whole album of songs preaching the 60's gospel: all poor people are infinitely deserving. But in the very next song, "Fast Car," she says goodbye to a down-and-out lover who's irresponsible and immature. The best rap album of the 80s, Public Enemy's *It Takes a Nation of Millions To Hold Us Back* (1988), takes a similar tack. "Clear the way/for the prophets of rage," they shout. But they direct part of their rage at unaware and uncaring black people—for example, mothers for whom "all their children/don't mean as much as the [TV] show."
- *Navigate the passage from rock's traditional language of yearning to a deeper language of personal maturity or political awareness.* Bruce Springsteen did it. His album *Born in the USA* (1984) ached with inchoate longings; *Tunnel of Love* (1987) revealed a steadier and more mature Bruce, ready to "walk like a man." U2 also did it. Their popular album *The Joshua Tree* (1987) ached with spiritual yearning; *Rattle and Hum* (1988) gave

that spirit flesh with soaring freedom songs, urgent pro-ecology songs, and protest songs laced with love.

Rock's insistence on helping us become "complete" in the 80s meant that at its best it generated a sensibility that was inclusive rather than self-righteous. Paul Simon captured that sensibility beautifully on his album *Graceland* (1986), in which he sings "These are the days of miracle and wonder" even as he comforts his lover, "Don't cry, baby don't cry." The Call, one of the most critically acclaimed new groups, gave us a primer on inclusiveness in their album *Let the Day Begin* (1989). The title song begins,

"Here's to the babies in a brand new world,
Here's to the beauty of the stars,
Here's to the travellers on the open road,
Here's to the dreamers in the bars,
Here's to the teachers in the crowded rooms,
Here's to the workers in the fields...."

If four kids in a rock band can weave together—in six simple lines—nature, workers, idealists, professionals and generativity ("babies"), surely we can create a world that's just as harmonious, just as diverse, just as complete. Rock in the 80s spelled out the tools we'd need: honesty, empathy, anger, self-criticism, personal maturity and political awareness. Put them all together and you have the caring individual.

IV. The caring individual and "higher" culture

"**Butterfly effect.**" They say that the spirit of an age can be found in its science. "Chaos theory" was the science of the 80s, and its spirit elevated the caring individual.

The most popular science book of the 80s was James Gleick's exquisitely written introduction to chaos theory, *Chaos* (1987). According to chaos theory, scientists are now able to see order and pattern where before they saw only randomness. A central component of chaos theory is what Gleick calls the "butterfly effect," after the "notion that a butterfly stirring the air today in Peking can transform storm systems next month in New York." The butterfly effect is technically known as "sensitive dependence on initial conditions." According to Gleick, it had a place in folklore:

194

"For want of a nail, the shoe was lost;
For want of a shoe, the horse was lost;
For want of a horse, the rider was lost;
For want of a rider, the battle was lost;
For want of a battle, the kingdom was lost!"

The spirit-of-the-age message of the butterfly effect is obvious. It is that everything each of us does—even the smallest things— are laden with long-term significance. This is not compatible with the outlook of rugged individuals, who figure their deeds are more significant than those of others. Nor is it compatible with the outlook of collective individuals, who don't feel personally that significant and don't spend much time thinking about themselves. It is perfectly compatible with the outlook of caring individuals, who are committed to self-discovery and self-development in part because they sense their actions have a ripple effect on life.

Two self-exams. It's rare for a decade to produce one truly outstanding analysis of the American condition. The 1980s produced two, and both were widely read: Tom Wolfe's *The Bonfire of the Vanities* (1987) and Anthony Lukas's *Common Ground* (1985).

Wolfe's novel tells you all you ever wanted to know about rugged individuals and collective individuals. It isn't pretty. Sherman McCoy, the Wall Street bond salesman, is the very embodiment of rugged-individual-Americanus. Reverend Bacon, the black activist/hustler, is the rugged individual who uses collective-individual rhetoric to enrich himself. Larry Kramer, the crummy assistant D.A., is the collective individual striving to become a rugged individual. They're all trapped by the same hell, our relentlessly status-driven society. None of them thinks about it much.

Lukas's book follows three Boston families through 10 years of the school busing wars. It's nonfiction, but it's as intimately revealing as Wolfe's book and its canvas is as broad: the Divers are upper-middle-class, the McGoffs are Irish working class, and the Twymons poor and black. At different times, various people in each family take steps toward transcending their stations in life (e.g., Lisa McGoff begins to question some of the prejudice she was brought up with), but you aren't advised to hold your breath. The title is ironic: there's nothing holding these Americans together.

Both authors served up bleak visions. But they did raise our awareness—and accurate observation is essential for effective social change. And like Spike Lee in *Do the Right Thing,* they refused to offer us The One Correct Answer. Instead, they made us think. . .and care. In a way, the heroes of both books were the authors themselves, with their courage to see things truly. That courage is one mark of the caring individual.

Equal, but different. The dominant feminism in the 1960s and 70s was what political scientist Naomi Black called "equity feminism." It emphasized how similar women are to men, and demanded equality for women on that basis. It envisioned a world in which women and men would become much more androgynous.

The dominant feminism in the 80s emphasized women's differences from men. It focused on women's "specificity"— women's characteristic values and perspectives—and demanded equality for women precisely because women's values and perspectives were so desperately needed by society as a whole.

Theorist upon theorist presented a vision not of a pallid and politically correct androgynous society, but of a society in which "female nature" was understood and appreciated—and fully incorporated into public life. Jean Elshtain, in *Public Man, Private Woman* (1981), suggested that women who entered the "rat race" should not try to be like men, but should resolve to bring their learned values of nurturance and community with them. Carol Gilligan, in *In a Different Voice* (1982), contrasted men's "ethics of justice" with women's "ethics of care," and argued that the world needs a big dose of both.

Marilyn French, in *Beyond Power* (1985), argued that society desperately needs the feminine world's values of pleasure-with and power-to, as distinct from power-over. Sara Ruddick, in *Maternal Thinking* (1989), argued that the everyday practices of mothers, which she summed up in the phrase "caring labor," can give rise to new ways of thinking about public policy.

For many women and men, there was something mechanistic and forced about equity feminism. But you couldn't read the feminists of the 80s without being moved by their commitment to the true personhood of women—or suspecting that the archetype of the "caring individual" is one they'd easily recognize!

The carceral society. In the 60s, Jean-Paul Sartre was all the rage on college campuses, and no wonder. His existentialism appealed to the rugged individual in us. His Marxism appealed to the collective individual in us. In the 80s, the philosophy shelves in college bookstores groaned under the weight of books by and about Michel Foucault, a philosopher of the caring individual.

Consider his political philosophy. In the conventional wisdom, we are ruled by massive institutions from the top down. In Foucault's view, the rule we are subjected to is both more subtle and more effective. It is exercised by means of a "network of disciplines" that entraps everyone. The ideas, routines, mores, etc., that we learn (often subconsciously) in schools, hospitals, prisons, armies, asylums, factories, etc., all work to turn us not into "free agents" but "useful subjects," useful, that is, to keeping the whole thing going. Foucault's terrible name for this is the "carceral society," with its echo of the word "incarceration."

If we live in a society that's run by rugged individuals from the top down, then social change means either replacing one set of rugged individuals with another, or inspiring the "masses," the collective individuals, to revolt. But neither strategy seems to bring real change. If, however, we live in a society that rules us primarily through its local and immediate institutions, and especially through the ideas, concepts, etc., that those institutions put into our minds—then a liberating strategy would have us constantly question (as Foucault urges) all our routines, all our assumptions, and our very identities; and seek to vitalize our communities.

In the 60s, we felt we had to choose between the Rolling Stones' message to be "street fighting men" and the Beatles' message that the battle was within. Foucault's work smashed that phony dichotomy by showing just how intimately connected are the "without" and the "within." Read Foucault and you'll see clearly why a new politics can only be built by self-aware *and* socially conscious individuals—caring individuals.

That's the spirit. Millions of us left the mainline churches during the 1980s. But we weren't becoming less religious or spiritual—according to a Gallup poll, 84% of us believed in the divinity of Christ in 1988, up from 78% in 1978. Instead, we were pouring into evangelical churches and taking up "new age" spiritual disciplines.

We left the mainline churches because we felt they were becoming spiritually hollow. "Spiritual uplift no longer appeared to be the mainline churches' top priority," wrote *Time* magazine associate editor Burton Pines in his popular book *Back to Basics* (1982).

A staggering 40 to 60 million Americans called themselves evangelical Christians in the 80s, and no wonder. The evangelical churches challenged us to take God back into our lives. "[Evangelicals] proclaim that finding God is not easy," Pines wrote. "It requires extraordinary effort and commitment. The required belief in Christ is intense, the profession of faith public and frequent, the lifestyle morally rigorous and the missionary obligation serious."

According to John Naisbitt and Patricia Aburdene in *Megatrends 2000* (1990), 10 to 20 million Americans identified with the "new age" movement in the 80s. Many new agers were drawn to yoga, meditation and other spiritual disciplines. Many were also drawn to such concepts as "global mind change" and the "intimate Earth community."

Most people suppose that evangelicals and new agers are poles apart. Naisbitt and Aburdene know better: "[They're both seeking] a link between their everyday lives and the transcendent." To that extent, they're both seeking to become caring individuals.

The new heroes. Traditional history books are about "great men," presidents and military commanders, rugged individuals. Beginning in the 1960s, a new wave of history books focused on masses, movements and classes. Free will was out, determinism was in. Narrative was out, statistics were in. The individual mattered little except to illustrate some larger point grounded in sociology or social psychology.

The 1980s saw the phenomenal commercial and critical success of three books that offered a third approach to American history. Taylor Branch's *Parting the Waters* (1988) and David Garrow's *Bearing the Cross* (1986) were histories of the U.S. in the 50s and 60s; Neil Sheehan's *A Bright Shining Lie* (1988) was a history of the U.S. in Vietnam. But their focus was neither on presidents nor masses. Instead, they focused on *one key person interacting with others*. Specifically, Branch and Garrow focused on Martin Luther King, Jr., and his relationships with other civil rights leaders; Sheehan focused on Lt. Col. John Paul Vann and his relationships with other military personnel and with the press.

This choice of focus allowed Branch, Garrow and Sheehan to make an important political point. They showed that history is created neither by Supermen nor masses, but by key people working within networks or webs. (A little free will, a little determinism, a lot of pluck.) That is, of course, how caring individuals hope to do social change.

V. A caring constituency?

The 1980s was not only the decade of glitz and greed. It was also the decade when the archetype of the caring individual broke into the mainstream. In science, the environment, movies, religion, rock music, business—in virtually every area of modern life—the caring individual was recognized, catered to.

There is a constituency of caring individuals now, and it is increasingly (albeit imperfectly) showing up in social surveys. In 1980, SRI International's Values and Lifestyles Program found that 10% of us are either "societally conscious" or "integrated." Before the 1988 election, the Times-Mirror Co. reported that 16% of us are caring types. That's 40 million people.

While caring individuals are wary of pat ideologies and One Correct Answers, they have the makings of a political agenda. From our brief review we can glean that they support, among other things, self-esteem training to create confident and caring young people; social programs that are self-help-oriented, not top-down and paternalistic; economic policies that foster community economic vitality, not GNP growth per se; and foreign aid programs that bypass governments and channel seed money to individuals and small groups in the Third World.

But if there is one area of life in the U.S. in which the caring individual is manifestly not recognized or catered to, it is electoral politics.

The Republicans continue to promote a politics of the rugged individual; the Democrats, of the collective individual. Among our (potential) third parties, only the U.S. Greens have the makings of a politics of the caring individual. And they are too weak and inept to matter much for now.

In the short run, the political prospects for the caring individual in the U.S. are less than glowing. But only in the short run. For if the caring individual is emerging as a new American archetype, as this article argues—and if that archetype models the hopes and dreams of anything like 40 million people—then it is only a matter of time before a major national movement or competent third party begins to articulate a politics of the caring individual. The challenge of the 90s is to ensure that that happens sooner rather than later; and that it happens with integrity.

22 The New Age Comes to Congress

March 1989

Over 70 bills expressing parts of the NEW OPTIONS/Greenish/ post-liberal political philosophy were introduced into the last session of Congress.

Few of those bills passed—or even made it to a vote. But a small group of Congresspeople consistently supported them.

The mainstream and traditional left media almost never told you about those bills. And the media rarely focused on the Congresspeople who supported them. Have you ever heard *anything* about the most supportive five—Chet Atkins, Barbara Boxer, George Brown, Claudine Schneider and Ted Weiss?

But just because the media doesn't see a phenomenon doesn't mean it isn't there.

This month we completed the New Options Inc. Congressional scorecard for the 100th Congress (1987 and 1988).

Previous editions of the scorecard have been favorably discussed by periodicals as diverse as *Common Cause Magazine* and the toney-conservative *Washington Dossier.* And we think this is our best one yet.

• Most scorecards highlight the negative. For example, last year the Coalition for a New Foreign Policy scored Congresspeople on 18 defense and foreign policy issues, and on 13 of them Congresspeople were awarded a plus if they *opposed* things. The vast majority of the votes and resolutions we looked at were in *favor* of some life-giving new policy or program.

• Most scorecards focus on bills that would do more (or, less) of the same. Left-wing voting indexes typically celebrate Congresspeople who'd spend less on defense and more on social services; right-wing indexes, the reverse. Our index pays very little attention to bills that would do more (or, less) of the same. It focuses instead on proposals that would change the way we do things.

• Most scorecards focus on 20-40 key bills. Ours focuses on *74;* more than any scorecard we've ever seen.

Why so many? We wanted to track Congressional support for *most* of the legislation that we felt deserved the label "decentralist/globally responsible."

And we wanted to come up with a truly accurate reading of who the Congressional supporters are...as definitive a list as possible.

We spent months tracking down legislation that reflected post-liberal priorities and values. In the process, we spoke with literally dozens of the groups we've reported on over the years. Not a few of them helped write some of the bills, and lobby for them.

Although we found almost nothing that might have been written by visionaries like James Robertson (Chapter 6) or Marilyn Ferguson, we found plenty of bills that could take us part of the way toward the world they envision.

We found bills that reflect ecological wisdom.

We found bills that promote economic sustainability.

We found bills that empower people and communities.

We found bills that boost world order.

We found bills that help Third World countries become self-reliant.

We found bills that promote nonviolent and democratic solutions to international disputes.

I. The "New Age 21"

Very few Congresspeople did well on our scorecard. Only 81—out of 535—scored better than 50%. (By contrast, 276 scored better than 50% on the Americans for Democratic Action scorecard.)

But some did very well indeed.

Nineteen members of the House of Representatives scored *80% or more*. That's phenomenal when you consider that most of our bills didn't come to a vote, so we were mostly looking at people who'd offered to become co-sponsors of bills.

Two members of the Senate scored 70% or more. That's just as impressive, given the fact that Senators had fewer good pieces of legislation to sign on to.

Here are those 21 Congresspeople, "post-liberal" (or "Green" or "New Age") in fact if not yet in the eyes of the media:

Rep. Chet Atkins (D-Mass.), 100%;
Rep. Barbara Boxer (D-Calif.), 100
Rep. Claudine Schneider (R-R.I.), 100
Rep. Ted Weiss (D-N.Y.), 100
Rep. George Brown (D-Calif.), 95
Rep. Gary Ackerman (D-N.Y.), 90
Rep. Ron Dellums (D-Calif.), 90
Rep. Bob Mrazek (D-N.Y.), 90
Rep. Jim Bates (D-Calif.), 85
Rep. Mel Levine (D-Calif.), 85
Rep. Howard Berman (D-Calif.), 80
Rep. John Conyers (D-Mich.), 80
Rep. Robert Garcia (D-N.Y.), 80
Rep. Matthew Martinez (D-Calif.), 80
Rep. Bruce Morrison (D-Conn.), 80
Rep. Major Owens (D-N.Y.), 80
Rep. Nancy Pelosi (D-Calif.), 80
Rep. Edolphus Towns (D-N.Y.), 80
Rep. Howard Wolpe (D-Mich.), 80
Sen. John Kerry (D-Mass.), 75
Sen. Mark Hatfield (R-Ore.), 70

What can we say about the "New Age 21," besides the obvious fact of their support for decentralist/ecological/globally responsible legislation?

For the most part, they are not your flaming liberals. The composite score of our Top 10 on the 1988 ADA index would place them exactly *111*th.

What they are is Congress' rainbow. Ironically, the multiracial, multiethnic coalition that Jesse Jackson wants to weld together on behalf of left-liberalism has *already* come together... albeit unknowingly... on behalf of a *post*-liberal, *post*-socialist politics.

Four of the 21 are black males.

Two are Hispanic males.

Five are Jewish males.

Three are white females—two Catholic, one Jewish.

One is a white male Catholic.

Only six are white male Protestants. And they are more diverse than meets the eye. Brown grew up in a Quaker household. Atkins is Unitarian Universalist. Hatfield is an evangelical. Mrazek is no WASP.

But black or white, male or female, Jewish or Christian, nearly all of them are bound together by two powerful, defining experiences.

All six racial "minorities" were born between 1929-35. Twelve of the other 15 Congresspeople were born between 1939-48.

In other words, *all six Congresspeople of color were in their 20s when Rosa Parks refused to get up from her seat* on that bus in Montgomery.

And *12 of the 15 others were in their 20s during the war on Vietnam.*

II. A few good bills

Here are some examples of the 74 bills (and resolutions and amendments) we focused on.

Deep ecology. The most extraordinary piece of legislation in the 100th Congress may have been Rep. Claudine Schneider's (R-R.I.) bill to prevent the greenhouse effect. John Chafee (R-R.I.) sponsored an identical bill on the Senate side.

Talk about "holistic"! The bill would have forced the Department of Energy to rank energy options according to cost— and to pursue the most cost-effective options. (Goodbye, nuclear; goodbye, oil.) It would have required new cars to get 45 miles per gallon by 1999. It would have established a program to promote reforestation. And it would have done much, much more. (Psst—Amory Lovins, author of *Soft Energy Paths,* 1977, was consulted several times by Rep. Schneider's office.)

There were several other global warming bills in Congress. but none were as comprehensive as Schneider's—and most included funding for nuclear power! *Five Senators and 39 Representatives were co-sponsors.*

Empower us. Rep. Chet Atkins (D-Mass.) sponsored a bill requiring the Secretary of Education to help elementary and secondary schools use volunteer teachers (including students, retirees and businesspeople). A "National Center" would provide money to train them and provide technical assistance to schools so they'd make good use of them. *Thirteen Representatives were co-sponsors.*

World order. Sen. Charles Grassley (R-Iowa) and Rep. Jim Leach (R-Iowa) sponsored resolutions establishing a U.S. Commission on Improving the Effectiveness of the U.N. The Commission would explore such things as creating a standing U.N. peacekeeping force; making better use of the World Court; and implementing the "binding triad" voting system in the General Assembly (see Chapter 18). *Five Senators and 39 Representatives were co-sponsors.*

Self-reliant development. Rep. George Crockett (D-Mich.) sponsored a bill promoting "equitable and participatory development" in the Caribbean. Among its provisions: "Priority...shall be given to supporting indigenous Caribbean institutions (including farmers' unions, cooperatives, labor organizations, women's groups, and community organizations) that represent, work with, and benefit the poor." Do you detect the hand of The Development GAP (Chapter 17) in any of this? *Twenty Representatives were co-sponsors.*

•   •   •

A copy of New Options Inc.'s scorecard—describing all 74 bills and recording the positions taken by all 535 Congresspeople—is available for $2 from NEW OPTIONS.

Copies of our scorecards from the 97th through 99th Congresses complete are available for $6.

Read those scorecards. Then, *use* them to hold your local, state and national legislators accountable.

Use them to demand that your local newspapers and TV stations pay more attention to the kinds of positive, life-affirming measures we list there.

Use them to come up with ideas for a political campaign of your own.

23 Four Groups Launching That Second Experiment

July 1985–March 1989

Thousands of groups are launching the Second American Experiment; we've mentioned nearly 100 in this book alone (see Appendix). The four we profile here—RESULTS, Listening Project, Center for Economic Conversion and Social Investment Forum—reflect the Experiment's staggering diversity and are particularly effective at what they do. They represent the wave of the future, if there is to be one.

I. This group gets RESULTS

Not unlike the Miami music teacher he used to be, Sam Harris, 38, with his dark red tie, paces back and forth in front of the 21 unusually attentive Washington, D.C. residents who've come to hear him speak about RESULTS, the "citizens' lobby on hunger" he's founded and directs (for something like 90 hours every week).

It's a hot June evening, and people are still straggling in from outside. We're in the basement of a church that could be anywhere: fake wood on the walls, faded rug on the floor. But we're 2½ blocks from the U.S. Capitol building. Like that red tie, the site was chosen to make a point.

Harris smiles. "My first purpose," he tells the assembled health professionals, lawyers, secretaries, activists, and city administrators (who include two blacks from Mayor Barry's office), "is to inspire you about the impact you can have working with others to create the political will to end hunger."

Some of us notice that we've chosen to sit two or three seats away from each other.

"My second purpose is to help us dissolve the separateness we feel from government."

His energy is lively, assertive—and highly contagious. Everybody's listening. Everybody seems to be rooting for him to do well.

"I want there to be three outcomes from tonight. I want you to finish a letter to one of your appointed representatives [supporting continued U.S. funding for the International Fund for Agricultural Development]. I want you to start a D.C. RESULTS group. And I want to give you an opportunity to participate financially."

Three remarkably fast-paced hours later, all three outcomes have been achieved.

•   •   •

For years post-liberal political activists have been trying to create effective social change organizations. Unfortunately, most of our efforts have been so mistrustful of leadership and hierarchy and "structure" in general that they have been utterly ineffective politically. On the other hand, many apparently "effective" national organizations have failed to educate or mobilize their grassroots members. In 1985, it is an open question which approach is the more irresponsible.

The genius of Harris's RESULTS organization is that it has managed to combine effective national leadership and structure with effective grassroots education and mobilization. In fact, it has come up with an eminently *replicable* way of organizing around decentralist/globally responsible issues and concerns. Harris himself says, "We have found a format that is usable by any group working to create the political will to accomplish anything."

And make no mistake, RESULTS' approach does produce results. Last year the group almost singlehandedly succeeded in generating $50 million from the U.S. Congress for global primary health care. ("We couldn't have done it without you," Rep. Tony Hall wrote RESULTS afterwards.) Now they're putting their weight behind another supposedly impossible goal: immunizing all children against the six "killer diseases" by the year 1990. Last month they played a key role not only in arranging a briefing for Congresspeople on the issue, but in getting five House Republicans (as well as five House Democrats) to sign the invitation to the briefing. Their "secret weapon": grassroots pressure, applied sensitively but firmly by a committed and aware membership.

At the D.C. chapter organizing meeting, Harris made no bones about it: participation in RESULTS requires a significant time commitment—even a certain amount of (gasp!) discipline. "We're trying to shift the model," Harris told NEW OPTIONS, "from 'the lobbyists live in Washington' to a model that says, 'If you bring the right structure and a sense of genuine empowerment to Denver, Kansas City, wherever, you'll end up with the best lobbyists in the country—citizens acting responsibly in their home towns.'"

All "partners" in RESULTS groups are expected to attend three meetings per month. The goals:

• **Learn to express yourself on the issues.** "People aren't inspired to do anything if they're going to be embarrassed," Harris told NEW OPTIONS. "So once a month we get people to learn to *deliver* and not just understand issues." At group meetings, members get together to study an issue. Then one member speaks for two minutes on the issue. Then members pair up and give talks to each other. Then they ask each other questions and pair up to speak again. "In the end," says Harris, "*you're* the one that needs to meet with your Senator, you're the one that'll be meeting with the editorial writers of your local newspaper, you're the one that needs to be brilliant."

• **Learn to feel part of the dialogue.** "Another reason people don't bother to do anything is they feel out of it," Harris says. "So we have our members participate in a telephone conference call each month" with a key player on the hunger issue. Recent conference callers: the executive director of UNICEF, the president of International Fund for Agricultural Development, the former head of the food stamp program, the chief of staff of the

House Select Committee on Hunger. "It's basically an extension course once a month by telephone."

• **Do letter-writing.** At this pleasant session, usually held on a Sunday afternoon, RESULTS members write letters to various officials—especially their own elected representatives. According to Harris, letter-writing can be surprisingly effective. For example, RESULTS members from Honolulu and Maui wrote letters and made phone calls to Hawaii Rep. Don Akaka about the African Famine and Relief Act of 1985. Akaka had said he would not co-sponsor the bill, but RESULTS' focused activity reportedly changed his mind.

These three meetings provide a kind of ground for the many other activities that take place in RESULTS. Among them:

• RESULTS members are now generating editorials, op-ed pieces and letters to the editor at the astonishing rate of *one per day!*

• RESULTS sponsors an annual national conference in Washington, D.C. The 1985 conference, held two months ago, was attended by over 160 participants from 30 states. As a built-in part of the conference, all participants are expected to lobby their Congresspeople—and report back to the group.

• RESULTS is committed to spending more of its income on phone calls than on salaries, more on travel than on printing. As a result, Harris has been able to start 50 RESULTS groups in 33 states (through meetings very similar to the one we attended in Washington, D.C.)—and to remain in constant touch with them.

The strategy of many citizens' groups has been to convince people that government *doesn't* work. The idea is to empower people by making them angry enough to want to take power "for themselves." But too often this strategy backfires: leads to feelings of powerlessness or despair. All people are easily co-opted when they discover that, hey, this *is* a democracy.

Harris's approach is the polar opposite. It's to convince people that government *does* work, but that we're too ill-informed or fearful—too caught up in negative self-images or a lack of self-worth—to *make* it work. In other words, the onus is on us—rather than on our supposedly antagonistic institutions.

"If we look around," says Harris, "we see that very few of the people we know spend any time communicating with their elected representatives about their concerns. Against the background of this silent indifference, the voices of committed citizens can make an enormous difference. Yet very few of us have spoken out.''

Harris told us about the meeting a RESULTS member had with her U.S. Senator on the final day of the national RESULTS conference. "It was her first face-to-face meeting with the senator who had co-sponsored the Global Primary Health Initiative eight months earlier. The initiative gave additional funding for oral rehydration therapy (ORT), among other things. She asked her senator if he knew what oral rehydration therapy was. When he said 'No,' she said she got goose bumps handing him a packet of ORT formula and telling him what it was.''

Would you exchange that scene for a thousand angry placards?

II. Relationships first!

The main way activists reach new people these days is by canvassing door to door. "From Boston to Los Angeles,'' SANE/FREEZE boasts, "[our] canvassers knock on 6,000 doors every night to encourage Americans to join the fight against nuclear weapons.''

Many of us have canvassed to the point of exhaustion. But how much good are we doing, really? Are we really *reaching* people—or are we just weeding out those who (superficially) "agree'' with us from those who don't? And how many people are we alienating in the process? *Ring! Ring! It's those canvassers again. They're here to tell us why they're smarter and more caring than we are, again.*

Over the last five years, in rural western North Carolina, a new kind of canvass has been developed. Called "the Listening Project,'' its practitioners don't proselytize so much as listen and ask questions. They're willing to spend an hour or more on each house call. Their method is designed to change *themselves* as much as those they're listening to.

The Listening Project is quietly having an impact on organizing efforts all over the Southeast. More and more local groups are bringing Project staffers in to consult with them and train their canvassers.

When word of the Project spread to us, it sounded too good to be true. So one day last week we took the Trailways out to Asheville, North Carolina, to see for ourselves.

•   •   •

The Listening Project's director, Herb Walters, was waiting at the bus station to drive us to his office, an hour further into the countryside.

Walters is a tall, casually dressed 36-year-old with long dark-blond hair, striking angular features and kind eyes. I suppose he has charisma, but his most notable (and winning) characteristic is his lack of pretense. His seven-year-old daughter wanted us to be sure to include the fact that, whatever others might say about him, to his family he is "King of Farts."

On the drive out he tells us what it's like growing up on army bases in places like Augusta, Georgia, and trying—hard—to communicate with parents who don't understand or empathize with your life choices (anti-Vietnam activism, college courses at the Institute for Social Ecology). It occurs to us that Walters's organizing strategy is that of a person who's spent his last few years trying to reconcile with his parents, rather than rebel against them.

"I think the peace movement has committed itself to confrontational tactics that won't carry us very far," he says as our car winds through the Black Mountains. "I think basically the only thing that will carry us are relationships—building relationships and trust and understanding between opposing sides."

•   •   •

We are sitting with Walters and Judy Scheckel in the long, wooden building that serves as Listening Project headquarters (Scheckel, Walters's co-worker, had previously been a Nuclear Weapons Freeze organizer in New England). We're on a land trust with greenhouses, pottery studio, health food stores—and good ol' boys waving from their pickup trucks.

"We try to train canvassers to not just deal with issues on an intellectual level," Scheckel is saying, "but to try to make a human connection with the person."

210

"It's almost like a therapeutic process we're going through with people," Walters says. "There's a whole process of helping them feel safe and secure, so they can open up and really say what they think and feel.

"Usually people won't open up—not in a normal canvass. They're just telling you sort of easy things to say. Stuff on the surface. Or stuff from TV. What we're out for is to get a person to go much deeper, so where they're speaking from is more heart centered and really at the center of what their values and beliefs are."

To lead people into their deeper beliefs, each listening project designs a sequence of questions—a "survey"—for canvassers.

Each community group works out its questions in consultation with Walters and Scheckel. But in *no* community will canvassers begin with political statements or with questions like, What do you think about such-and-such a policy? They'll always begin with questions like, "How long have you lived in this community?" "What kind of work do you do?" "What are some of the things you like most about living here?"

Canvasser training also involves teaching listening and communications skills. Chief among them: empathize, empathize, empathize.

"Suppose you're in an interview with someone," says Walters, "and they say something like, 'The blacks always trash the neighborhoods they move into.'. . . What can you empathize with in that statement?"

Scheckel: "That it's important to have a neighborhood where your kids can feel secure?"

Walters: "Yeah. Well, in canvasser training we make a list of what people can empathize with in that statement. And then we list the negatives. And—this is the key to the Listening Project—then we say, These are your two choices. Do you focus on the positive feeling behind the statement, or do you focus on the negative?

"If you focus on the positive, you focus on the humanity of that other person. And you gain trust. And once you've done that you can begin to look at differences and challenge the person. . . . But if you just do the negative, you've lost them immediately. So it's a process."

Even the way Walters and Scheckel challenge people is different from most. Instead of hectoring, they ask what they call clarifying questions. "In that example," says Walters, "a clarifying question might be, Where have you seen this happening? Why do you think this happens?"

Just sitting down and asking questions and caring about the answers "is an empowering experience for poor and working-class people," says Walters. "They can't believe that someone would really want to sit there and listen to them go on and on. . . .

"But the most important empowerment thing is in the follow-up. We identify people who are interested in more information or who are interested in possibly getting involved in some of the issues the canvasser discussed. So the second part of the process is to return to them and find some way to involve them, or help them get organized, or help them do what they want to do."

The Listening Project can do just as much for the canvassers—the activists—themselves.

"It has helped give me more self-confidence," says Scheckel. "I know, now, that I can talk to someone who is really angry or upset on the opposite side of the issue from me."

"Many activists have a real basic fear of those people 'out there' that they've always been trying to reach," says Walters.

"One of our stereotypes is that the masses out there are mad at us and don't believe what we believe. Another stereotype is that people really don't care about the issues.

"If you went out and did a normal survey, that's probably what you would get back. But when people get to a deeper level of what they think and feel, and they feel safe talking to you, you know, what you find out is that people really care. *Mainstream America really does care.*"

III. Conversion to what?

For 20 years now, "economic conversation" advocates have been urging the conversion of defense plants to civilian use (e.g., General Dynamics switching from submarines to subways). Sounds great, but it is fair to say that the conversion movement has hardly gotten off the ground. What's the problem?

To the political left, "the problem" is simple: people are afraid of losing their jobs, and/or their communities' tax bases. For Michael Closson, tall, strawberry-blond executive director of the California-based Center for Economic Conversion (CEC), the problem is not in the movement's would-be supporters but in the movement itself. It is not visionary enough...not bold enough.

"The conversion of individual defense plants remains a valid concern," Closson told us last week from CEC's cluttered offices in the San Francisco Bay area. "But it is problematic, too. Plant level conversion does not capture the public imagination. It tends to lock proponents into stressing the need to preserve the aerospace behemoths which dominate defense industry.... It tends to equate conversion with job insurance. Not to put that down—but we feel it's critical to have a much broader definition of what conversion means and who can benefit.

"We believe economic conversion must be broadly defined to include not only the conversion of defense plants, but also the *diversification of defense-dependent communities,* and the *transformation of our overall economy....* Encompassing both of these is the values issue. Some of the values which served us quite well when we were an immature country settling a continent are no longer functional—rugged individualism, resource exploitation and material acquisitiveness. Now our central role in the world community compels us to encourage social responsibility, conservation, and personal development for ourselves and others...."

In addition, Closson speaks of the need to promote positive defense policies (and not be merely anti-defense), and the need to appeal to business people, professionals and local officials, "not just the traditional progressive constituency."

How did an activist in a very traditionally left- and labor-based movement come to embrace a holistic, post-materialist world view? "Part of it has been the inability to effectuate change at the plant level," Closson told NEW OPTIONS. "But the other part is just the recognition that we have to *open our eyes* and perceive that we have to create a positive future! And that means being really imaginative and innovative.

"Another part of it is that we want to have a real impact. We've reached a new era. There are limits to growth, there are limits

213

to the old industrial model, we have to talk about quality rather than quantity...."

And another part of it is, surely, more personal. Closson, 48, is an Ivy League Ph.D.; he came to the West Coast to be an assistant dean at Stanford. "But all of that stuff is a little too mainstream for me....

"What it comes down to is we're trying to move out of the 60s into the 90s—leapfrogging the 70s and 80s a little bit." He looks around, sees clutter all over the office, and laughs: "Well, we're trying to move out of the 60s programmatically, but office-wise we still have some of the flavor of the 60s intact...."

• • •

Like other economic-conversion groups, CEC produces a fistful of literature. But its activities go far beyond the literary. "We are taking a two-track approach in our program," says Closson. "We are providing organizing assistance in military-dependent communities, primarily through our workshops and model conversion ordinances. At the same time, we are promoting positive alternatives to the military economy."

• **Workshops.** "We're about to take our workshop to San Diego," Closson told NEW OPTIONS. "We've got some interesting people coming: one of the mayor's top aides, a Congressman's aide, the head of the local enterprise board....

"We'll be talking about the need to build healthy diversified local economies, and we'll be giving concrete examples of what cities could do instead. A lot of these examples are already out there—community self-reliance strategies, community loan funds—the work of the Institute for Local Self-Reliance.... We're going to basically give an array of options to choose from so cities will know they *don't* have to stay locked in to the military economy. More than the examples, we'll be conveying a mindset, a recognition that WE CAN RE-CREATE our communities—that we don't have to fall back on federal spending whether it's military or non-military...."

• **Ordinances.** "We have developed a model conversion ordinance," says Closson. "It could be instituted by city councils or through the initiative process.

214

"There's a group meeting next month in San Jose to start an initiative campaign. I have mixed feelings about that. The advantage is that you get a lot of publicity right away. The disadvantage is that you move into adversarial modes right away."

Closson helped write the San Jose initiative—which closely resembles CEC's model conversion ordinance. "It would do three things," he says. "The first is conventional conversion stuff— job retraining, employment assistance, that sort of thing. But the second would be helping companies develop *strategies* for diversifying and moving away from defense dependency. And the third is having the city develop strategies to diversify the *whole local economy.*"

• **Alternatives.** Closson and CEC are—increasingly— promoting positive alternatives to the military economy for the U.S. as a whole, not just for individual cities.

These alternatives are anything but tepid. In one recent article in CEC's newspaper, EXPRO co-founder Mark Sommer suggests "reclaiming the natural environment" and "developing alternative energy sources." In another, Urban Ecology founder Richard Register argues that "creating 'ecocities' is an adventure more exciting than war."

Closson calls this kind of thinking "demand side conversion" because it focuses upon "the wide array of critical unmet human and environmental needs and the 'real security' which can be achieved by addressing them. . . . These needs can and *should* be perceived as opportunities. . . . We are operating on the assumption that Star Wars lacks not for cogent critiques but for compelling rivals. We are starting to create those rivals."

IV. "Money is power"

Most people know Gordon Davidson as the laid-back co-founder of Sirius Community, one of North America's most successful alternative communities (pop. 25). He takes pride in giving a constant flow of visitors the "grand tour" of the place: the old farmhouse, the vegetable gardens, the llamas, and one strikingly beautiful new house that he built for himself and his wife largely with his own two hands.

But twice a week Davidson wakes up early, puts on an impressive-looking suit and tie and drives to a converted brick warehouse in Boston, where he reigns as the executive director of the Social Investment Forum—the recently founded professional association for brokers, bankers, investors, and all those who believe in applying social as well as financial criteria to their investments (i.e. all those who'd think twice about investing in companies that do business with South Africa; that have poor environmental records; that have poor employer-employee relations...). Groups like the U.S. Greens tend to garner the attention of the alternative press, but according to Davidson the Social Investment Forum may be the most significant social change group of our time.

"The Forum gives its members news about social investing," Davidson told NEW OPTIONS from his living room (with the sun streaming in through three huge hand-wrought windows). "We have a quarterly newsletter, we have quarterly meetings in different locations around the country.... We had our first annual 'national conference and expo' earlier this year—right on Wall Street—over 500 people attended—there were panels and speakers and dozens of booths where our members put out their literature and talked with the public....

"We publicize social investing. And we help all the people that are starting up, brokers from all over the country who want to help their clients do social investing.... Most of the major players in the social investment field are members, Calvert Fund, Working Assets, South Shore Bank, Institute for Community Economics, National Association for Community Development Loan Funds.... There are a lot of women members, a lot more than you'd find in a typical brokerage office!...

"We publish a directory, *Social Investment Services,* which lists and describes all our members [in often fascinating detail–ed.]—so when the public writes to us and says, I want to do social investing, we can send them that directory and they can go through it and find a broker or mutual fund or newsletter or whatever in their geographic area...."

This is all well and good, we tell Davidson (while staring out his windows at the gardens and forest). But how can you say you're working for a social change group? You know what Murray

Bookchin would say: Guilty capitalists aren't going to change the world.

"The Fund has not only brought together all these individuals and groups," Davidson replies. "It's helped them see themselves as part of a coherent movement.

"We've created a national presence around social investing, and the social investment route is moving very intensively right now—about $400 billion is currently invested with some kind of 'social screen' attached, as compared to $40 billion just three years ago. I think one of the most significant things about social investing is the impact it actually has on companies' policies. You can significantly affect what even the biggest companies are doing— they *change their policies* as a result of these kinds of pressures.

"Social investing is becoming a mass movement. It's open to anybody who has money. Many social investment funds will permit you to join if you invest as little as $250, and that's a pretty minimal amount for a lot of people in this society.

"Right now the Forum is encouraging people to move away from divestment—what you *don't* want your money to be doing— and to begin thinking about what you positively *want* your money to be doing, how you're going to positively 'reinvest' your money. We've really been beating on that drum! We're trying to be out front of where social investing is for the mainstream, we're all trying to think about how we can lead this thing on to the next step. . . .

"I think the political implications of all this are fairly obvious. One of the things that's fueling the social investment movement is the fact that people from the Sixties are getting to be in their 30s and 40s—I mean, their 40s and 50s—and coming into professional positions and professional salaries. These people have got to recognize that they have power with their money. Our bottom line on the first piece of literature we send out to people is, 'Money is power and our task is to learn to use it wisely.'"

Down at the old farmhouse, someone rang the bell. The communal meal was ready.

24   Win Every "Battle"—or Change the Discourse?

July 1989

When we Americans disagree over issues like abortion or gun control, typically we'll "battle it out" until one side "wins." But one side rarely "wins" for long. The losing side always seems to come back with reinforcements, ready for more.

For most Americans, this constant battling is the very essence of politics. But more and more of us are beginning to suspect that the battling, itself, is part and parcel of what we need to overcome.

It keeps our spokespeople from ever letting down their guard—from ever admitting doubt and uncertainty. It keeps most of the rest of us partisans from carefully considering what "the other side" has to say. No wonder the policies we adopt are rarely inclusive or wise.

Many political activists are now giving lip service to such values as "humility" and "process." But like the U.S. Greens (Chapters 3 and 20), most of them are still eager to stake out their own "politically correct" positions.

Among some activists, however, another approach is gaining ground. The idea here is not so much to come up with a better political *platform* as it is to come up with a better political *discourse*. . .one that forces all "sides" to listen to and learn from each other. Out of this new discourse, a better political platform may emerge.

Three organizations are currently promoting this new discourse, and this month we spoke with leaders of each of them:

• **Thomas Crum,** 44, is founder and president of Aiki Works, Inc., based in Colorado, and author of *The Magic of Conflict* (1987);

• **John Marks,** 46, is founder and president of Search for Common Ground, based in Washington, D.C.;

• **Craig Schindler,** 42, is co-founder and president of Project Victory, based in California, and co-author of *The Great Turning: Personal Power, Global Victory* (1989).

There's nothing wishy-washy about any of these non-adversarial types. Crum is a multi-sport athlete (skiing, aikido, even boxing); Marks is co-author of one of the best exposes of the CIA (*The CIA and the Cult of Intelligence,* 1974); Schindler has a law degree from Stanford.

All three want the rhetoric of escalation to give way to true communication—and creative problem solving—among people of divergent views.

"We don't advocate any 'content' solution," Schindler told us. "What we strongly advocate is a shared commitment to change the process by which we make political decisions...."

"The participant in a true dialogue may prefer a certain position at the outset. But he or she must be willing to listen to other perspectives.... The intent is to learn, to increase mutual understanding, to discover new ways of working together so we can deal effectively with the long-term threats to our future."

"It's not that people are going to look deeply into each other's eyes and agree that, yes, they are all human beings," Marks told us. "But there are things they agree on. And as it is now, they have virtually no chance to come together on them.

"If the new discourse really works, instead of people facing each other as adversaries they'd start sitting together facing the problem. They'd start sitting on the same *side* of the table facing the problem, which is on the other side of the table."

I. "Mediated dialogue"

Crum, Marks and Schindler are all practical people, and each has worked out a concrete dialogue *process* that, if adopted widely—in church basements and candidate forums, in social change groups and on national television—could achieve their ends.

They think it could transform the nature of political discourse in this country. And the nature of the solutions offered.

Schindler speaks of it as "mediated dialogue," Marks as "the search process," Crum simply as "putting it all together." But it's basically the same process, and has five key steps:

• Get prominent people from different "sides" of an issue to agree to sit down together. Provide a mediator and an audience.

"The environment should be conducive to cheerfulness, peace and understanding," says Crum.

• Ask one participant to state his or her position on the issue. Then ask the other(s) to restate that position to the first participant's satisfaction. Keep going until everyone's positions have been satisfactorily restated. "This means they have to *listen*," says Marks, "which in the kinds of polarized exchanges we have now doesn't happen very often. Usually people are thinking ahead to what they're going to say next, rather than listening to the other person."

• Ask the participants to clarify their basic disagreement, and other disagreements. "The mediator has got to make sure that the questioning is informative and not argumentative," says Schindler.

• Ask the participants to identify any areas of agreement they might have. Schindler: "The mediator notes where there is agreement, often on a 'scoreboard' of some kind, and has participants expand on those areas."

• Encourage the participants to discuss whether there are any areas of agreement in which their groups might work together after the conclusion of the dialogue. "I think the agreements, while interesting, become a lot more interesting if you can get the participants working together," says Marks.

This spring Marks's group taped a series of 10 mediated dialogues between well-known antagonists. Among the topics covered: abortion, gun control, energy, human rights, the Middle East, and the U.N. This fall all 10 dialogues will be shown on over 100 public television stations nationwide—easily the biggest exposure yet for the new kind of political discourse.

To bring the new discourse to life for you, we've taken two excerpts from the dialogue on abortion. Participants are John Willke, president of the National Right to Life Committee, and Kate Michelman, director of the National Abortion Rights Action League. John Marks is mediator.

•   •   •

In our first excerpt, Marks tries to get his guests to clarify their basic disagreement.

Marks: What do you think the fundamental disagreement is between the two of you?

Willke: Pro-abortion advocates deny the humanity of the unborn child, or at least deny the rights of the unborn human boy or girl inside. And they give the woman's social and economic concerns prioritization—simply stating that in order to solve those concerns as they see them, she has the right to directly take the life. . .the word there biologically is kill. . .this developing baby inside of her.

We say, No way.

Marks: What is the fundamental disagreement in your view?

Michelman: [sighs] Well I think there are several fundamental disagreements. But the one Dr. Willke was just speaking about. . .there's a moral decision making that was missed here.

We believe that fetal life has value. But there are times in hard situations when there are higher values to consider. And a woman has to *decide* which are the higher values, fetal life or the value of bringing. . .the immorality of bringing a child into the world that could be abused, live in poverty. . .or carry on her life.

Willke: I don't think the big should kill the little, the mighty should kill the weak, the rich should kill the. . .and so forth.

Marks: Yeah. So the fundamental disagreement, as I understand it, is that *[to Willke]* you're saying that all life is equal. Fetal life and not fetal life.

And *[to Michelman]* you're saying that there can be circumstances in which the rights of the mother, the rights of the woman, have priority over fetal rights.

Michelman: That's right.

Willke: I'll accept that.

In our second excerpt, Marks's guests easily managed to find common ground on a very important point.

Marks: Would you both agree that adoption should be a viable alternative for every woman who doesn't want to keep her baby?

Michelman: Absolutely!

Marks: And you?

Willke: Absolutely! But I must make a comment. Planned Parenthood has done a real number on adoption, nationwide. They have taught a generation of children that adoption is a fate worse than death. . . .

Marks: But would you. . .would your group and your group, perhaps, be willing to have some talks about adoption [in hopes of making it an even more] viable alternative?

Willke: I certainly would.

Michelman: Absolutely. We're willing to talk about anything that serves the well-being of women and their families.

•   •   •

As you can tell from the above, staging a "mediated dialogue"—centerpiece of the new political discourse—is no easy matter. But all three of our activists are convinced the difficulties are worth the candle.

Mark's reasoning is pragmatic. "I don't think you can solve the basic disagreement on abortion or any other major issue," he told us. "I don't think that people who are pro-life or pro-choice are going to say the others are right and change their position.

"But what you can do is find a whole range of options on which they could work together—and which might decrease the *need* for abortion.

"For instance, at the end of our mediated dialogue on abortion, the leaders of the two groups agree they could work together to prevent unwanted pregnancies. Now, there are a million and a half unwanted pregnancies every year. Let's just say that through a campaign of that sort, a million could be eliminated. That would eliminate the need for most of those abortions!

"So abortion would be less of a national issue—without even *getting into the question* of when does life begin."

Schindler and Crum go further. They think the new discourse will not only help us find "common ground," but go beyond our old solutions and find new ones.

"When you change the rules in the way we suggest, "Schindler told us, "you allow the different parties to talk *candidly* about their *real* concerns. Because they have a different commitment— which is to think together, to actually look for a meeting of the minds.

"And in that process they'll come up with options that are more inclusive. As we've seen again and again, in our own work in more than 40 cities around the country, new ideas—literally, 'new options'—will come into view."

II. Three strategies

Each of the three activists has devised a strategy for spreading the new kind of political discourse. And each hopes to carry it out.

Crum has developed what might be called a *workshop strategy*. "I've been developing workshops and materials," he told us, "different modules people can use, you know, videotapes, books, audiotapes. I'm developing workbooks for families, businesses and schools and I'm also working with corporations. . . . I think enough of us doing this work in a quality way will build up a critical mass."

Marks has developed what might be called a *national strategy*. "I'd like to do follow-up on some of the 10 issues we covered in our PBS series," he told us. "When you have two people like Michelman and Willke, you can be pretty sure that, even though they've just agreed to [cooperate on] six things, they're going to go back to their offices and do exactly what they did the day before *[laughs]*. There's not gonna be much change, right?

"So it seems to me that, to keep the process going, somebody needs to keep inviting them back, or if not them then their friends, representatives, other people in their groups. And you need some staff support to keep the process going. You need to invite people to meetings, you need to set up agendas and all of that.

"If you could do all that, I think you could put together some national coalitions across ideological lines—you could put together an adoption coalition, for example.

"And if you wanted to get into local coalition-building, you could just show a videotape of people like Willke and Michelman agreeing to work together on various issues. It sort of gives permission to people on the local level to cooperate in some of the same ways.

"The problem is, who's going to build those coalitions locally? Nobody's got an organizational stake in these new possibilities. All the organizational energy is in the old argument."

Schindler's strategy—call it a *populist strategy*—speaks to just that question. "During the decade of the 90s," he told us, "I envision a 10 year, two-tiered campaign for a 'great turning.'

"The first tier is thousands of people taking on a personal practice in their lives to make small changes that have to do with conflict management and environmental restoration as well as personal well-being.

"The second tier is building an 'ethical alliance' among all those who are committed to changing the *way* we address the issues that threaten our future."

How to begin building that alliance? "People could use mediated dialogues to address issues of concern in their local communities. For example, a community group might decide to organize a series of mediated dialogues on a local environmental dispute, or on how to reduce violent crime...."

•   •   •

Let's say that, like most of the readers of this newsletter, you support such "Green" or "New Age" values as decentralism, deep ecology, global responsibility, human growth and voluntary simplicity. Why should you be content to work for a world in which your views would merely be part of an ongoing dialogue (however public and "sincere" that dialogue might be)? Why shouldn't you fight for the imposition of your views, as radicals have from time immemorial?

After listening to Crum, Marks and Schindler at length, I believe there are two good answers:

• The new kind of political discourse will, itself, win people over to sustainable ways of thinking... because it virtually demands that we learn to take everyone's perspectives (and feelings) into account. And that will help generate the empathy out of which Green solutions can and must come.

• The whole notion of one political viewpoint "winning" and the others all "losing" may be an anachronism. As Schindler puts it, in a dangerous, complex and interdependent world "it is in our own best interests to turn our conflicts into *mutual* gain."

PART SIX

POLITICS IS NOT ENOUGH

After I'd written all the pieces above, I set off to write a brief cover story on female prostitution, and more specifically on the ways three prostitutes' rights groups look at prostitution.

But it quickly took on a life of its own. I found it difficult to believe any of the prostitutes' rights groups, and realized I had to discover for myself what prostitution is all about. That meant I had to get to know some prostitutes.

And then, without my fully realizing it, the theme of the piece shifted. On one level it is still about prostitutes. But on another level it is about our need for love, and about what happens when many of us are incapable of love.

25 Some of Our Daughters, Some of Our Lovers

November 1990

We've all seen them, stared at them, wondered about them, more than we like to admit.

Short-skirted, high-heeled women endlessly walking certain streets in our cities and towns. Heavily painted women in too-tight

225

jeans asking if you want a "date." Women with sad crazy smiles saying they want you *now* and adding that they won't charge much.

In Washington, on the blocks around 13th and N Streets (10 minutes' walk from the White House), you can see them getting into mens' cars; going down stairwells with men; taking men into alleys. You can see them kibitzing with each other on the street corners. You can see them sipping soft drinks to wash away the aftertaste of their last man.

And as a matter of fact, they don't charge much: $25 for a b.j., $50 for a half-and-half. And even that is negotiable.

The best guess is that there are a million homeless people in the U.S. For whatever good it does them, they are a constant media concern. They are "news."

The best guess (by the most competent prostitute advocates) is that there are a million female prostitutes in the U.S.—a million women who earn at least part of their income by having sex for pay. But they are not a media concern. They are not "news." They are simply *there,* like the weather.

It is very convenient to treat issues like homelessness as news but issues like prostitution as not-news. Homelessness is a relatively easy problem to solve. We can solve it with some clever combination of money and policy. But prostitution cannot be addressed so easily.

We've always had prostitutes; perhaps we always will. Their presence, therefore, does not just say something about our nation's policies or leaders. It also says something fundamental about us.

And not the kind of thing you want to dwell on, on the six o'clock news.

I. Whores R us

What it says about us begins (but does not end) with the fact that prostitutes are not some mysterious and distant Other. They are deeply implicated in our lives. They are *many* of our daughters; they are *many* of our lovers, or our husbands' lovers.

If a million U.S. women work as prostitutes in any one year, and the turnover is 10% a year—then at any one time, *five million U.S. women* either are or have been prostitutes.

Nobody knows how many men use prostitutes. From talking with men, I'd estimate that one out of five of us sees prostitutes in any one year. That's *20,000,000 adult men.*

That is not an implausible figure. We know that the average adult street prostitute sees 1,500 men a year (women working in massage parlors, or as call girls, or out of their homes, may see fewer). We know that most of these men go to prostitutes more than once a year. But even if the ratio goes down dramatically— to 20 men per prostitute—with a million prostitutes that works out to 20,000,000 men.

That is a lot of women and men.

II. Three "explanations"

So—what does prostitution say about us? What's it *really* all about?

To come up with a convincing answer, I thought I'd have to look no farther than the three major prostitutes' rights organizations. But they do not agree among themselves as to the answer. Each is promoting a different "line":

• **It's about women's freedom.** According to COYOTE (acronym for "Call Off Your Old Tired Ethics"), the important thing is that "women have the right to determine, for themselves, how they will use their bodies," as COYOTE co-director and lesbian activist Priscilla Alexander puts it. For Alexander and COYOTE, prostitution is just another kind of work—"sex work" is the politically correct designation.

In Alexander's anthology *Sex Work* (1987), she adopts an unusually matter-of-fact and surprisingly accepting tone: "Some [women] get to like the work as they become skilled at it. Other women hate it from the beginning to the end. And still others like some aspects of the job while hating parts of it." Similar sentiments abound in a more recent anthology, Gail Pheterson's *A Vindication of the Rights of Whores* (1989).

• **It's about economics.** Another leading prostitutes' rights group, the U.S. Prostitutes' Collective (U.S. PROS—terrific double entendre), argues that the economy encourages and even forces some women to become prostitutes. "Prostitution is about money," says U.S. PROS spokeswoman Rachel West. "If women's basic economic situation does not change, then women will continue to work as prostitutes."

• **It's about male oppression.** The third major prostitutes' rights group, WHISPER (Women Hurt in Systems of Prostitution Engaged in Revolt), believes that no woman ever really *chooses* to work as a prostitute—that prostitution is an institution created by men to control and exploit women.

"There has been a deliberate attempt to validate men's perceived need, and self-proclaimed right, to buy and sell women's bodies for sexual use," says Sarah Wynter, founder and editor of WHISPER's national newsletter. "This has been accomplished, in part, by euphemizing prostitution as an occupation. . . .

"Both the conservative right and the liberal left male hierarchies collude to teach and keep women in prostitution. . . ."

All three organizations are doing good work. But I did not trust their politically correct positions on prostitution. They seemed too shallow and pat.

I mistrusted those politically correct anthologies, too. Behind both of them I detected a pernicious assumption: *The sexual love relationship between men and women is neither sacred nor special.*

A spokeswoman for the Women's Organization for Equality (WOE) let that assumption out of the bag in Pheterson's anthology: "What's the difference between being promiscuous and being paid for it, and just being all free and not being paid for it? . . . . I can't see any difference." *You can't?* Priscilla Alexander also made that assumption explicit when she wrote, in the introduction to her anthology. "[M]oney has become the main factor that distinguishes prostitution from marriage." The *main* factor?

III. "Community of complicity"

All of a sudden, an article that may have been relatively easy to write became much harder. If I could not rely on the major prostitutes' rights groups and the standard anthologies on the subject, there was only one thing left to do. I would have to interview some prostitutes myself.

I began hanging out in the neighborhood around 13th and N Streets—a neighborhood full of streetwalkers. At first I was even afraid to approach them. So I spent some time just observing. . . and plotting my strategy.

I had noticed that all the prostitutes whose words found their way into the Alexander and Pheterson anthologies sounded just like they were talking to—and for—radical-feminist and lesbian activists. I was sure that, to some extent, the prostitutes had shaped what they said and wrote in order to meet the expectations of their anthologists, and I was deeply committed to not making that same mistake. The last thing that I wanted was for the prostitutes I interviewed to shape their thoughts and feelings in order to please me, a male journalist and "concerned professional."

So standing there on the streets at night, watching the prostitutes get in and out of their customers' cars, I realized that if I wanted to come close to anything like the truth about their lives, I'd have to break down, as much as humanly possible, the barriers between us. To the greatest extent possible I'd have to come across to them not as an ideologue and not as a Journalist, but as just another flawed and vulnerable person.

I further realized that there was only one way to do this and maintain their interest. I'd have to come up to them like any other trick and ask to have sex with them.

The way I liked to put it to myself was I'd be entering into a "community of complicity" with them.

I was too afraid of catching sexually transmitted diseases to propose having intercourse with them, but I figured I could ask them to whip me or something. And then—so I thought—at some point I'd interrupt the proceedings, say I didn't feel in the mood that night, mention I'm a journalist, and ask if they'd mind being interviewed—if not that night, then sometime soon.

It was an unorthodox approach, I know. But it worked.

Over the course of the last two months, I spoke with 15 prostitutes, and conducted long and searching interviews with six of them. (I confined myself to whites, whom I felt I'd be able to understand better, and confined myself further to those who didn't look completely blown away by drugs or suffering.)

Most of the interviews lasted several sessions and all took place in my apartment. Each of the prostitutes got to know me first as a (very) flawed and (very) vulnerable human being, and only then as a Professional Journalist. And each of them, in turn, revealed themselves to me in ways that were touching and illuminating and even, I believe, accurate (I checked parts of their stories with *other* streetwalkers—they gossip incessantly about each other—just to make sure I wasn't being led astray).

Of course, 15 white D.C. streetwalkers is hardly a representative sampling of all the prostitutes in the nation. But I think they conveyed enough of the depth and texture of their lives to allow me to begin to understand prostitution beyond the "correct lines" of the ideologues.

IV. Beginner's luck

I wasn't real successful with the first prostitute I tried to take home. But the experience unforgettably confirmed for me the limitations of all three correct lines on prostitution.

I'd seen Amy in the neighborhood for weeks. She was hard to miss. She usually dressed in a black leather jacket and rode a bike, pedalling right up to cars and asking guys if they wanted a date. (If they did, she excused herself while she chained her bike to a post.) A Green prostitute!, I thought, with my heart on my sleeve. And she was a genuinely attractive woman, small but well-built, with soft cheeks and big brown eyes and a mouth that puckered expressively and often.

Around midnight I was walking in a particularly run-down part of the neighborhood when I saw Amy on the corner. I walked by her slowly and tentatively and she asked if I wanted a date. My heart was pounding wildly. I said I was just walking around but she looked so attractive I was willing to change my mind.

Her mouth puckered. What was I into?, she wanted to know.

I'd like to be abused, I said, trying to follow my "strategy."

I thought you might be into that, she said, 'cause of the leather you're wearing.

I only have $25, I said, but I have a nice place we can go to.

Well, I live just down the street, she said. And she took my hand and started leading me there. *What do I do now?*, I thought.

Maybe just play along with her for a while, then invite her to my place some other time?

Do you share the place?, I asked, terrified I might be jumped by some pimp. No way, she said, relax, it's all mine.

I continued trying to figure out how to get out of the situation without making it impossible to see her again. Meanwhile, she kept walking—faster and faster, it seemed—and began telling me about herself. She was 24 years old, born and bred in Baltimore, had been "tricking" two years, and also had a straight job (her phrase!) as a hairdresser in a suburban mall.

We got to her apartment building—one of those new but already shoddy-looking tall buildings around 14th and N with 24-hour security downstairs. The security guard glared at us as she whisked me into the elevator.

Now I was really panicky. *What was I doing? How could I stop this?* She got off on the third floor and yelled into her apartment, "Is anybody there?" But I thought you said it was yours, I said. Be quiet! she said. Stand here in the hall. My girlfriend might be visiting.

She walked inside. Hello! she said; and a thick male voice said something drowsy and unintelligible. I can't stay now, she said, and went out to me again.

Let's go up to the seventh floor landing, she said, and she led me up the stairs. Nobody ever goes up there, she said. I've taken plenty of dates up there, and they have a great time. Once a guy spread a blanket on the floor and we stayed there for nearly an hour!

The seventh floor landing was dingy and cold, and it didn't look private to me. And I didn't want to be there in the first place! Amy, I said, listen, I'm too nervous to do anything here, it's not private at all. Let's go to my place. I'll pay for the cab.

She looked at me directly for the first time, and her big brown eyes turned cold as ice. She demanded the $25 that I "promised" her. But you promised to take me to your *apartment,* I said.

Then she draws the knife, with a motion so swift and smooth I can hardly follow. It's got a nasty curl at the tip of the blade, and an eagle's head on the handle, and she's holding it in a way that makes it clear she knows how to use it.

I can tell my knees are beginning to buckle, from the fear. I'm sorry, I say to Amy. Of course I'm gonna pay you. Here!

She takes the money and mercifully, miraculously, puts the knife away. She's only had to use it once, she says—on a guy who tried to take his money back from her. She slashed his face and chest, she says, "but didn't jab it in"; she is very proud of that fact.

She goes to the foot of the next flight of stairs and gets down on her knees. Now that you've paid you can finish your date, she says. She pulls up her sweater, revealing a red see-through brassiere. Her nipples are taut. She puckers her lips suggestively.

Uh, Amy, I say, thanks a lot. But after seeing that knife I no longer feel like it. Why don't we just go now?

She gets back on her feet. How much money do you have left?, she asks. Just enough for cab fare, I say. Yeah, well your place is walking distance, she says, and pulls out the knife again.

My eyes become as big as hers. She sees this and says she needs the $4 because she has $1 of her own plus my $25, and $30 will allow her to buy a "D" (for "dilaudid"—a potent drug). Unhesitatingly, I hand it over.

When we go out she's all charm. She thanks the security guard for watching her bike (which had been sitting in the lobby). She tells me to get my hair done at her studio sometime. I tell her I'm a journalist and might like to interview her, and she puckers her lips and gives me her phone number. Then she gets up on her bike and is gone.

I begin to walk home and realize I'm trembling. I walk the streets for hours, thinking about all that happened.

I knew I didn't have any idea why Amy was working the streets. But I'd already seen enough to know that all three of the "correct lines" on prostitution were useless as guides to understanding her.

It was inconceivable to me that she was living that life by choice. She claimed to have a job as a hairdresser (something I later confirmed), so she didn't need to sell herself to make a living. And she had too much spunk to be purely a victim—of men, "the patriarchy," or anything else.

V. Heart of darkness

If Amy definitively taught me the limitations of the three "correct lines," Beth helped point me toward a better, deeper understanding of prostitution.

I often saw Beth sitting on the stone wall at the corner of 13th and N—a thin woman with an intelligent, angular face overlaid by pimples and pock marks. We talked occasionally; I'm sure she thought I was a regular. One day I went to the neighborhood hoping to bring someone home for an interview, and there Beth was, sitting on her stone wall in a short denim skirt. Although it was bitter cold, she wasn't wearing underwear.

I told her I was looking for someone to beat me, and she told me she was real good at that. In the cab she held my hand, then started rubbing my thigh.

By the time I got her upstairs, though, I began dreading any kind of physical contact with her. Something was off about her— something was not quite right.

So what would you like?, she asked me.

You're the expert, I told her. And besides, I've never been beaten before. I'd just like to feel less. . .*responsible* for a while. (I thought that sounded pretty realistic.)

She seemed to be spacing out; she was clearly on some kind of drug. Lemme think about this, she said. You're different. I wanna come up with the right thing for you.

Her head began weaving back and forth. Are you all right?, I asked.

Am I all right?, she said, mimicking me. Lemme tell you something. You don't know shit about problems. I don't have nothin' but what I've got on my back. I don't even know where I'm gonna sleep tonight.

Look at my legs!, she says. She pulls up her skirt and I see that they're covered with cuts and bruises. My body can't heal itself anymore!, she shouts.

She leaves her skirt up. I'm finding it hard to look at her, and she knows it.

I'm a heroin addict! she shouts, knowing it'll horrify me to hear it.

You want a little ass-whipping? That's nothing—nothing. Lemme tell you something. I've had three coathangers stuck up my ass! I've had a red-hot poker up there!. . .

You are so lucky you chose me! There's bitches out there who'd see this place and stake it out! There's girls out there with the AIDS virus! I was sitting with one this morning. . . .

I really wanted to calm her down. I brought her some After the Fall sparkling fruit juice and asked if she'd ever been to college. It wasn't a spurious question; there was an intelligence in there somewhere.

Yeah, she says, finally covering her legs. I spent a semester at Stanford. At 18. My dad had lots of money, she says—virtually spitting out the words "dad" and "money."

I had a great advisor there, she says. She thought I'd be a real good psychologist. But I dropped out to be with my boyfriend, and he had a drug habit. And I've been into drugs for 10 years now.

She clutches her side and puts a bit of lower-class-black intonation into her voice. Now the doctor say I'm gonna die in two or three months. From cancer!

Oh my God, I think—instantly suspecting that her "cancer" is, in reality, AIDS. Beth, I say, listen: I can't ask you to abuse me.

I am abusing you, she says. And you lovin' it!

She launches into a long explanation of why men feel they're raping her when she's whipping them. Her advisor was right, I think: she *would* have made a good psychologist.

Then she launches into a long rap that sounds like she picked it up verbatim from the black pimps she claims to have had.

Whites are mad at black pimps for pimping their white women, she declares. But blacks are just pimping to get some money to build up their own economy. That's how everybody does it!

Your landlord pimps you for rent, right? Boss pimps his workers. Whites pimp blacks every day....

Sure, the blacks are pimping our bodies. But that's *all* they're pimping. You go to work, the white man is pimping your body *and your mind*....

After I got Beth out of there, I bolted the door and sat down on the rug—once again, trembling.

She certainly sounded "politically correct" at times. Parts of her rap would have been great in the Alexander or Pheterson anthologies. But seeing and hearing it all in context gave a different impression entirely.

Beth's anger was real. But it was also a protective coating. Beneath it I sensed (I could almost reach out and touch) an emotional pain so great that to have felt it fully might have killed her. In fact, I was sure that it *was* killing her, no less stealthily than the AIDS or cancer or whatever.

234

You could hear the pain in her voice. You could see it in her face, in her eyes. Doesn't it come bouncing off the page at you?

I didn't understand the ultimate source of the pain—though when she spoke of her dad with contempt, I felt I was getting a clue.

But I did understand one thing. Beth's emotional hurt was the key to *why* she was on the streets. It was a lot more key than all her politically correct insights about the universality of pimping.

After talking with Beth I realized my task would be even harder than I thought.

It wasn't enough to take prostitutes home and ask them the questions a reporter might ask. I had to talk with them long enough—and listen to them closely enough—to detect where they hurt, and why...to uncover what Hemingway used to call the "broken places."

That became the purpose of my taped interviews. The first were with Nancy.

VI. Getting to Nancy

I'd seen Nancy around for years—as a 19-year-old she'd been tricking near our first office—and if you met her at a party or something you'd have never guessed she was a prostitute. She looked like your typical corn-fed Midwesterner, straw-colored hair, winning smile, slightly overweight but almost intimidatingly wholesome-looking. Acted like your storybook Midwesterner too—"nice" almost to a fault.

The first time I took her home she had her clothes off before we'd hardly said a word. I'm more comfortable this way, she said, smiling and laughing and sitting with her legs crossed on my couch. It was genuinely hard for her to get into the whipping, and after I told her to stop she spent a lot of time in my bathroom, fixing her make-up, combing her hair, trying to look wholesome again.

"Why do you choose this way of life?" I shouted, over the running water.

"Money," she said. "No boss, I can work for myself. I can work when I want...."

"Were you a happy kid?"

"Very! I come from a very good family."

Damn, I thought. I've done this whole thing with her and she's still talking to me like I'm a do-gooder. But after a few weeks she came over again, more ready to be real.

"I *was* a real happy kid," she said, sitting at my big kitchen table in an oversized knit sweater. "I had everything I wanted, I had a lot of friends in school, I made good grades.

"Uh—my father wasn't around much. But my mother and I were very, very close. My mom and him were total opposites. She was very caring and understanding, gave people a million and one chances."

Tell me about your dad, Nancy.

"My father owns a car business, an auto body repair shop and a car rental service. And he's doing very, very well for himself. But my mother passed away four years ago—she was only 41. That was real hard, when she passed away.

"He's remarried now. I don't know how long it's gonna last *[laughs]*. My father's not the marrying type...."

Why wasn't your father around much? "He was more into workin', trying to make money. We didn't communicate much. *[Voice is flat, no emotion.]* We still don't. Even when I was in rehab and had to stay with him it was hard.

"Now don't get me wrong. There's nothing my father wouldn't do for me. As far as money's concerned, I could have whatever I wanted, as much as I wanted. He gave me a beautiful car; he gave me a beautiful home, in Virginia, I had a four-bedroom house all by myself. But *[laughs]* I don't have it any more."

Can you sum it up, Nancy? "He gives me a lot of material things. That's it. As far as being there when you need someone emotionally, uh, you know, he's just not there."

Was he like that with your mom, too? "Yeah."

Nancy can't seem to stop scratching her wrist; I pretend not to notice.

Nancy was introduced to drugs in junior high school, and by high school she was hooked. "Back when I was growing up," she says, "there wasn't all this talk about drugs. People just overlooked it. And I just said, Oh, I don't have a problem" *[laughs]*.

236

Her drugs of choice were (and still are) dilaudids and cocaine, and they are not cheap. She says that's why she took a job at a massage parlor—the one just across the street from the Washington Hilton, where President Reagan was shot. "I made anywhere from three to five hundred dollars a day, and spent it all, every day," on drugs. But she didn't get along with the owner, and "had to" start turning tricks on the street. She was 19 years old.

Then she went into rehab. "I stayed off drugs for about a year and nine months after going through treatment. And then my mother passed away, and my boyfriend and I broke up, and, um, I don't know; I didn't really like myself that much; I turned to food to feel good, and I overdid it; and I knew in back of my mind, well, if people use drugs they lose weight real fast; so I started using drugs again. And that's when I went back out into the street. And then I went back into treatment, but I left again.

"You have to have the will power to say no. It's kind of hard when you're working out on the street."

Nancy smiled sadly and looked down at the table.

Nancy's love life is no happier than her mother's was. "In two relationships I've come close to getting married. And then something along the line causes me to relapse. *[Voice goes way down.]* And I start using drugs again. And the relationship ends. . . .

"I don't have a boyfriend when I'm doing this kind of work. . . ."

But there is one special person in her life, and don't you dare call him a pimp. "I have someone that I hang out with who—he's not a pimp, but a lot of the pimps will think that he is, because he's black. So they leave me alone.

"He's a real good friend. And he doesn't let anything happen to me *[laughs]*. You know, we don't always get along too well. But uh *[her voice trails off]*.

"One thing my friend does do is he follows me. You know, the person I'm with won't know he's following me. Once in a while they'll see; but if they're not up to anything it shouldn't bother them."

Oh God, I think. "Is that guy out there now?"

"No," she says, "he dropped me off and left. I'll have to catch a cab."

What does he get out of the relationship, Nancy?

"It depends. Like say I get a hundred dollar date, you know, I'll give him twenty bucks for his time. Or I'll give him gas money, you know? But it's not like I give him all my money! I don't believe in that."

How did you meet this nice man? "He helped me out and gave me some money one time *[laughs]*. So I went ahead and dated him. But this was before I *knew* him. And then I saw him a couple of months later, and, you know, he just started helpin' me out with rides and stuff, and we started talking. And we just ended up getting close after a while.

"He's a nice person, but—if and when I finish school and I'm not out here any more, I don't really think I'm gonna hang around him *[laughs],* to be honest. . . ."

I thought back to Beth and some other prostitutes I'd talked with who sounded like they were repeating lines fed to them by their black male "friends," and I asked Nancy what was going on. "Most of these black guys have no job," she said. "Most of them want to get high themselves. So these girls—I don't want to say they've been brainwashed, but a lot of them have [been], in my opinion.

"And my friend tells me the same thing. He knows a lot of black guys who live with some of those white girls. And they tell them how much they love them, and all that. He says it's a crock of shit, you know."

For years Nancy has been in and out of a community college. Currently she's studying business administration. "Eventually I want to be a legal assistant," she told me bravely.

But she has a hard time envisioning even that for herself. "A lot of time I put myself down and I think I'm not good enough," she says. "Like, I'm thinking I could start out as a receptionist, although I have a lot more skills than what's required for a receptionist. . . ." She's scratching her wrist so hard I get up and bring her some lotion.

Did you ever *want* to do anything, Nancy?, I ask. "I wanted to be a lawyer *[laughs]*. Yeah! I did real well in school. My grandfather [on my mother's side] always said I'd make a good lawyer. And, uh, *he* was a lawyer.

238

That's what I wanted to do. But—it's kind of strange how things happen. You know, how it progresses. Drugs—being out on the street—.''

No, Nancy, I thought, it's all too predictable how things happen. If your parents don't love each other, and your dad doesn't communicate with you, then once you become a teen-ager it's hard to imagine being or doing anything special; and the temptation to abuse and obliterate yourself can be overwhelming.

I didn't know how to communicate any of that to Nancy, and in any event I wouldn't get the chance. Someone called up on the phone from the lobby. It was Nancy's "friend," and he was hopping mad. Something about her taking too long. Something about another trick waiting.

Like a good soldier, I insisted on going down with her. By the time the elevator brought us down there he was already in his car. It was a real nice car, and he was dressed like someone out of *Gentlemen's Quarterly.*

"C'mon shorty!" he hissed at me. "Let's go!" he shouted at her in a menacing voice.

Nancy tried to flash me her patented wholesome smile. I have to catch my cab now, she said.

It was only then that I realized how massive her denial of her reality was. She's not only tried to put me on about certain things. She also tried—needed—to put herself on. If that wasn't really a cab out there, then by God she'd make it one. For both of us.

The receptionist in my lobby wasn't fooled a bit. She glared at me every day for weeks afterwards.

VII. Getting to Gail

If Nancy was pretty representative of the (formerly) middle-class streetwalkers I met, Gail was pretty representative of the lower-middle-class ones.

It's hard to miss Gail when you go down to 13th and N. She's the short woman with the semi-punk haircut and the rebellious scowls. She's the woman bursting with so much energy that she sometimes seems to be dancing on the sidewalk, and always seems to enjoy the banter with the drivers in the passing cars.

She's even harder to miss these days. She's six months pregnant.

I didn't have it in me to ask a pregnant woman to whip me. So I haggled over price with Gail a couple of times—just to establish that "community of complicity" with her. Then one day I saw her sitting quietly (!!!) on a brick wall, and asked her to come to my apartment to be interviewed. She looked kind of skeptical, but said sure.

Her first words could have come straight from Alexander or Pheterson: "I used to think hookers were low-life women who thought nothing of their bodies. And that's not so, that's not so...." But as the interview progressed her doubts and unhappiness became more pronounced, until the whole thing resembled a symphony of sadness.

"I'm 25," Gail is telling me, "I'm from Florida, was born and raised in St. Petersburg. I haven't seen my father since I was 15.

"My mother is what they call a 'transit informant.' A snitch for the po-lice [Gail always puts the emphasis on the first syllable of "po-lice"]. Yeah.

"Evidently—what I found out happened was—our house burned down when she was living in Ohio. And to my surprise, I had a younger brother *[laughs]*, and he burned up in the fire. She was [off getting] some drugs for herself. And [becoming an informant is how she was able to] beat that rap, you know.

"She kidnapped my two kids. She set me up on 14th and W to go to jail, and I went back to get my kids, 'cause I was moving them away from her; and all my shit was on the porch *[lowers voice]*, and they were gone.

"And the po-lice here won't let me press kidnapping charges even though I have legal custody. It's not the fact that I'm a hooker, it's that she's a snitch! Evidently she says she wants her grandkids otherwise she's stoppin' [being an informant]. And she's good, she's real good at snitchin'; at bein' naive and playin' the game."

And what about your father, Gail? "He used to be car parts, auto parts, something like that." Did your parents get along? "Naw, they divorced when I was 12.

"And then my mother remarried. A man named Larry Osha. And he was molesting me an' she didn't *believe* it, you know *[smiles].* And I went to the state, you know, the authorities, and they didn't do anything because he was so 'respectable'—he was production manager [on a kids' TV show down there, and] up here he worked for public television.

"He died of a heart attack, thank God!"

Gail loves to speak of her "wild" (her term) childhood. "When I was 13 I always ran away, I was ungovernable. I got expelled from school *[switches to a seductive sing-song voice]* 'cause I was in the boys' bathroom smokin' pot and drinkin' beer, the only girl in there, you know *[raucous laughter].* Got expelled. Failed the eighth grade three times."

She eventually did graduate, went to Tampa College for a while, and learned to type 90 words a minute. But to no avail. "Secretary is boring," she says now. "And I can't stand bein' told what to do. I'm very rebellious. I'm like a cat in a corner, I come out scratching... So rather than do that, I started dancing.

"People liked the way I danced, and I made a lot of money, and it made me *feel good.* And I didn't have people telling me to do this and do that. Cause when you dance, you know, you do it the way *you* want to do it. You come at 11, you leave at seven, you dance for 10 minutes an hour and that's it."

Gail also started doing hard drugs. "A girl down in Florida [got me involved]. She was quote-unquote a friend of mine. Anybody who knows what this shit can do to yuh and would then turn you on to it, after sayin' they're your friend, is nothin' but scum."

And then one day "I was hitchhikin' down the street, a guy picked me up an' offered me money an'—it just went on from there...

"I was in a situation where I needed money. I'd lost my ID, I didn't have my birth certificate to get another ID, somebody'd stole my [dancing] costumes. And my kids needed to eat, and I needed to eat and pay rent...

"And then I came up here. I'd sent my kids up here to be with my mom, cause I knew jail and all that would come real quickly. And then I was hooking up here. And a year later my mom took my kids, and *[a stillness comes over her voice]*—here I am now."

I asked Gail if she'd ever been in love with a man, and, softly, she answered "No." Had she ever loved a woman? "Nope. Never been with a woman. Never *be* with one...."

What about the fathers of your kids? "It was very short, I just couldn't get into it. I just couldn't let my feelings out....

"I've come closer with some black guys. The father [of the baby inside me]!"

Are you still seeing him? "I see him all the time. He's the one that brought me back here" [Gail had excused herself at one point during our interview to go off and buy drugs].

Another nice guy, I thought. Uh, Gail, I said. Do you really want to do hard drugs when you're six months pregnant? "Please, no lectures. Ple-e-eze! Hey!

"Not every baby born is gonna be a crack baby! I was shooting up a lot when I was pregnant with my first baby. And I gained five pounds the whole pregnancy. And they told me if she came out with 10 fingers, 10 toes, and could spell her name by the time she was 20, she'd be lucky. They expected a mute, a total nothin'. And she came out an' she was so healthy, and she was so-o-o smart. Oh! She was smart! Disney Duck Tales, who-o-o, she knows the whole song; every day, got to watch it. I mean she's very, very smart."

Will her friend be helping her raise their baby? "I'll take care of this baby by myself. I love this baby enough for the both of us!

"The father *chooses* not to be around! I *chose* to keep it! It's what I want! I don't need a father who don't want to be a father. I'm not gonna make a man do something he don't wanna do."

Gail's defiant personality serves a very practical purpose: It keeps her going. But talk with her long enough and a more reflective, more self-critical side comes to the fore.

"At first it's the excitement," she told me toward the end of our afternoon together. "I mean, the thrill of breakin' the law and getting away with it. I love doing that! But after a while it gets old....

"If I had a real boyfriend—my ex-boyfriend is a kingpin drug dealer, you know *[laughs]*, I mean he didn't live the normal 9-to-5 life.... Um, lemme think, can't put this into words.... I *miss* bein' a square—they call 'em a 'square,' you know, normal life...."

Yes, Gail, I do know. I used to use that language too. My friends and I once tried to give intellectual legitimacy to the kind of visceral rebellion your life seems—on the surface—to be about.

And to whatever extent we helped put you in the bind you're in, I am truly sorry.

VIII. Brutes and boors?

Many of the pieces in the Alexander and Pheterson anthologies imply that the clients of prostitutes are dangerous or pathetic or both.

And that's not just the left's correct line. The tone *most* of us adopt when discussing men who use prostitutes is one of disdain and contempt. We seem to want to feel they're all brutes and boors—the better to put distance between them and us, perhaps.

I knew enough before I started this article to be skeptical of that attitude. Still, it was a big revelation for me to hear my prostitutes talk about how *ordinary* most of their customers are—and how starved for affection most of them are.

"Most of the people I date are middle class," Nancy told me. "Most of them work with computers, or in an office, you know. Accountants. I've met a lot of lawyers. . . .

"There's a few young people I date, but I'd say most of them are over 30 and are married" *[laughs]*.

"They're all different kinds," Gail told me. "Most of 'em are married. And married men come out and pay for what their wives won't give them.

"If the wife don't give head, that's what they come out and pay for. The wife cut 'em off completely, they'll come out and pay for pussy. . . . It's all whatever they don't get at home."

"Most of them are very nice," Nancy says. "They just wanna be with someone young, I guess" *[laughs]*.

"I have a guy who just likes to hug and hold, you know," Gail says. "Affection! Another guy who just likes to talk."

Don't they have you do weird things sometimes? "Oh, I've jacked a guy off with my feet," says Gail, laughing. "Yeah. I date a CIA guy who likes to be ripped right before he goes in for the kill, cause he's a pussycat, and—you know—all kinds of stuff."

"I try to make friends with them," says Lisa, interviewed below. "And sometimes I get into 'em, you know?"

"I get to know a lot of 'em," says Gail, "cause you get what you call 'regulars.' They keep coming back. You know, if you like the way I give head, you come back and see me knowin' I'm not gonna rip you off. And you get to *know* me, I mean, person-to-person.

"I have guys who are fallin' in love with me, literally. And some of 'em, they start to feel like I'm their daughter, I'm part of their family. They come close to me and feel like they're committing incest" *[laughs]*.

"I've met a few who are real jerks, really nasty," says Nancy. "But when they get nasty with you, you have to get really nasty right back, you know, and you have to act like you're not scared."

"I gave a guy head right back in the alley on 14th and Rhode Island," says Gail. "And, uh, after I was done datin' him he starts pullin' my hair; he was gonna take my money back. An' there was a mickey bottle, Budweiser, unopened. And I took the bottle and hit him over the head and knocked him out. . . .

"And I dated this other guy for over a year. He was a regular. And then one time he hit me over the head with a lead pipe, and I had to have stitches. . . . "

So the prostitutes have to be constantly on guard. But the politically incorrect fact is that the vast majority of their clients are *not* brutes or boors. Most of them are just like you and me, and desperate for female affection or attention of a kind that they can't get in real life.

Or that they don't know *how* to get.

IX. Getting to Lisa

The first time I saw Lisa I knew she had a very revealing story to tell. It was midnight, and she was *limping* up and down N Street in a yellow jogging suit; she was a pretty sorry sight. But her thin, angular face was alert and incredibly expressive—I knew there was a sensitive being in there somewhere.

We talked several times over the next couple of weeks, and other times I sort of spied on her. Once I saw her hobbling down the street with the help of a metal walker; another time I saw her sitting in her beat-up old Chevy, presumably waiting for tricks she knew. Finally I asked her to come punish me, and she said she'd drive over that night, and asked me to wait for her outside since she might need help crossing the street.

She arrived half an hour late (on a very cold night), and she looked worse than I'd ever seen her. Her yellow jogging suit was stained all over, and she couldn't even get out of the car without my help. Also, she was trembling. I put my jacket around her shoulders and my arm around her waist, and guided her across the street and past an appalled receptionist in my lobby. She apologized to me for going so slow.

I sat her down on the couch in my apartment, made her some coffee, brought her an ashtray. She apologized for asking me to bring the ashtray. She tried to relax and asked me to tell her what I wanted her to do. I was sweating—Christ!, I didn't want to go through with this. But I felt I had to. She apologized for asking me to help her take her shoes and pants off.

Even getting them off was painful for her, and I soon saw why. Her arms and legs had been chewed up by something; they were covered with deep scars. I tried to not let her see my horror. I gave her my belt and let her beat me a little, and then told her I just wasn't into it that night.

Then we just sat there on the couch, both of us half-naked, both of us uncontrollably trembling. She apologized for what she feared was the poor quality of her discipline. I asked if she'd mind being interviewed.

Truly, life is more astonishing than fiction. I have confirmed that Lisa, 33, is the daughter of a man who was once one of a Southern state's most ambitious conservative politicians, an outspoken foe of abortion and the Equal Rights Amendment. Lisa remembers seeing Jack Kemp and operatives from the first Reagan campaign in her father's home.

"I do come from a nice family," she began. "Just because I've tricked and all of that. . . .

"You know, my father was in the [legislature]. But my mother drank a little bit, and that caused problems between them. And there was a divorce. I was seven years old. . . .

"I couldn't take my mother's drinking and depression and stuff. So I moved in with my father. He got married to someone 12 years younger. . . .

"Eventually we got on pretty well. [But then] he turned Christian. One day he was going to the races and having a lot of fun. Drinking but not abusing it. And the next day it was church, church, church; I mean, everything was Jesus Christ this and Jesus Christ that, and I don't mean in vain. . . .

"My mother committed suicide a couple years back. She never got over that my father remarried. . . .

"My father wanted me to go to college, and I mean I tried, but it just seemed like [I was having] more and more problems. [My father and stepmother] didn't have a lot of patience, and they just go tired of it all. And I felt deserted and alone. . . .

"If I really need money I can get it from him. As far as going [home] Christmas and Thanksgiving, no. And he calls himself one of these Christian people. That's what gets me. . . . I mean, there's no second chances."

Now Lisa stays with her uncle, who's in advertising. "I can be honest with him. But he gets mad. And I'll take the car for a couple of days [and go on binges], because I have a hard time living with him. I can't live in clutter, with food around. . . .

"He kind of gets off hearing about the dates where I've beat and yelled at people."

Lisa is still sitting on my couch, pants off, belt in hand. The words come cascading out of her, she's totally caught up in what she's saying.

"I got married when I was about 19. Had a baby when I was 24. My husband was into drugs. He got into drugs in the service, in Germany, before I met him, but I thought the problem was over.

"I used to watch him get high. But I never did. For like years. And then it was like, I'll try it [coughs].

"He would use heroin and I would use coke. And then he got into trouble, you know, real trouble to support his habit, stealing and so forth. And he got locked up.

"I waited [for him] as long as I could. And then I just got tired of it. And—I always pick the druggies for some reason. I don't know why. I mean, I think I can make them better, or change them, or *[voice deepens and thickens here]*—and it just doesn't work that way.

"So I came [to D.C.] with this other guy that I was involved with. And then I was down in [the N Street neighborhood] and I ran into a girl friend and I think she was tricking for money.

"And then one day I was going to job interviews and stuff, and I went down there to talk to her. And I was dressed in a nice suit and stockings and high heels, and looked fine. I was just standing on the corner, looking for her. And some man just propositioned me. And that was it. I just got into it, off and on.

"Sometimes I thought it was a joke. I'd gone to an all-girls Catholic high school and was deprived of being around men, you know *[laughs]*.

"But then I went to jail—prison—for this. And my daughter went to court with me. And I got 45 days. And that guy I was with took my daughter to my father. And I haven't seen her since...."

Two years ago another disaster befell Lisa. "I was coming [in] from Virginia, on the last [subway] train to MacPherson Square. I was the only one to go [up the escalator], they closed and locked the gate, and I got on there and they turned it off and on, and it shimmied and shook. Next thing I knew I was unconscious. Ate my arms and legs up."

An orthopedic surgeon installed an artificial hip. And that was only the beginning. "I got better—I was in a wheelchair, and then I could walk. And then, out of the blue, I dislocated it.

"And I've dislocated it two or three times [since then]. I've been having operations every three or four months! I'm just beginning to think that my body can't adjust to it. You know, some people just can't."

Oh, Lisa, I thought. How *could* your body adjust to it, given your lifestyle?

The last time I spoke with Lisa she was in the hospital, awaiting yet another operation. I was going to go see her, but at the last minute she got some terrible news. The surgeon had decided to remove the artificial hip. If she couldn't stop him, she'd be confined to a wheelchair for the rest of her life.

She was in no mood for visitors.

247

More than any of the other prostitutes I talked with, Lisa is *continuously* aware of what it is she's missing—of what she needs to (begin to) be happy and whole.

"Hey, everybody needs a family, huh?," she told me on the couch, her scarred legs drawn up under her body.

Some of what Lisa cried out to me when she was whipping me was clearly meant for her father and ex-husband, and I've been playing it back in my mind ever since:

"You think you're something, don't you? Well, let me tell you you're shit! You're good for nothing! You always let me down!

(CRACK!)

"How come you always let me down? How come you're never there when I need you?

(LASH!)

"You're never there when I need you! Never there when I need you!"

X. The problem revealed

The prostitutes' rights organizations I mentioned at the beginning of this article see prostitution as an economic problem, or a civil liberties problem, or both. After spending hours and hours with all kinds of prostitutes, I certainly agree that there are economic and civil liberties issues that need to be addressed. But I also see, now, that prostitution is an even larger problem, one that speaks volumes about who we are *as human beings*.

Most of the prostitutes I talked with had marketable skills. Certainly most of them could have made it economically in "straight" society.

Most of my prostitutes had good relations with the police. "If you're honest with them, they're there for you," Gail told me.

But none of my prostitutes—not one—had ever been exposed to a healthy male-female sexual love relationship.

None of their parents had had one.

And none of them had ever managed to achieve one on their own, either with their husbands or with any of their boyfriends.

And we should not forget that their clients are—for the most part—ordinary men who simply aren't able to meet all their needs for female affection.

The largest cause of female prostitution, then, isn't sexual discrimination, economic exploitation or male oppression.

It is that too many of us do not know how to love.

Husbands and wives, parents and children, boyfriends and girlfriends, same-sex partners—for too many of us, it's just not all there.

XI. Old options, new options

Of course, the way you define a problem determines what you'll want to do about it.

If you see prostitution as largely a civil liberties or economic problem, then you'll feel comfortable with the agendas of the three prostitutes' rights organizations.

COYOTE wants to decriminalize prostitution.

U.S. PROS wants to abolish all laws against prostitution (it suspects that "decriminalization" would still allow the state to control prostitutes' working conditions). In addition, it supports "economic independence" for all women—by which it means bigger welfare checks and fewer immigration laws.

WHISPER wants the state to stop arresting prostitutes and *start* arresting their clients, and all other "men who traffic in women's bodies for their own pleasure and profit."

If you see prostitution as largely a problem of lack of love, you'll be drawn to a different agenda.

You might support decriminalization, but *not* legalization. You'll want cities to determine where women can and cannot solicit tricks, for example. And you'll want to prosecute the pimps and hangers-on, the *real* exploiters.

And you *won't* support decriminalization because you see "sex work" as just another kind of work. As this article makes crystal-clear, it isn't! Your rationale will be more pragmatic—nothing is being gained by having *the police* try to stop it. "They're out there tryin' to bust the hookers," Gail said knowingly. "As long as there's a man willing to pay for pussy, there's gonna be a woman to take the money."

You'll certainly support greater economic security—but not just for welfare mothers, or illegal immigrants, or whomever. If our problem is lack of love, you won't want to exacerbate a situation in which interest groups brutally fight each other for resources. Instead, you'll want to support some of the *universal* economic-security schemes we've discussed in NEW OPTIONS: the Universal Stock Ownership Plan, for example, or the idea of separating work from income.

In addition, you'll want to support decriminalization of drugs. With decriminalization, prostitutes won't have to earn nearly as much money to support their drug habits.

Above all, however, you'll want to support measures that can build a society in which people *learn to love* each other...and themselves.

There are such measures; NEW OPTIONS has written about a number of them.

Some *pre-schools* are making training in social and emotional skills a regular part of their curriculum.

Parental leave, family counseling and new-parent programs are helping us "rear gentler and more compassionate people."

Empowered teachers, visual/spatial teaching methods and democratic classrooms are helping schools reach the "whole person" and not just the left brain.

Multicultural trainings—often held at the workplace—are helping to foster solidarity across ethnic and racial lines.

Finally, John Vasconcellos's *Self-Esteem Task Force* has come up with a myriad of suggestions for promoting self-esteem.

These approaches do not offer a "quick fix" for prostitution. But nothing can. The problem does not exist only in the prostitutes and their clients, but in nearly all of us to some degree. We're each going to have to clean up our acts.

XII. Afterword

When I started this article, I still had a romantic view of prostitutes and prostitution. A couple of years ago I'd have gone as far as prostitutes' rights activist Lynn Hampton when she said, in the Pheterson anthology, "I think that the woman who defies her family, her country, her religion—and often, her husband— and becomes a prostitute by choice is the most liberated of all women."

Now that I've finished this article I have a very different view. There is nothing I can say that can fully convey the pain, the sadness, and the futility of the lives of the women I interviewed. And most of them claim that their stories are typical.

I've spent many nights wanting to go back to 13th and N and talk with some of them again. I want to see if Lisa escaped that wheelchair. And I want to bring Gail—now in her seventh month—some hot chocolate. I wonder if she drinks the stuff.

But I know enough, now, to know that there's nothing I can do for them, really. And I know they know that, too. So I have kept my distance...a "journalist," at last.

I've also spent many nights thinking about this: That in my own life I have not made room for the love, the intimacy, the generativity, that I claim This Society so desperately needs.

I am still working 80 hours a week, for a pittance. Still trying to save the world. I do not have time to love someone fully. I do not have the resources to be a good provider. I do not have the psychic space to be a father.

Now that I've written this article, I notice these things more. And they make me very sad.

What I am saying is that writing this article has made me want to change my life in ways that will allow me to get married and have children, and love my family with my every breath. It has made me realize that that is a good and important and even (may Alexander and Pheterson forgive me) necessary thing, a major clause in the human contract.

Appendix

Addresses of Groups Mentioned in the Text

All numbers in parentheses refer to the chapters in which the groups are mentioned.

The Advocate (#15)
6922 Hollywood Blvd., 10th
   Floor
Los Angeles CA 90028

African Development
   Foundation (#16)
1400 "I" St. NW, 10th
   Floor
Washington DC 20005

Afro-American Resource
   Center (#15)
Howard University
PO Box 441
Washington DC 20059

Aiki Works, Inc. (#24)
PO Box 7845
Aspen CO 81612

American Holistic Medical
   Assn (#13)
4101 Lake Boone Trail, #201
Raleigh NC 27607

Americans for the
   Universality of UNESCO
   (#18)
PO Box 18418
Asheville NC 28814

Arab-American Institute (#15)
918 16th St. NW, #601
Washington DC 20006

Assn for Humanistic
   Psychology (#2)
1772 Vallejo St., #3
San Francisco CA 94123

Buy Freedom (#4)
1501 Broadway, #2014
New York NY 10036

Calvert Social Investment
   Fund (#23)
1700 Pennsylvania Ave. NW
Washington DC 20006

Campaign for U.N. Reform
   (#18)
418 Seventh St. SE
Washington DC 20003

Center for Collaborative
   Education (#11)
1573 Madison Ave., #412
New York NY 10029

Center for Economic
   Conversion (#23)
222-C View St.
Mountain View CA 94041

Center for Innovative
Diplomacy (#2)
17931-F Sky Park Circle
Irvine CA 92714

Center for Rural Affairs (#7)
PO Box 405
Walthill NE 68067

Center for Science in the
Public Interest (#10)
1501 16th St. NW
Washington DC 20036

Center for Self-Care Studies
(#10)
3805 Stevenson Ave.
Austin TX 78703

Center for Urban Affairs
(#11)
2040 Sheridan Road
Evanston IL 60208

Center for War/Peace Studies
(#18)
218 E. 18th St.
New York NY 10003

Citizens for a Sound
Economy (#9)
470 L'Enfant Plaza "E"
SW, #7112
Washington DC 20024

Coalition on Smoking OR
Health (#10)
1615 New Hampshire Ave.
NW, 2nd Floor
Washington DC 20009

Community Capital Bank
(#8)
111 Livingston St.
Brooklyn NY 11201

Community Regeneration
(#7, 10)
222 Main Street
Emmaus PA 18049

Conf. Group on
Transformational Politics
(#1)
c/o Dept. of Government
School of Public Affairs
American University
Washington DC 20016

Co-op America (#2)
2100 "M" St. NW, #403
Washington DC 20063

Council for a Black
Economic Agenda (#21)
1367 Connecticut Ave. NW
Washington DC 20036

COYOTE (#25)
333 Valencia, #101
San Francisco CA 94103

Cultural Survival (#2)
53-A Church St.
Cambridge MA 02138

Development GAP (#17)
1400 "I" St. NW, #520
Washington DC 20005

East/West Report (#19)
4 Embarcadero Center,
 #2150
San Francisco CA 94111

Education-with-Production
 Network (#11)
c/o Chris Hennin
1818 "H" St. NW, #J-3028
Washington DC 20433

Elmwood Institute (#2)
PO Box 5805
Berkeley CA 94705

Equity Institute (#15)
48 N. Pleasant St.
Amherst MA 01002

EXPRO (#23)
1601 Connecticut Ave. NW,
 #500
Washington DC 20009

Global Education Associates
 (#19)
475 Riverside Dr., #456
New York NY 10115

Global Tomorrow Coalition
 (#17)
1325 "G" St. NW, #915
Washington DC 20005

Grameen Trust (#8, 21)
Mirpur Two
Dhaka 1216 Bangladesh

Green Committees of
 Correspondence [aka U.S.
 Green] (#3, 20)
PO Box 30208
Kansas City MO 64112

Greenpeace (#2)
1436 "U" St. NW
Washington DC 20009

HEMP (#14)
5632 Van Nuys St., #210
Van Nuys CA 91401

Holistic Education Review
 (#11)
PO Box 1476
Greenfield MA 01302

Hoover Institution (#9)
Stanford CA 94305

Human Economy Center
 (#10)
Box 14, Economics
 Department
Mankato State University
Mankato MN 56001

In Context Magazine (#1)
PO Box 11470
Bainbridge Island WA 98110

Institute for Community
 Economics (#23)
57 School Street
Springfield MA 01105

Institute for Cultural Affairs
(#1)
206 E. Fourth St.
New York NY 10009

Institute for Local Self-
Reliance (#23)
2425 18th St. NW, 2nd Floor
Washington DC 20009

Institute for Social Ecology
(#23)
PO Box 89
Plainfield VT 05667

Inter-American Foundation
(#16)
1515 Wilson Blvd.
Rosslyn VA 22209

Land Institute (#7)
2440 E. Water Well Rd.
Salina KS 67401

Left Green Network (#3)
PO Box 5566
Burlington VT 05402

Listening Project (#23)
1901 Hannah Branch Rd.
Burnsville NC 28714

NAACP (#21)
4805 Mt. Hope Drive
Baltimore MD 21215

National Abortion Rights
Action League (#24)
1101 14th St. NW, 5th Floor
Washington DC 20005

National Assn of Community
Development
Loan Funds (#23)
924 Cherry St., 4th Floor
Philadelphia PA 19107

National Assn of Railroad
Passengers (#12)
236 Massachusetts Ave. NE,
#603
Washington DC 20002

National Center for
Employee Ownership (#10)
2201 Broadway, #807
Oakland CA 94612

National Center for
Neighborhood Enterprise
(#21)
1367 Connecticut Ave. NW
Washington DC 20036

National Coalition Building
Institute (#15)
172 Brattle St.
Arlington MA 02174

National Right to Life
Committee (#24)
419 Seventh St. NW
Washington DC 20004

Natural Resources Defense
Council (#17)
1350 New York Ave. NW,
#300
Washington DC 20005

New Horizons for Learning
(#11)
4649 Sunnyside St. North
Seattle WA 98103

New Options Newsletter
PO Box 19324
Washington DC 20036

New Synthesis Think Tank
(#1)
c/o Center for Urban
   Community Development
929 No. Sixth St.
Milwaukee WI 53202

NORML (#14)
1636 "R" St. NW, 3rd
   Floor
Washington DC 20009

NOW (#20)
1000 16TH St. NW, #700
Washington DC 20009

The Other Economic Summit
(#6, 10, 19)
1442 Harvard St. NW
Washington DC 20009

Overseas Development
   Council (#16)
1717 Massachusetts Ave.
   NW, #501
Washington DC 20036

PACE Group (#11)
School of Education
Oakland University
Rochester MI 48309

Peer Research Lab (#11)
25 W. 43rd St., #620
New York NY 10036

People for the Ethical
   Treatment of Animals (#2)
PO Box 42516
Washington DC 20015

Post-Industrial Future Project
(#11)
PO Box 2699
Canmore, Alta. TOL-OMO
   Canada

Project Victory (#24)
560 Oxford, #1
Palo Alto CA 94306

Radical Faeries (#15)
5343 La Cresta Court
Los Angeles CA 90038

RAPID (#14)
1340 Valley Pl. SE
Washington DC 20020

Renew America (#2)
1001 Connecticut Ave. NW,
   #719
Washington DC 20036

RESULTS (#23)
236 Massachusetts Ave. NE,
   #110
Washington DC 20002

Rocky Mountain Institute
(#10)
1739 Snowmass Creek Rd.
Snowmass CO 81654

SANE/FREEZE (#23)
711 "G" St. SE
Washington DC 20003

Search for Common Ground
(#24)
2005 Massachusetts Ave.
NW, lower level
Washington DC 20036

Second Thoughts Project (#1)
c/o National Forum
Foundation
107 Second St. NE
Washington DC 20002

Self-Esteem Central (#5)
PO Box 277877
Sacramento CA 95827

Seventh Generation Fund
(#15)
PO Box 10
Forestville CA 95436

Sierra Club (#20)
730 Polk St.
San Francisco CA 94109

Sirius Community (#23)
Baker Rd.
Shutesbury MA 01072

Social Investment Forum
(#23)
711 Atlantic Ave.
Boston MA 02111

South Shore Bank (#8)
71st & Jeffery Blvd.
Chicago IL 60649

U.N. Association-USA (#18)
300 E. 42nd St.
New York NY 10017

US Association for the Club
of Rome (#18)
1325 "G" St. NW, #1003
Washington DC 20005

U.S. PROS (#25)
333 Valencia
San Francisco CA 94103

Urban Ecology (#12)
PO Box 10144
Berkeley CA 94709

WHISPER (#25)
PO Box 8719
Lake Street Stn.
Minneapolis MN 55408

Women's World Banking
(#1)
104 E. 40th St., #607
New York NY 10016

Working Assets Money Fund
(#23)
230 California St.
San Francisco CA 94111

APPENDIX

World Constitution and
  Parliament Assn (#18)
1480 Hoyt St., #31
Lakewood CO 80215

World Federalist Assn (#18)
418 Seventh St. SE
Washington DC 20003

World Order Models Project
  (#18)
475 Riverside Dr., #460
New York NY 10115

World Policy Institute (#16,
  19)
777 U.N. Plaza, 5th Floor
New York NY 10017

Worldwatch Institute (#10,
  12)
1776 Massachusetts Ave.
  NW, #701
Washington DC 20036

Afterword

In 1982 while I was dean of the School of Arts and Humanities at California State University, Fresno I decided to found a University Press. Since the California State University System has no budgetary provision for university presses, I realized that I would have to publish books by recognized authors if my Press were to survive as a self supporting enterprise. Scholarly books on miniscular topics vital to twelve people simply wouldn't cut it.

Since 1982 I have published seven books by Frank Lloyd Wright, all derived from his near inexhaustible archive in Arizona. I have published Francoise Gilot's artistic autobiography (Mme. Gilot, presently Mrs. Jonas Salk, was Picasso's companion for 17 years and is a significant artist in her own right). I have published five plays by William Saroyan never before in print, including the last two plays he ever wrote, the "cosmic vision" ones. A two volume set of 18 one-act unpublished Saroyan plays, curiously interlinked, is scheduled for May 1991 under the rubric, "The Spring of '75." I have translated and published Federico Fellini's comments on film and a history of flamenco by Juan Serrano, hailed by the San Francisco Chronicle as "the greatest flamenco guitarist of our day." And as you can see I have also published NEW OPTIONS FOR AMERICA by Mark Satin.

In the 1960s Mark Satin was recognized as one of the most significant voices of his generation. In the 1980s he founded the newsletter *New Options,* which the *Washington Post* has hailed as "one of the top four publications spearheading the ideology shuffle" and the *Whole Earth Review* described as "A highly influential newsletter that tracks transformational social change, while avoiding the usual dogmas of the left, the new age, or the fading '60s.''

In 1985 the US Association for The Club of Rome, voting on the Best Problematique Reporting in Print among all the periodicals in the world, selected *New Options* fourth, behind the *Christian Science Monitor*, the *New York Times* and *The Economist*. In 1989 *New Options* was awarded the *Utne Reader*'s Alternative Press Award for General Excellence (Best Publication from 10,000 to 30,000 Circulation). The essays in the preceding pages of this book give ample testimony as to why. What I am trying to say is that I would have proposed the publication of NEW OPTIONS FOR AMERICA whether or not Mark Satin was my son.

But I'm very glad he is.

Joseph Satin, Director
California State University Press
Fresno, CA